ORTHODOXY
and the Religion of the Future

BY FR. SERAPHIM ROSE

Fifth Edition

SAINT HERMAN OF ALASKA BROTHERHOOD

2023

St. Herman of Alaska Brotherhood
P. O. Box 70
Platina, California 96076

www.sainthermanmonastery.com

First Printing: April 1975
Second Printing: August 1975
Third Printing: May 1976
Fourth Printing (Second Edition): March 1979
Fifth Printing (Second Edition): February 1983
Sixth Printing (Third Edition): January 1990
Seventh Printing (Fourth Edition): December 1996
Eighth Printing (Fourth Edition): January 1999
Ninth Printing (Fifth Edition): December 2004
Tenth Printing (Fifth Edition): September 2008
Eleventh Printing (Fifth Edition): July 2013
Twelfth Printing (Fifth Edition): May 2018
Thirteenth Printing (Fifth Edition): January 2021
Fourteenth Printing (Fifth Edition): March 2023

Printed in the United States of America.

Front cover: The triumph of the Archangel Michael over the antichrist, who is shown falling into the abyss together with the cities of this world at the Last Judgment. Fresco by Pimen Maximovich Sofronov in the Sepulchre of St. John (Maximovitch) of Shanghai and San Francisco, below the Mother of God "Joy of All Who Sorrow" Cathedral in San Francisco.

Publishers Cataloging-in-Publication

Rose, Hieromonk Seraphim, 1934–1982.
    Orthodoxy and the religion of the future / by Fr. Seraphim Rose.—5th ed.
        p. cm.
    Includes bibliographical references and index.
    ISBN: 1–887904–00–X
    1. Orthodox Eastern Church. 2. Christianity and other religions. 3. Pentecostalism. I. Title

BX324.R67 2004
281.9—dc22   75–16940

ORTHODOXY AND THE RELIGION OF THE FUTURE

HIEROMONK SERAPHIM ROSE
1934–1982

HOW NARROW IS THE GATE, and strait is the way that leadeth to life: and few there are that find it! Beware of false prophets, who come to you in the clothing of sheep, but inwardly they are ravening wolves. By their fruits ye shall know them.... Not everyone that saith to Me, Lord, Lord shall enter into the Kingdom of heaven: but he that doeth the will of My Father Who is in heaven, he shall enter into the Kingdom of Heaven. Many will say to Me in that day: Lord, Lord, have we not prophesied in Thy name, and cast out devils in Thy name, and done many miracles in Thy name? And then will I profess unto them, I never knew you: depart from Me, ye that work iniquity. Every one therefore that heareth these My words, and doeth them, shall be likened to a wise man that built his house upon a rock.

—Matthew 7:14–16, 21–24

Contents

Preface to the Fifth Edition xi

Preface xix

Introduction xxiii

    1. The "Dialogue with Non-Christian Religions" xxiii

    2. "Christian" and Non-Christian Ecumenism xxix

    3. "The New Age of the Holy Spirit" xxxii

    4. The Present Book xxxix

I. The "Monotheistic" Religions: *Do We Have the Same God that Non-Christians Have?* 1

II. The Power of the Pagan Gods: *The Assault Upon Christianity* 7

    1. The Attractions of Hinduism 8

    2. A War of Dogma 13

    3. Hindu Places and Practices 15

    4. Evangelizing the West 21

    5. The Goal of Hinduism: The Universal Religion 26

III. A Fakir's "Miracle" and the Prayer of Jesus 30

IV. Eastern Meditation Invades Christianity 36

    1. "Christian Yoga" 38

    2. "Christian Zen" 42

    3. Transcendental Meditation 45

V. The "New Religious Consciousness": *The Spirit of the Eastern Cults in the 1970s* 52

vii

1. Hare Krishna in San Francisco — 54
2. Guru Maharaj-ji at the Houston Astrodome — 56
3. Tantric Yoga in the Mountains of New Mexico — 59
4. Zen Training in Northern California — 62
5. The New "Spirituality" vs. Christianity — 67

VI. "Signs from Heaven": *An Orthodox Christian Under standing of Unidentified Flying Objects (UFOs)* — 70
1. The Spirit of Science Fiction — 72
2. UFO Sightings and the Scientific Investigation of Them — 77
3. The Six Kinds of UFO Encounters — 85
4. Explanation of the UFO Phenomena — 98
5. The Meaning of UFOs — 108

VII. The "Charismatic Revival" as a Sign of the Times — 115
1. The 20th-century Pentecostal Movement — 116
2. The Ecumenical Spirit of the "Charismatic Revival" — 119
3. "Speaking in Tongues" — 124
4. "Christian" Mediumism — 128
5. Spiritual Deception — 143
   A. Attitude toward "Spiritual" Experiences — 146
   B. Physical Accompaniments of "Charismatic" Experiences — 151
   C. "Spiritual Gifts" Accompanying "Charismatic" Experiences — 158
   D. The New "Outpouring of the Holy Spirit" — 163

VIII. Conclusion: The Spirit of the Last Times — 169
1. The "Charismatic Revival" as a Sign of the Times — 169
   A. A "Pentecost without Christ" — 170

B. The "New Christianity" 173
C. "Jesus Is Coming Soon" 175
D. Must Orthodoxy Join the Apostasy? 179
E. "Little Children, It is the Last
    Hour" (I John 2:18) 183
2. The Religion of the Future 187

Epilogue: Jonestown and the 1980s 195

Epilogue to the Fifth Edition: Further Developments
    in the Formation of the Religion of the Future 201
1. The New Age Movement 201
2. The Revival of Paganism 203
3. The Rise of Witchcraft 204
4. The Leaven of New Age Spirituality 208
5. The Toronto Blessing 212
6. UFOs in the Contemporary Mind 219
7. The Plan for the New Age 223
8. Globalism 227
9. Denatured Christianity 231
10. The Vague Expectancy of the "New Man" 235
11. Conclusion 238

General Index 241
Scripture Index 255

14,000-foot Mount Shasta in northern California.

Preface to the Fifth Edition

ON May 10, 1976, Fr. Seraphim Rose was driving home to the St. Herman Monastery in the mountains of northern California. He was coming from Oregon, where he had just picked up a shipment of his first published book, *Orthodoxy and the Religion of the Future*—a book that would one day become spiritual dynamite, especially in Russia. The book was an examination of contemporary religious phenomena, symptoms of the "new religious consciousness" which prepared the way for one world religion and marked the beginning of a "demonic pentecost" in the last times. Never before had such a penetrating analysis of 20th-century spiritual currents been written, for until now no one had studied them so closely according to the timeless wisdom of the Holy Fathers.

In the early to mid-1970s, when Fr. Seraphim was writing his book, much of the phenomena he was describing was considered part of an aberrant "fringe." But he saw what was coming: he saw that the fringe would become more and more the mainstream. He saw the frightening unity of purpose behind a wide range of outwardly disparate phenomena, and saw the end result looming over the horizon. As he travelled southward with this book which was to blow the mask off the most subtle forms of demonic deception in our times, it was appropriate that he should stop at a nucleus of neo-paganism in America:

Mount Shasta. Considered by some to have been a holy mountain of the original Indian inhabitants, Mount Shasta had long been a center of occult activities and settlements, which were now on the increase there. Fr. Seraphim drove part way up with his truckload of books. Standing in the shadow of the immense mountain, on a spot where neo-pagan festivals were commonly held, he sang Paschal chants, sang of Christ's Resurrection and His victory over satan and the law of death. A thought arose in his mind which had come to him before: "An Orthodox priest should come and bless this mountain with holy water!"* Later, after his ordination to the priesthood, he would return to bless the mountain. But his book would do more: it would move mountains.

1. How This Book Was Born

The seeds of *Orthodoxy and the Religion of the Future* had been with Fr. Seraphim for quite some time. In the early 1960s he had begun a monumental work, *The Kingdom of Man and the Kingdom of God,* which would trace the philosophical, spiritual and social currents of the last 900 years, and would include a large section entitled "Orthodox Christian Spirituality and the 'New Spirituality.'" For years his monastic co-laborer, Fr. Herman, had been urging him to complete his *magnum opus,* but Fr. Seraphim had balked on the grounds that it was too big a job to undertake along with all the other tasks of their St. Herman Brotherhood, and that, besides, it was too intellectual and abstract. "We need something more practical," he said. By this time his understanding of Orthodox Christianity had

---

* From Fr. Seraphim's Chronicle of the St. Herman Brotherhood, entry for May 10, 1976.

deepened considerably, both from study and from personal struggle, and he was better able to contrast pseudo-spirituality with a commanding view of true, sober and salvific spiritual life. Ironically, as he had grown in both inward and outward knowledge since the early 1960s, his writings had grown not more complex and abstruse, but more accessible, understandable, basic and to-the-point.

In 1971, Fr. Seraphim began to write and compile chapters for *Orthodoxy and the Religion of the Future*, serializing them in the Brotherhood's journal *The Orthodox Word*. Four years later, on Bright Friday, May 9, 1975, the fathers finished printing the first edition of the book. It sold out so quickly that they had to do another printing in August, and then again the following May. An expanded edition was published in 1979. The book had struck a responsive chord; the monastery received letters and visits from several people who had been delivered from spiritual deception after reading it.*

2. The Clarity of a Patristic Mind

In the last century, the Russian Orthodox philosopher Ivan Kireyevsky explained how the acquisition of the Patristic mind enables one to see what others cannot: "An Orthodox mind stands at the point where all roads cross. He carefully looks down each road and, from his unique vantage point, observes the conditions, dangers, uses, and ultimate destination of each road. He examines each road from a Patristic viewpoint as his personal convictions come into actual, not hypothetical, contact with the surrounding culture." These words exactly

---

* Some of these encounters are described in *Father Seraphim Rose: His Life and Works,* St. Herman of Alaska Brotherhood, Platina, Calif., 2003, pp. 688–90.

describe Fr. Seraphim and explain why his writings now seem so prophetic. It was not that he was a divinely inspired prophet to whom the mysteries of the future were revealed. Rather, it was that he had acquired the Orthodox Patristic mind, the mind of the ancient Holy Fathers; and with this he discerned where the road of his surrounding culture—its general spiritual trend—was headed.

When Fr. Seraphim was writing in the mid-1970s about the dangers of the neo-pagan cults, there were other "cult-watchers" around (although then they were not so widely listened to as when the "cult-scare" hit America in 1979, in the wake of the Jonestown massacre). Without the Patristic principles of spiritual life, however, they were not able to perceive the underlying unity behind the phenomena of UFOs, Eastern religions, *and* the "charismatic revival"—all of which possess mediumistic techniques for getting in contact with fallen spirits under different guises.

Now that the New Age movement has become so visible and powerful, a number of "warning" books by Christian authors have become available. In 1983, a year after Fr. Seraphim's death, one of these books became a number one bestseller among Protestant Christians: *The Hidden Dangers of the Rainbow: the New Age Movement and Our Coming Age of Barbarism,* by Attorney Constance E. Cumbey. Although this book is also not informed by Patristic principles and may include some exaggerations, it came as a much-needed eye-opener to the Christian world, revealing little-known facts about the roots of the New Age movement, and about the co-operating religious, political, economic, health and environmental organizations working toward the "New World Order." After the book came out, Constance Cumbey went on a speaking tour, appearing many times on television and radio, giving interviews and debating such prominent New Age leaders as Benjamin Creme. Then, in 1988, she came across *Orthodoxy and the Religion of the Future*. This book by a predecessor in her field was like a revelation to her. To the St. Herman Brotherhood she wrote: "An unknown benefactor sent me a copy of Fr. Rose's book approximately one year ago, and I consider it the most important book I have read on the subject to date. Reading Fr. Rose is like drinking pure water after wading in muck! I have recommended it to many people in my public talks and radio interviews."*

3. The Impact of This Book in Russia and throughout the World

Of the forty books which the St. Herman Brotherhood published during Fr. Seraphim's lifetime—twenty in English and twenty in Russian—*Orthodoxy and the Religion of the Future* was the most popular. At the time of this writing, it is in its ninth English printing.

In Russia the impact of the book has been far greater than it has in America. During his lifetime Fr. Seraphim learned that the book had been translated into Russian behind the Iron Curtain, but he was never to know the astounding results. After his death it became known that the Russian translation (or a number of translations) had been secretly distributed among believers all over Russia in the form of countless typewritten manuscripts. The lives of untold thousands were changed as this book awakened them to the spiritual dangers of their times. The book is particularly relevant to Russia today, where

---

* Letter of Constance E. Cumbey to the St. Herman of Alaska Brotherhood, July 8, 1988.

a society deprived by seventy years of enforced materialism is falling prey to the growing influence of fraudulent spiritual trends.

With the "opening up" of Eastern European countries, portions of the widely known "underground" manuscript of *Orthodoxy and the Religion of the Future* were published in newspapers inside Russia. The chapters on "The Fakir's Miracle and the Prayer of Jesus" and on the UFO phenomenon appeared, introduced by biographical information on Fr. Seraphim. In both cases the articles were deliberately published to fulfill a specific need, since Eastern religions and UFO experiences have attracted tremendous interest in Russia. As the newspaper publishers stated, Fr. Seraphim's explanation of these phenomena has proven more plausible than any other theory. One believer in Russia, Mikhail Scherbachev of the Moscow Patriarchate Publishing Department, has said it well: "Fr. Seraphim's books demonstrate that these seemingly 'inexplicable' phenomena *can* be explained according to the stable, secure, precise theory of Orthodox Patristic doctrine."

Finally, in 1991, the entire book was published in mass quantities inside Russia. Since then, several Russian editions have been printed and distributed. Along with Fr. Seraphim's *The Soul After Death,* this book is one of the most widely read spiritual books in Russia today. It has been sold not only in bookstores and churches throughout the country, but even in the subway (Metro) and on book tables in the streets.

Beginning in the mid-1990s, *Orthodoxy and the Religion of the Future* began to be published in other countries, as well—primarily in Orthodox countries, where it has generated widespread interest. There are now editions in Greek, Serbian, Romanian, Bulgarian, Georgian, Latvian and French. The seventh chapter of the book, on the "charismatic revival," has also been translated into the Malayalam (south Indian) language and published in India.

4. Uncompromising Witness

Although Fr. Seraphim was generally understated in his deliberate avoidance of sensationalism, some readers may find the conclusions he draws in this book to be unnecessarily severe. In this, as in all his published writings, he was not one to soften his punches. Since betrayals of Christian truth—from the blatant to the highly subtle—were going on everywhere, he felt he could not afford to put on kid gloves; he had to be uncompromising in print.

Despite his severity when it came to writing about demonic deceptions which could lead the well-meaning to eternal perdition, Fr. Seraphim was loving and compassionate when it came to his pastoral approach to individual people. This personal, one-on-one care for people can be seen in his letters, journals and counsels which are cited in his biography, *Father Seraphim Rose: His Life and Works.* The present book, on the other hand, is an unequivocal statement, written for the world at large with a specific purpose in mind. Because Fr. Seraphim adhered to this purpose without sidestepping in the least, his book has over the years succeeded in jarring countless people out of complacency, making them take spiritual life more seriously, and giving them a firm push on the right path. It has challenged them with the reality that there is indeed a spiritual war going on, a battle for souls, and that they must *walk circumspectly* (Eph. 5:15) so as not to lose the grace of God which leads them heavenward.

May God continue to use this book to enlighten those wandering in darkness, and to remind those walking in the light how straight and narrow is the path they are to tread—the path to eternal life.

Hieromonk Damascene
St. Herman of Alaska Monastery
Platina, California
September 2004

Preface

EVERY HERESY has its own "spirituality," its own characteristic approach to the practical religious life. Thus, Roman Catholicism, until recently, had a clearly distinguishable piety of its own, bound up with the "sacred heart," the papacy, purgatory and indulgences, the revelations of various "mystics," and the like; and a careful Orthodox observer could detect in such aspects of modern Latin spirituality the practical results of the theological errors of Rome. Fundamentalist Protestantism, too, has its own approach to prayer, its typical hymns, its approach to spiritual "revival"; and in all of these can be detected the application to religious life of its fundamental errors in Christian doctrine. The present book is about the "spirituality" of Ecumenism, the chief heresy of the 20th century.

Until recently it appeared that Ecumenism was something so artificial, so syncretic, that it had no spirituality of its own; the "liturgical" agenda of Ecumenical gatherings both great and small appeared to be no more than an elaborate Protestant Sunday service.

But the very nature of the Ecumenist heresy—the belief that there is no one visible Church of Christ, that it is only now being formed—is such that it disposes the soul under its influence to certain spiritual attitudes which, in time, should produce a typical Ecumenist "piety" and "spirituality." In our day this seems to be happening at last, as the Ecumenical

xix

attitude of religious "expectancy" and "searching" begins to be rewarded by the activity of a certain "spirit" which gives religious satisfaction to the barren souls of the Ecumenist wasteland and results in a characteristic "piety" which is no longer merely Protestant in tone.

This book was begun in 1971 with an examination of the latest "Ecumenical" fashion—the opening of a "dialogue with non-Christian religions." Four chapters on this subject were printed in *The Orthodox Word* in 1971 and 1972, reporting chiefly on the events of the late 1960s up to early 1972. The last of these chapters was a detailed discussion of the "charismatic revival" which had just then been taken up by several Orthodox priests in America, and this movement was described as a form of "Ecumenical spirituality" inclusive of religious experiences which are distinctly non-Christian.

Especially this last chapter aroused a great deal of interest among Orthodox people, and it helped to persuade some not to take part in the "charismatic" movement. Others, who had already participated in "charismatic" meetings, left the movement and confirmed many of the conclusions of this article about it. Since then the "charismatic revival" in "Orthodox" parishes in America, judging from Fr. Eusebius Stephanou's periodical *The Logos,* has entirely adopted the language and techniques of Protestant revivalism, and its un-Orthodox character has become clear to any serious observer. Despite the Protestant mentality of its promoters, however, the "charismatic revival" as a "spiritual" movement is definitely something more than Protestantism. The characterization of it in this article as a kind of *"Christian" mediumism,* which has been corroborated by a number of observers of it, links it to the new "Ecumenical spirituality" out of which is being born a new, non-Christian religion.

Preface

In the summer of 1974, one of the American monasteries of the Russian Orthodox Church Outside of Russia was visited by a young man who had been directed to one of its monks by the "spirit" who constantly attended him. During his brief visit the story of this young man unfolded itself. He was from a conservative Protestant background which he found spiritually barren, and he had been opened up to "spiritual" experiences by his Pentecostalist grandmother: the moment he touched a Bible she had given him, he received "spiritual gifts"—most notably, he was attended by an invisible "spirit" who gave him precise instructions as to where to walk and drive; and he was able at will to hypnotize others and cause them to levitate (a talent which he playfully used to terrorize atheist acquaintances). Occasionally he would doubt that his "gifts" were from God, but these doubts were overcome when he reflected on the fact that his spiritual "barrenness" had vanished, that his "spiritual rebirth" had been brought about by contact *with the Bible,* and that he seemed to be leading a very rich life of prayer and "spirituality." Upon becoming acquainted with Orthodoxy at this monastery, and especially after reading the article on the "charismatic revival," he admitted that here he found the first thorough and clear explanation of his "spiritual" experiences; most likely, he confessed, his "spirit" was an evil one. This realization, however, did not seem to touch his heart, and he left without being converted to Orthodoxy. On his next visit two years later this man revealed that he had given up "charismatic" activities as too frightening and was now spiritually content practicing Zen meditation.

This close relationship between "Christian" and "Eastern" spiritual experiences is typical of the "ecumenical" spirituality of our days. For this second edition much has been added concerning Eastern religious cults and their influence today, as well as concerning a major "secular" phenomenon which is helping to form a "new religious consciousness" even among non-religious people. None of these by itself, it may be, has a crucial significance in the spiritual make-up of contemporary man; but each one in its own way typifies the striving of men today to find a new spiritual path, distinct from the Christianity of yesterday, and the sum of them together reveals a frightening unity of purpose whose final end seems just now to be looming above the horizon.

Shortly after the publication of the article on the "charismatic revival," *The Orthodox Word* received a letter from a respected Russian Orthodox ecclesiastical writer who is well versed in Orthodox theological and spiritual literature, saying: "What you have described here is the religion of the future, the religion of antichrist." More and more, as this and similar forms of counterfeit spirituality take hold even of nominal Orthodox Christians, one shudders to behold the deception into which spiritually unprepared Christians can fall. This book is a warning to them and to all trying to live a conscious Orthodox Christian life in a world possessed by unclean spirits. It is not an exhaustive treatment of this religion, which has not yet attained its final form, but rather a preliminary exploration of those spiritual tendencies which, it would indeed seem, are preparing the way for a true religion of anti-Christianity, a religion outwardly "Christian," but centered upon a pagan "initiation" experience.

May this description of the increasingly evident and brazen activity of satan, the prince of darkness, among "Christians," inspire true Orthodox Christians with the fear of losing God's grace and turn them back to the pure sources of Christian life: the Holy Scriptures and the spiritual doctrine of the Holy Fathers of Orthodoxy!

Introduction

1. The "Dialogue with Non-Christian Religions"

OURS is a spiritually unbalanced age, *when many Orthodox Christians find themselves tossed to and fro, and carried about with every wind of doctrine, by the sleight of men, and cunning craftiness, whereby they lie in wait to deceive* (Eph. 4:14). The time, indeed, seems to have come when men *will not endure sound doctrine, but after their own lusts shall they heap to themselves teachers, having itching ears; and they shall turn away their ears from the truth, and shall be inclined unto fables* (II Tim. 4:3–4).

One reads in bewilderment of the latest acts and pronouncements of the ecumenical movement. On the most sophisticated level, Orthodox theologians representing the American Standing Conference of Orthodox Bishops and other official Orthodox bodies conduct learned "dialogues" with Roman Catholics and Protestants and issue "joint statements" on such subjects as the Eucharist, spirituality, and the like—without even informing the heterodox that the Orthodox Church is the Church of Christ to which all are called, that only her Mysteries are grace-giving, that Orthodox spirituality can be understood only by those who know it in experience within the Orthodox Church, that all these "dialogues" and "joint statements" are an academic caricature of true Christian discourse—a discourse which has the salvation of souls as its aim. Indeed, many of the Orthodox participants in these "dialogues" know or suspect that this is no place for Orthodox witness, that the very atmosphere of ecumenical "liberalism" cancels out whatever truth might be spoken at them; but they are silent, for the "spirit of the times" today is often stronger than the voice of Orthodox conscience. (See *Diakonia*, 1970, no. 1, p. 72; *St. Vladimir's Theological Quarterly*, 1969, no. 4, p. 225; etc.)

On a more popular level, ecumenical "conferences" and "discussion" are organized, often with an "Orthodox speaker" or even the celebration of an "Orthodox Liturgy." The approach to these "conferences" is often so dilettantish, and the general attitude at them is so lacking in seriousness, that rather than advance the "unity" their promoters desire, they actually serve to prove the existence of an impassible abyss between true Orthodoxy and the "ecumenical" outlook. (See *Sobornost*, Winter, 1978, pp. 494–98, etc.)

On the level of action, ecumenical activists take advantage of the fact that the intellectuals and theologians are irresolute and unrooted in Orthodox tradition, and use their very words concerning "fundamental agreement" on sacramental and dogmatic points as an excuse for flamboyant ecumenical acts, not excluding the giving of Holy Communion to heretics. And this state of confusion in turn gives an opportunity for ecumenical ideologists on the most popular level to issue empty pronouncements that reduce basic theological issues to the level of cheap comedy, as when Patriarch Athenagoras allows himself to say: "Does your wife ever ask you how much salt she should put in the food? Certainly not. She has the infallibility. Let the Pope have it too, if he wishes" (*Hellenic Chronicle*, April 9, 1970).

The informed and conscious Orthodox Christian may well ask: where will it all end? Is there no limit to the betrayal, the denaturement, the self-liquidation of Orthodoxy?

It has not yet been too carefully observed where all this is leading, but logically the path is clear. The ideology behind ecumenism, which has inspired such ecumenistic acts and pronouncements as the above, is an already well-defined heresy: the Church of Christ does not exist, no one has the Truth, the Church is only now being built. But it takes little reflection to see that the self-liquidation of Orthodoxy, of the *Church of Christ*, is simultaneously the self-liquidation of Christianity itself; that if no one is *the* Church of Christ, then the combination of all sects will not be *the* Church either, not in the sense in which Christ founded it. And if all "Christian" bodies are relative to each other, then all of them together are relative to other "religious" bodies, and "Christian" ecumenism can only end in a syncretic world religion.

This is indeed the undisguised aim of the masonic ideology which has inspired the Ecumenical Movement, and this ideology has now taken such possession of those who participate in the Ecumenical Movement that "dialogue" and eventual union with the non-Christian religions have come to be the logical next step for today's denatured Christianity. The following are a few of the many recent examples that could be given that point the way to an "ecumenical" future *outside of Christianity*.

1. On June 27,1965, a "Convocation of Religion for World Peace" was held in San Francisco in connection with the 20th anniversary of the founding of the United Nations in that city. Before 10,000 spectators there were addresses on the "religious" foundation of world peace by Hindu, Buddhist, Moslem, Jewish, Protestant, Catholic, and Orthodox representatives, and hymns of all faiths were sung by a 2,000-voice "interfaith" choir.

2. The Greek Archdiocese of North and South America, in the official statement of its 19th Clergy-Laity Congress

(Athens, July 1968), declared: "We believe that the ecumenical movement, even though it is of Christian origin, must become a movement of all religions reaching towards each other."

3. The "Temple of Understanding, Inc.," an American foundation established in 1960 as a kind of "Association of United Religions" with the aim of "building the symbolic Temple in various parts of the world" (precisely in accord with the doctrine of Freemasonry), has held several "Summit Conferences." At the first, in Calcutta in 1968, the Latin Trappist Thomas Merton (who was accidentally electrocuted in Bangkok on the way back from this conference) declared: "We are already a new unity. What we must regain is our original unity." At the second, at Geneva in April 1970, eighty representatives of ten world religions met to discuss such topics as "The Project of the Creation of a World Community of Religions;" the General Secretary of the World Council of Churches, Dr. Eugene Carson Blake, delivered an address calling on the heads of all religions to unity; and on April 2 an "unprecedented" supra-confessional prayer service took place in St. Peter's Cathedral, described by the Protestant Pastor Babel as "a very great date in the history of religions," at which "everyone prayed in his own language and according to the customs of religion which he represented" and at which "the faithful of all religions were invited to coexist in the cult of the same God," the service ending with the "Our Father" (*La Suisse*, April 3, 1970). Promotional material sent out by the "Temple of Understanding" reveals that Orthodox delegates were present at the second "Summit Conference" in the United States in the autumn of 1971, and that Metropolitan Emilianos of the Patriarchate of Constantinople is a member of the Temple's "International Committee." The "Summit Conferences" offer Orthodox delegates the opportunity to

enter discussions aiming to "create a world community of religions," to "hasten the realization of mankind's dream of peace and understanding" according to the philosophy of "Vivekananda, Ramakrishna, Ghandi, Schweitzer," and the founders of various religions; and the delegates likewise participate in "unprecedented" supra-confessional prayer services where "everyone prays according to the customs of the religion he represents." One can only wonder what must be in the soul of an Orthodox Christian who participates in such conferences and prays together with Moslems, Jews, and pagans.

4. Early in 1970 the WCC sponsored a conference in Ajaltoun, Lebanon, between Hindus, Buddhists, Christians, and Moslems, and a follow-up conference of twenty-three WCC "theologians" in Zurich in June declared the need for "dialogue" with the non-Christian religions. At the meeting of the Central Committee of the WCC at Addis Ababa in January of this year, Metropolitan Georges Khodre of Beirut (Orthodox Church of Antioch) shocked even many Protestant delegates when he not merely called for "dialogue" with these religions, but left the Church of Christ far behind and trampled on nineteen centuries of Christian tradition when he called on Christians to "investigate the authentically spiritual life of the unbaptized" and enrich their own experience with the "riches of a universal religious community" (Religious News Service), for "it is Christ alone who is received as light when grace visits a Brahmin, a Buddhist, or a Moslem reading his own scriptures" (*Christian Century*, Feb. 10, 1971).

5. The Central Committee of the World Council of Churches at its meeting in Addis Ababa in January 1971, gave its approval and encouragement to the holding of meetings as regularly as possible between representatives of other religions, specifying that "at the present stage priority may be given to

bilateral dialogues of a specific nature." In accordance with this directive a major Christian-Moslem "dialogue" was set for mid-1972 involving some forty representatives of both sides, including a number of Orthodox delegates (*Al Montada*, January–February 1972, p. 18).

6. In February 1972, another "unprecedented" ecumenical event occurred in New York when, according to Archbishop Iakovos of New York, for the first time in history, the Greek Orthodox Church (Greek Orthodox Archdiocese of North and South America) held an official theological "dialogue" with the Jews. In two days of discussions definite results were achieved, which may be taken as symptomatic of the future results of the "dialogue with non-Christian religions": the Greek "theologians" agreed "to review their liturgical texts in terms of improving references to Jews and Judaism where they are found to be negative or hostile" (Religious News Service). Does not the intention of the "dialogue" become ever more obvious?—to "reform" Orthodox Christianity in order to make it conformable to the religions of this world.

These events were the beginnings of the "dialogue with non-Christian religions" at the end of the decade of the 1960s and the beginning of the 1970s. In the years since then such events have multiplied, and "Christian" (and even "Orthodox") discussions and worship with representatives of non-Christian religions have come to be accepted as a normal part of contemporary life. The "dialogue with non-Christian religions" has become part of the intellectual fashion of the day; it represents the present stage of ecumenism in its progress towards a universal religious syncretism. Let us now look at the "theology" and the goal of this accelerating "dialogue" and see how it differs from the "Christian" ecumenism that has prevailed up to now.

2. "Christian" and Non-Christian Ecumenism

"Christian" ecumenism at its best may be seen to represent a sincere and understandable error on the part of Protestants and Roman Catholics—the error of failing to recognize that the visible Church of Christ already exists, and that they are outside it. The "dialogue with non-Christian religions," however, is something quite different, representing rather a conscience departure from even that part of genuine Christian belief and awareness which some Catholics and Protestants retain. It is the product, not of simple human "good intentions," but rather of a diabolical "suggestion" that can capture only those who have already departed so far from Christianity as to be virtual pagans: worshippers of the *god of this world*, satan (II Cor. 4:4), and followers of whatever intellectual fashion this powerful god is capable of inspiring.

"Christian" ecumenism relies for its support upon a vague but nonetheless real feeling of "common Christianity" which is shared by many who do not think or feel too deeply about the Church, and it aims somehow to "build" a church comprising all such indifferent "Christians." But what common support can the "dialogue with non-Christians" rely on? On what possible ground can there be any kind of unity, however loose, between Christians and those who not merely do not know Christ, but—as is the case with all the present-day representatives of non-Christian religions who are in contact with Christianity—decisively *reject* Christ? Those who, like Metropolitan Georges Khodre of Lebanon, lead the avant-garde of Orthodox apostates (a name that is fully justified when applied to those who radically fall away from the whole Orthodox Christian tradition), speak of the "spiritual riches" and "authentic spiritual life" of the non-Christian religions; but it is only by doing great violence to the meaning of words and by reading his own fantasies into other people's experience that he can bring himself to say that it is "Christ" and "grace" that pagans find in their scriptures, or that "every martyr for the truth, every man persecuted for what he believes to be right, dies in communion with Christ."* Certainly these people themselves (whether it be a Buddhist who sets fire to himself, a Communist who dies for the "cause" in which he sincerely believes, or whoever) would never say that it is "Christ" they receive or die for, and the idea of an unconscious confession or reception of Christ is against the very nature of Christianity. If a rare non-Christian does claim to have experience of "Christ," it can only be in the way which Swami Vivekananda describes: "We Hindus do not merely tolerate, we unite ourselves with every religion, praying in the mosque of the Mohammedan, worshipping before the fire of the Zoroastrian, and kneeling to the Cross of the Christian"—that is, as merely one of a number of equally valid spiritual experiences.

No: "Christ," no matter how redefined or reinterpreted, cannot be the common denominator of the "dialogue with non-Christian religions," but at best can only be added as an afterthought to a unity which is discovered somewhere else. The only possible common denominator among all religions is the totally vague concept of the "spiritual," which indeed offers religious "liberals" almost unbounded opportunity for nebulous theologizing.

The address of Metropolitan Georges Khodre to the Central Committee meeting of the WCC at Addis Ababa in January 1971, may be taken as an early, experimental attempt to

---

* *Sobornost,* Summer 1971, p. 171.

xxx

set forth such a "spiritual" theology of the "dialogue with non-Christian religions."[*] In raising the question as to "whether Christianity is so inherently exclusive of other religions as has generally been proclaimed up to now," the Metropolitan, apart from his few rather absurd "projections" of Christ into non-Christian religions, has one main point: it is the "Holy Spirit," conceived as totally independent of Christ and His Church, that is really the common denominator of all the world's religions. Referring to the prophecy that *I will pour out My Spirit upon all flesh* (Joel 2:28), the Metropolitan states, "This must be taken to mean a Pentecost which is universal from the very first.... The advent of the Spirit in the world is not subordinated to the Son.... The Spirit operates and applies His energies in accordance with His own economy and we could, from this angle, regard the non-Christian religions as points where His inspiration is at work" (p. 172). We must, he believes, "develop an ecclesiology and a missiology in which the Holy Spirit occupies a supreme place" (p. 166).

All of this, of course, constitutes a heresy which denies the very nature of the Holy Trinity and has no aim but to undermine and destroy the whole idea and reality of the Church of Christ. Why, indeed, should Christ have established a Church if the Holy Spirit acts quite independently, not only of the Church, but of Christ Himself? Nonetheless, this heresy is here still presented rather tentatively and cautiously, no doubt with the aim of testing the response of other Orthodox "theologians" before proceeding more categorically.

In actual fact, however, the "ecclesiology of the Holy Spirit" has already been written—and by an "Orthodox" thinker at that, one of the acknowledged "prophets" of the

---

[*] Full text in *ibid.,* pp. 166–74.

xxxi

"spiritual" movement of our own day. Let us therefore examine his ideas in order to see the picture he gives of the nature and goal of the larger "spiritual" movement in which the "dialogue with non-Christian religions" has its place.

3. "The New Age of the Holy Spirit"

Nicholas Berdyaev (1874–1949) in any normal time would never have been regarded as an Orthodox Christian. He might best be described as a gnostic-humanist philosopher who drew his inspiration rather from Western sectarians and "mystics" than from any Orthodox sources. That he is called in some Orthodox circles even to this day an "Orthodox philosopher" or even "theologian," is a sad reflection of the religious ignorance of our times. Here we shall quote from his writings.*

Looking with disdain upon the Orthodox Fathers, upon the "monastic ascetic spirit of historical Orthodoxy," indeed upon that whole "conservative Christianity which ... directs the spiritual forces of man only towards contrition and salvation," Berdyaev sought rather the "inward Church," the "Church of the Holy Spirit," the "spiritual view of life which, in the 18th century, found shelter in the Masonic lodges." "The Church," he believed, "is still in a merely potential state," is "incomplete"; and he looked to the coming of an "ecumenical faith," a "fullness of faith" that would unite, not merely different Christian bodies (for "Christianity should be capable of existing in a variety of forms in the Universal Church"), but also "the partial truths of all the heresies" and "all the humanis-

---

* As cited in J. Gregerson, "Nicholas Berdyaev, Prophet of a New Age," *Orthodox Life,* Jordanville, New York, 1962, no. 6, where full references are given.

tic creative activity of modern man ... as a religious experience consecrated in the Spirit." A "New Christianity" is approaching, a "new mysticism, which will be deeper than religions and ought to unite them." For "there is a great spiritual brotherhood ... to which not only the Churches of East and West belong, but also all those whose wills are directed towards God and the Divine, all in fact who aspire to some form of spiritual elevation"—that is to say, people of every religion, sect, and religious ideology. He predicted the advent of "a new and final Revelation": "the New Age of the Holy Spirit," resurrecting the prediction of Joachim of Floris, the 12th century Latin monk who saw the two ages of the Father (Old Testament) and the Son (New Testament) giving way to a final "Third Age of the Holy Spirit." Berdyaev writes: "The world is moving towards a new spirituality and a new mysticism; in it there will be no more of the ascetic world view." "The success of the movement towards Christian unity presupposes a new era in Christianity itself, a new and deep spirituality, which means a new outpouring of the Holy Spirit."

There is clearly nothing whatever in common between these super-ecumenist fantasies and Orthodox Christianity, which Berdyaev in fact despised. Yet anyone aware of the religious climate of our times will see that these fantasies in fact correspond to one of the leading currents of contemporary religious thought. Berdyaev does indeed seem to be a "prophet," or rather, to have been sensitive to a current of religious thought and feeling which was not so evident in his day, but has become almost dominant today. Everywhere one hears of a new "movement of the Spirit," and now a Greek Orthodox priest, Father Eusebius Stephanou, invites Orthodox Christians to join this movement when he writes of "the mighty outpouring of the Holy Spirit in our day" (*The Logos,* January

1972). Elsewhere in the same publication (March 1972, p. 8), the Associate Editor Ashanin invokes not merely the name, but also the very program, of Berdyaev: "We recommend the writings of Nicholas Berdyaev, the great spiritual prophet of our age. This spiritual genius ... [is] the greatest theologian of spiritual creativeness.... Now the cocoon of Orthodoxy has been broken.... God's Divine Logos is leading His people to a new understanding of their history and their mission in Him. *The Logos* [is the] herald of this new age, of the new posture of Orthodoxy."

4. The Present Book

All of this constitutes the background of the present book, which is a study of the "new" religious spirit of our times that underlies and gives inspiration to the "dialogue with non-Christian religions." The first three chapters offer a general approach to non-Christian religions and their radical difference from Christianity, both in theology and in spiritual life. The first chapter is a theological study of the "God" of the Near Eastern religions with which Christian ecumenists hope to unite on the basis of "monotheism." The second concerns the most powerful of the Eastern religions, Hinduism, based on a long personal experience which ended in the author's conversion from Hinduism to Orthodox Christianity; it also gives an interesting appraisal of the meaning *for Hinduism* of the "dialogue" with Christianity. The third chapter is a personal account of the meeting of an Orthodox priest-monk with an Eastern "miracle-worker"—a direct confrontation of Christian and non-Christian "spirituality."

The next four chapters are specific studies of some of the significant spiritual movements of the 1970s. Chapters Four and Five examine the "new religious consciousness" with particular reference to the "meditation" movements which now claim many "Christian" followers (and more and more "ex-Christians"). Chapter Six looks at the spiritual implications of a seemingly non-religious phenomenon of our times which is helping to form the "new religious consciousness" even among people who think they are far from any religious interest. The seventh chapter discusses at length the most controversial religious movement among "Christians" today—the "charismatic revival"—and tries to define its nature in the light of Orthodox spiritual doctrine.

In the Conclusion the significance and goal of the "new religious consciousness" are discussed in the light of Christian prophecy concerning the last times. The "religion of the future" to which they point is set forth and contrasted with the only religion which is irreconcilably in conflict with it: true Orthodox Christianity. The "signs of the times," as we approach the fearful decade of the 1980s, are all too clear; let Orthodox Christians, and all who wish to save their souls in eternity, take heed and act!

I

The "Monotheistic" Religions

DO WE HAVE THE SAME GOD
THAT NON-CHRISTIANS HAVE?

By Fr. Basile Sakkas

"The Hebrew and Islamic peoples, and Christians ... these three expressions of an identical monotheism, speak with the most authentic and ancient, and even the boldest and most confident voices. Why should it not be possible that the name of the same God, instead of engendering irreconcilable opposition, should lead rather to mutual respect, understanding and peaceful coexistence? Should the reference to the same God, the same Father, without prejudice to theological discussion, not lead us rather one day to discover what is so evident, yet so difficult—that we are all sons of the same Father, and that, therefore, we are all brothers?"

Pope Paul VI, *La Croix,* Aug. 11, 1970

ON THURSDAY, April 2, 1970, a great religious manifestation took place in Geneva. Within the framework of the Second Conference of the "Association of United Religions," the representatives of ten great religions were invited to gather in the Cathedral of St. Peter. This "common prayer" was based

I

on the following motivation: "The faithful of all these religions were invited to coexist in *the cult of the same God!*" Let us then see if this assertion is valid in the light of the Holy Scriptures.

In order better to explain the matter, we shall limit ourselves to the three religions that have historically followed each other in this order: Judaism, Christianity, Islam. These three religions lay claim, in fact, to a common origin: as worshipers of the God of Abraham. Thus it is a very widespread opinion that since we all lay claim to the posterity of Abraham (the Jews and Moslems according to the flesh and the Christians spiritually), we all have as God the God of Abraham and all three of us worship (each in his own way, naturally) the *same God.* And this same God constitutes in some fashion our point of unity and of "mutual understanding," and this invites us to a "fraternal relation," as the Grand Rabbi Dr. Safran emphasized, paraphrasing the Psalm: "Oh, how good it is to see brethren seated together...."

In this perspective it is evident that Jesus Christ, God and Man, the Son Co-eternal with the Father without beginning, His Incarnation, His Cross, His Glorious Resurrection and His Second and Terrible Coming—become secondary details which cannot prevent us from "fraternizing" with those who consider Him as "a simple prophet" (according to the Koran) or as "the son of a prostitute" (according to certain Talmudic traditions)! Thus we would place Jesus of Nazareth and Mohammed on the same level. I do not know what Christian worthy of the name could admit this in his conscience.

One might say that in these three religions, passing over the past, one could agree that Jesus Christ is an extraordinary and exceptional being and that He was sent by God. But for us Christians, if Jesus Christ is not *God,* we cannot consider Him either as a "prophet" or as one "sent by God," but only as a great imposter without compare, having proclaimed Himself "Son of God," making Himself thus *equal* to God (Mark 14:61–62). According to this ecumenical solution on the supra-confessional level, the Trinitarian God of Christians would be the same thing as the monotheism of Judaism, of Islam, of the ancient heretic Sabellius, of the modern anti-Trinitarians, and of certain Illuminist sects. There would not be *Three Persons in a Single Divinity,* but a single Person, unchanging for some, or successively changing "masks" (Father-Son-Spirit) for others! And nonetheless one would pretend that this was the *"same God."*

Here some might naively propose: "Yet for the three religions there is a common point: all three confess *God the Father!"* But according to the Holy Orthodox Faith, this is an absurdity. We confess always: "Glory to the Holy, Consubstantial, Life-giving and *Indivisible* Trinity." How could we separate the *Father* from the *Son* when Jesus Christ affirms *I and the Father are One* (John 10:30); and St. John the Apostle, Evangelist, and Theologian, the Apostle of Love, clearly affirms: *Whosoever denieth the Son, the same hath not the Father* (I John 2:23).

But even if all three of us call God *Father:* of whom is He really the Father? For the Jews and the Moslems He is the Father of men in the plane of *creation;* while for us Christians He is, first of all, *before the foundation of the world* (John 17:24) *the Father of our Lord Jesus Christ* (Eph. 1:3), and through Christ He is our Father *by adoption* (Eph. 1:4–5) in the plane of *redemption.* What resemblance is there, then, between the Divine Paternity in Christianity and in the other religions?

Others might say: "But all the same, Abraham worshipped the true God; and the Jews through Isaac and the Moslems through Hagar are the descendants of this true worshipper of God." Here one will have to make several things clear: Abraham worshipped God not at all in the form of the unipersonal monotheism of the others, but in the form of the Holy Trinity. We read in the Holy Scripture: *And the Lord appeared unto him at the Oaks of Mamre ... and he bowed himself toward the ground* (Gen. 18:1–2). Under what form did Abraham worship God? Under the unipersonal form, or under the form of the Divine Tri-unity? We Orthodox Christians venerate this Old Testament manifestation of the Holy Trinity on the Day of Pentecost, when we adorn our churches with boughs representing the ancient oaks, and when we venerate in their midst the icon of the Three Angels, just as our father Abraham venerated it! Carnal descent from Abraham can be of no use to us if we are not regenerated by the waters of Baptism in the Faith of Abraham. And the Faith of Abraham was the Faith in Jesus Christ, as the Lord Himself has said: *Your father Abraham rejoiced to see My day; and he saw it and was glad* (John 8:56). Such also was the Faith of the Prophet King David, who heard the Heavenly Father speaking to His Consubstantial Son: *The Lord said unto my Lord* (Ps. 109:1; Acts 2:34). Such was the Faith of the Three Youths in the fiery furnace when they were saved by the *Son of God* (Dan. 3:25); and of the holy Prophet Daniel, who had the Vision of the two natures of Jesus Christ in the Mystery of the Incarnation when the Son of Man came to the Ancient of Days (Dan. 7:13). This is why the Lord, addressing the (biologically incontestable) posterity of Abraham, said: *If ye were the children of Abraham, ye would do the works of Abraham* (John 8:39), and these "works" are to *believe on Him Whom God hath sent* (John 6:29).

Who then are the *posterity* of Abraham? The sons of Isaac according to the flesh, or the sons of Hagar the Egyptian? Is Isaac or Ishmael the posterity of Abraham? What does the Holy Scripture teach by the mouth of the divine Apostle? *Now*

4

to Abraham and his seed were the promises made. He saith not, And to seeds, as of many; but as of one, And to thy seed: which is Christ (Gal. 3:16). *And if ye be Christ's, then are ye Abraham's seed, and heirs according to the promise* (Gal. 3:29). It is then in Jesus Christ that Abraham became *a father of many nations* (Gen. 17:5; Rom. 4:17). After such promises and such certainties, what meaning does carnal descent from Abraham have? According to the Holy Scripture, Isaac is considered as the *seed* or *posterity,* but only as *the image of Jesus Christ.* As opposed to Ishmael (the son of Hagar; Gen. 16:1ff), Isaac was born in the miraculous "freedom" of a sterile mother, in old age and against the laws of nature, similar to our Saviour, Who was miraculously born of a Virgin. He climbed the hill of Moriah just as Jesus climbed Calvary, bearing on His shoulders the wood of sacrifice. An angel delivered Isaac from death, just as an angel rolled away the stone to show us that the tomb was empty, that the Risen One was no longer there. At the hour of prayer, Isaac met Rebecca in the plain and led her into the tent of his mother Sarah, just as Jesus shall meet His Church on the clouds in order to bring Her into the heavenly mansions, the New Jerusalem, the much-desired homeland.

No! We do not have the same God that non-Christians have! The *sine qua non* for knowing the Father, is the Son: *He that hath seen Me hath seen the Father; no man cometh unto the Father, but by Me* (John 14:6,9). Our God is a God Incarnate, *Whom we have seen with our eyes, and our hands have touched* (I John 1:1). The immaterial became material for our salvation, as St. John Damascene says, and He has *revealed* Himself in us. But when did He reveal Himself among the present-day Jews and Moslems, so that we might suppose that they know God? If they have a full understanding of God outside of Jesus Christ, then Christ was incarnate, died, and rose in vain!

According to Christ's words, they have not yet fully *come to the Father.* They have *conceptions* about the Father; but those conceptions do not contain the ultimate, supra-rational revelation of God given to mankind through Jesus Christ. For us Christians God is *inconceivable, incomprehensible, indescribable,* and *immaterial,* as St. Basil the Great says. For our salvation He became (to the extent that we are united to Him) conceived, described and material, by *revelation* in the Mystery of the Incarnation of His Son. *To Him be the glory unto the ages of ages. Amen.* And this is why St. Cyprian of Carthage affirms that he who does not have the Church for Mother, does not have God for Father!

May God preserve us from the apostasy and from the coming of antichrist, the preliminary signs of which are multiplying from day to day. May He preserve us from the great affliction which even the elect would not be able to bear without the Grace of Him Who will cut short these days. And may He preserve us in the "small flock," the "remainder according to the election of Grace," so that we like Abraham might rejoice at the Light of His Face, by the prayers of the Most Holy Mother of God and Ever-Virgin Mary, of all the heavenly hosts, the cloud of witnesses, prophets, martyrs, hierarchs, evangelists, and confessors who have been faithful unto death, who have shed their blood for Christ, who have begotten us by the Gospel of Jesus Christ in the waters of Baptism. We are their sons—weak, sinful, and unworthy, to be sure; but we will not stretch forth our hands toward a *strange god!* Amen.

Fr. Basile Sakkas
La Foi Transmise, April 5, 1970*

---

* For this fifth edition, some theological clarifications have been made in this chapter by the editors.

II

The Power of the Pagan Gods

HINDUISM'S ASSAULT UPON CHRISTIANITY

By a Convert to Orthodoxy

All the gods of the pagans are demons.
Psalm 95:5

The following article comes from the experience of a woman who, after attending high school in a Roman Catholic convent, practiced Hinduism for twenty years until finally, by God's grace, she was converted to the Orthodox Faith, finding the end of her search for truth in the Russian Orthodox Church. She currently resides on the West Coast. May her words serve to open the eyes of those Orthodox Christians who might be tempted to follow the blind "liberal" theologians who are now making their appearance even in the Orthodox Church, and whose answer to the assault of neo-paganism upon the Church of Christ is to conduct a "dialogue" with its wizards and join them in worshipping the very gods of the pagans.

7

1. The Attractions of Hinduism

I WAS just sixteen when two events set the course of my life. I came to Dominican Catholic Convent in San Rafael (California) and encountered Christianity for the first time. The same year I also encountered Hinduism in the person of a Hindu monk, a Swami, who was shortly to become my guru or teacher. A battle had begun, but I wasn't to understand this for nearly twenty years.

At the convent I was taught the basic truths of Christianity. Here lies the strength of the humble and a snare to the proud. St. James wrote truly: *God resisteth the proud, and giveth grace to the humble* (James 4:6). And how proud I was; I wouldn't accept original sin and I wouldn't accept hell. And I had many, many arguments against them. One Sister of great charity gave me the key when she said: "Pray for the gift of faith." But already the Swami's training had taken hold, and I thought it debasing to beg anyone, even God, for anything. But much later, I remembered what she had said. Years later the seed of Christian faith that had been planted in me emerged from an endless sea of despair.

In time the nature of the books that I brought back to school with me, all in plain covered wrappers, was discovered. Books like the *Bhagavad Gita*, the *Upanishads*, the *Vedantasara*, the *Ashtavakra Samhita....* In part my secret was out, but nothing much was said. No doubt the Sisters thought it would pass, as indeed most of the intellectual conceits of young girls do. But one bold nun told me the truth. It's a very unpopular truth and one that is rarely heard today. She said that I would go to hell if I died in Hinduism after knowing the truth of Christianity. St. Peter put it this way: *For by whom a man is overcome, of the same also he is the slave. For if, flying from the pollutions of the world, through the knowledge of our Lord and Saviour Jesus Christ, they be again entangled in them and overcome, their latter state is become unto them worse than the former. For it had been better for them not to have known the way of justice, than after they had known it, to turn back from that holy commandment which was delivered to them* (II Peter 2:19–21). How I despised that Sister for her bigotry. But if she were alive today I would thank her with all my heart. What she told me nagged, as truth will, and it was to lead me finally to the fullness of Holy Orthodoxy.

The important thing that I got at the convent was a measuring stick, and one day I would use it to discover Hinduism a fraud.

The situation has changed so much since I was in school. What was an isolated case of Hinduism has developed into an epidemic. Now one must have an intelligent understanding of Hindu dogmatics if one is to prevent young Christians from committing spiritual suicide when they encounter Eastern religions.

The appeal of Hinduism is full spectrum; there are blandishments for every faculty and appeals to every weakness, but particularly to pride. And being very proud, even at sixteen, it was to these that I first fell prey. Original sin, hell, and the problem of pain troubled me. I'd never taken them seriously before I came to the convent. Then, the Swami presented an "intellectually satisfying" alternative for every uncomfortable Christian dogma. Hell was, after all, only a temporary state of the soul brought on by our own bad karma (past actions) in this or in a former life. And, of course, a finite cause couldn't have an infinite effect. Original sin was marvelously transmuted into Original Divinity. This was my birthright, and nothing I could ever do would abrogate this glorious end. I was Divine. I was God: "the Infinite Dreamer, dreaming finite dreams."

As for the problem of pain, the Hindu philosophy known as Vedanta has a really elegant philosophical system to take care of it. In a nutshell, pain was maya or illusion. It had no real existence—and what's more, the Advaitin could claim to prove it!

In another area, Hinduism appeals to the very respectable error of assuming that man is perfectible: through education (in their terms, the guru system) and through "evolution" (the constant progressive development of man spiritually). An argument is also made from the standpoint of cultural relativity; this has now assumed such respectability that it's a veritable sin (with those who don't believe in sin) to challenge relativity of any sort. What could be more reasonable, they say, than different nations and peoples worshipping God differently? God, after all, is God, and the variety in modes of worship make for a general religious "enrichment."

But perhaps the most generally compelling attraction is pragmatism. The entire philosophical construct of Hinduism is buttressed by the practical religious instructions given to the disciple by his guru. With these practices the disciple is invited to verify the philosophy by his own experience. Nothing has to be accepted on faith. And contrary to popular notions, there aren't any mysteries—just a tremendous amount of esoteric material—so there simply is no need for faith. You are told: "Try it, and see if it works." This pragmatic approach is supremely tempting to the Western mind. It appears so very "scientific." But almost every student falls right into a kind of pragmatic fallacy: i.e., if the practices work (and they do in fact work), he believes that the system is true, and, implicitly, that it is good. This, of course, doesn't follow. All that can really be said is: if they work, then they work. But missing this point, you can understand how a little psychic experience gives the poor student a great deal of conviction.

This brings me to the last blandishment that I'll mention, which is "spiritual experiences." These are psychic and/or diabolic in origin. But who among the practitioners has any way of distinguishing delusion from true spiritual experience? They have no measuring stick. But don't think that what they see, hear, smell and touch in these experiences are the result of simple mental aberration. They aren't. They are what our Orthodox tradition calls *prelest.* It's an important word, because it refers to the exact condition of a person having Hindu "spiritual experiences." There is no precise equivalent to the term *prelest* in the English lexicon. It covers the whole range of false spiritual experiences: from simple illusion and beguilement to actual possession. In every case the counterfeit is taken as genuine and the overall effect is an accelerated growth of pride. A warm, comfortable sense of special importance settles over the person in *prelest,* and this compensates for all his austerities and pain.*

In his first Epistle, St. John warns the early Christians: *Dearly beloved, believe not every spirit, but try the spirits if they be of God....* (I John 4:1).

St. Gregory of Sinai was careful to instruct his monks on the dangers of these experiences: "All around, near to beginners and the self-willed, the demons are wont to spread the nets of thoughts and pernicious fantasies and prepare moats for their

---

* Further on *prelest,* see below, p. 143ff.

downfall...." A monk asked him: "What is a man to do when the demon takes the form of an angel of light?" The Saint replied: "In this case a man needs great power of discernment to discriminate rightly between good and evil. So in your heedlessness, do not be carried away too quickly by what you see, but be weighty (not easy to move) and, carefully testing everything, accept the good and reject the evil. Always you must test and examine, and only afterwards believe. Know that the actions of grace are manifest, and the demon, in spite of his transformations, cannot produce them: namely, meekness, friendliness, humility, hatred of the world, cutting off passions and lusts—which are the effects of grace. Works of the demons are: arrogance, conceit, intimidation and all evil. By such actions you will be able to discern whether the light shining in your heart is of God or of satan. Lettuce looks like mustard, and vinegar in color like wine; but when you taste them the palate discerns and defines the difference between each. In the same way the soul, if it has discernment, can discriminate by mental taste the gifts of the Holy Spirit from the fantasies and illusions of satan."

The misguided or proud spiritual aspirant is most vulnerable to *prelest*. And the success and durability of Hinduism depends very largely on this false mysticism. How very appealing it is to drug-using young people, who have already been initiated into these kinds of experiences. The last few years have seen the flowering and proliferating of Swamis. They saw their opportunity for fame and wealth in this ready-made market. And they took it.

12

2. A War of Dogma

Today Christianity is taking the thrusts of a foe that is all but invisible to the faithful. And if it can, it will pierce to the heart before declaring its name. The enemy is Hinduism, and the war being waged is a war of dogma.

When Vedanta Societies were founded in this country around the turn of the century, first efforts were directed to establishing that there *was no real difference* between Hinduism and Christianity. Not only was there no conflict, but a good Christian would be a better Christian by studying and practicing the Vedanta; he would understand the real Christianity.

In early lectures, the Swamis attempted to show that those ideas which seemed peculiar to Christianity—like the Logos and the Cross—really had their origin in India. And those ideas which seemed peculiar to Hinduism—like rebirth, transmigration of the soul and samadhi (or trance) were also to be found in Christian scripture—when it was properly interpreted.

This kind of bait caught many sincere but misguided Christians. The early push was *against* what might be called "sectarian" dogmas, and *for* a so-called scientific religion based on a comparative study of all religions. Primary stress was always on this: there is no such thing as difference. All is One. All differences are just on the surface; they are apparent or relative, not real. All this is clear from published lectures that were delivered in the early 1900s. Today we are in great danger because this effort was so very successful.

Now common parlance has "dogma" as a derisive term. But this scorn could not have originated with those who know that it refers to the most precious heritage of the Church. However, once the bad connotation became fixed, the timid, who never like to be associated with the unpopular, began to speak of "rigid dogma," which is redundant but bespeaks disapproval. So the attitude was insidiously absorbed from "broad-minded" critics who either didn't know that dogma states what Christianity is, or simply didn't like what Christianity is all about.

The resulting predisposition of many Christians to back down when faced with the accusation of holding to dogma has given the Hindus no small measure of help. An aid from within had strategic advantages.

The incredible fact is that few see that the very power that would overturn Christian dogma is itself nothing but an opposing system of dogmas. The two cannot blend or "enrich" each other because they are wholly antithetical.

If Christians are persuaded to throw out or (what is tactically more clever) to alter their dogmas to suit the demand for a more up-to-date or "universal" Christianity, they have lost everything, because what is valued by Christians and by Hindus is immediately derived from their dogmas. *And Hindu dogmas are a direct repudiation of Christian dogmas.* This leads us to a staggering conclusion: *What Christians believe to be evil, Hindus believe to be good,* and conversely: *What Hindus believe to be evil, Christians believe to be good.*

The real struggle lies in this: that the ultimate sin for the Christian, is the ultimate realization of good for the Hindu. Christians have always acknowledged *pride* as the basic sin—the fountainhead of all sin. And Lucifer is the archetype when he says: *I will ascend into heaven, I will exalt my throne above the stars of God … I will ascend above the height of the clouds; I will be like the Most High* (Is 14:13–14). On a lower level, it is pride that turns even man's virtues into sins. But for the Hindu in general, and the Advaitin or Vedantan in particu-

14

lar, the only "sin" is not to believe in yourself and in Humanity as God Himself. In the words of Swami Vivekananda (who was the foremost modern advocate of Vedanta): "You do not yet understand India! We Indians are Man-worshipers after all. Our God is Man!" The doctrine of mukti or salvation consists in this: that "Man is to become Divine by realizing the Divine."

From this one can see the dogmas of Hinduism and Christianity standing face to face, each defying the other on the nature of God, the nature of man and the purpose of human existence.

But when Christians accept the Hindu propaganda that there is no battle going on, that the differences between Christianity and Hinduism are only apparent and not real—then Hindu ideas are free to take over the souls of Christians, winning the battle without a struggle. And the end result of this battle is truly shocking; the corrupting power of Hinduism is immense. In my own case, with all of the basically sound training that I received at the convent, twenty years in Hinduism brought me to the very doors of the love of evil. You see, in India "God" is also worshipped as Evil, in the form of the goddess Kali. But about this I will speak in the next section, on Hindu practices.

This is the end in store when there is no more Christian dogma. I say this from personal experience, because I have worshipped Kali in India and in this country. And she who is satan is no joke. *If you give up on the Living God, the throne is not going to remain empty.*

3. Hindu Places and Practices

In 1956 I did field work with headhunters in the Philippines. My interest was in primitive religion—particularly in what is termed an "unacculturated" area—where there had been few missionaries. When I arrived in Ifugao (that's the name of the tribe), I didn't believe in black magic; when I left, I did. An Ifugao priest (a munbaki) named Talupa became my best friend and informant. In time I learned that he was famous for his skill in the black art. He took me to the baki, which is a ceremony of ritualistic magic that occurred almost every night during the harvest season. A dozen or so priests gathered in a hut and the night was spent invoking deities and ancestors, drinking rice wine and making sacrifices to the two small images known as bulol. They were washed in chicken blood, which had been caught in a dish and used to divine the future before it was used on the images. They studied the blood for the size and number of bubbles in it, the time it took to coagulate; also, the color and configuration of the chicken's organs gave them information. Each night I dutifully took notes. But this was just the beginning. I won't elaborate on Ifugao magic; suffice it to say that by the time I left, I had seen such a variety and quantity of supernatural occurrences that any scientific explanation was virtually impossible. If I had been predisposed to believe anything when I arrived, it was that magic had a wholly natural explanation. Also, let me say that I don't frighten very easily. But the fact is that I left Ifugao because I saw that their rituals not only worked, but they had worked on me—at least twice.

I say all this so that what I say about Hindu practices and places of worship will not seem incredible, the product of a "heated brain."

Eleven years after the Ifugao episode, I made a pilgrimage to the Cave of Amarnath, deep in the Himalayas. Hindu tradition has it as the most sacred place of Siva worship, the place where he manifests himself to his devotees and grants boons. It is a long and difficult journey over the Mahaguna, a 14,000 foot pass, and across a glacier; so there was plenty of time to worship him mentally on the way, especially since the boy who led the pack pony didn't speak any English, and I didn't speak any Hindi. This time I was predisposed to believe that the god whom I had worshipped and meditated on for years would graciously manifest himself to me.

The Siva image in the cave is itself a curiosity: an ice image formed by dripping water. It waxes and wanes with the moon. When it is full moon, the natural image reaches the ceiling of the cave—about fifteen feet—and by the dark of the moon almost nothing of it remains. And so it waxes and wanes each month. To my knowledge, no one has explained this phenomenon. I approached the cave at an auspicious time, when the image had waxed full. I was soon to worship my god with green coconut, incense, red and white pieces of cloth, nuts, raisins and sugar—all the ritually prescribed items. I entered the cave with tears of devotion. What happened then is hard to describe. The place was vibrant—just like an Ifugao hut with baki in full swing. Stunned to find it a place of inexplicable wrongness, I left retching before the priest could finish making my offering to the great ice image.

The facade of Hinduism had cracked when I entered the Siva Cave, but it was still some time before I broke free. During the interim, I searched for something to support the collapsing edifice, but I found nothing. In retrospect, it seems to me that we often know something is really bad, long before we can really believe it. This applies to Hindu "spiritual practices" quite as much as it does to the so-called "holy places."

When a student is initiated by the guru, he is given a Sanskrit mantra (a personal magic formula), and specific religious practices. These are entirely esoteric and exist in the oral tradition. You won't find them in print and you are very unlikely to learn about them from an initiate, because of the strong negative sanctions which are enforced to protect this secrecy. In effect the guru invites his disciple to prove the philosophy by his own experience. The point is, these practices do in fact work. The student may get powers or "siddhis." These are things like reading minds, power to heal or destroy, to produce objects, to tell the future and so on—the whole gamut of deadly psychic parlor tricks. But far worse than this, he invariably falls into a state of *prelest,* where he takes delusion for reality. He has "spiritual experiences" of unbounded sweetness and peace. He has visions of deities and of light. (One might recall that Lucifer himself can appear as an angel of light.) By "delusion" I don't mean that he doesn't really experience these things; I mean rather that they are not from God. There is, of course, the philosophical construct that supports every experience, so the practices and the philosophy sustain each other and the system becomes very tight.

Actually, Hinduism is not so much an intellectual pursuit as a system of practices, and these are quite literally—black magic. That is, if you do x, you get y: a simple contract. But the terms are not spelled out and rarely does a student ask where the experiences originate or who is extending him credit—in the form of powers and "beautiful" experiences. It's the classical Faustian situation, but what the practitioner doesn't know is that *the price may well be his immortal soul.*

There's a vast array of practices—practices to suit every temperament. The chosen deity may be with form: a god or goddess; or formless: the Absolute Brahman. The relationship to the chosen Ideal also varies—it may be that of a child, mother, father, friend, beloved, servant or, in the case of Advaita Vedanta, the "relationship" is identity. At the time of initiation the guru gives his disciple a mantra, and this determines the path he will follow and the practices he will take up. The guru also dictates how the disciple will live his everyday life. In the Vedanta (or monistic system) single disciples are not to marry; all their powers are to be directed towards success in the practices. Nor is a sincere disciple a meat eater, because meat blunts the keen edge of perception. The guru is literally regarded as God Himself—he is the disciple's Redeemer.

At base, the many "spiritual" exercises derive from only a few root practices. I'll just skim over them.

First, there's idolatry. It may be the worship of an image or a picture, with offerings of light, camphor, incense, water and sweets. The image may be fanned with a yak tail, bathed, dressed and put to bed. This sounds very childish, but it is prudent not to underestimate the psychic experiences which they can elicit. Vedantic idolatry takes the form of self-worship—either mentally or externally, with all the ritualistic props. A common aphoristic saying in India epitomizes this self-worship. It is *So Ham, So Ham,* or "I am He, I am He."

Then there's Japa, or the repetition of the Sanskrit mantra given to the disciple at his initiation. In effect, it's the chanting of a magic formula.

Pranayama consists in breathing exercises used in conjunction with Japa. There are other practices which are peculiar to the Tantra or worship of God as Mother, the female principle, power, energy, the principle of evolution and action. They're referred to as the five Ms. They're overtly evil and rather sick-making, so I won't describe them. But they, too, have found their way to this country. Swami Vivekananda prescribed this brand of Hinduism along with the Vedanta. He said: "I worship the Terrible! It is a mistake to hold that with all men pleasure is the motive. Quite as many are born to seek after pain. Let us worship the Terror for Its own sake. How few have dared to worship Death, or Kali! Let us worship Death!" Again, the Swami's words on the goddess Kali: "There are some who scoff at the existence of Kali. Yet today She is out there amongst the people. They are frantic with fear, and the soldiery have been called to deal out death. Who can say that God does not manifest Himself as evil as well as Good? But only the Hindu dares worship Him as Evil."*

The great pity is that this one-pointed practice of evil is carried on in the firm conviction that it's good. And the salvation that is vainly sought through arduous self-effort in Hinduism can only be wrought by God through Christian self-effacement.

---

* *Editor's note:* Few, even of those most desirous of entering into "dialogue" with Eastern religions and of expressing their basic religious unity with them, have any precise conception of the pagan religious practices and beliefs from whose tyranny the blessed and light yoke of Christ has liberated mankind. The goddess Kali, one of the most popular of Hindu deities, is most commonly depicted in the midst of a riot of blood and carnage, skulls and severed heads hanging from her neck, her tongue grotesquely protruding from her mouth thirsting for more blood; she is appeased in Hindu temples by bloody offerings of goats. (Swami Vivekananda justifies this: "Why not a little blood to complete the picture?") Of her, Swami Vivekananda, as recorded by his disciple 'Sister Nivedita,' said further: "I believe that she guides me in every little thing that I do, and does with me what she will," and at every step he was conscious of her presence as if she were a person in the room with him. He invoked her: "Come, O mother, come! For Terror is thy name;" and it was his religious ideal "to become one with the Terrible forevermore." Is this, as Metropolitan Georges Khodre tries to persuade us, to be accepted as an example of the "authentic spiritual life of the unbaptized," a part of the spiritual "riches" which we are to take from the non-Christian religions? Or is it not rather a proof of the Psalmist's words: *The gods of the pagans are demons?*

4. Evangelizing the West

In 1893 an unknown Hindu monk arrived at the Parliament of Religions in Chicago. He was Swami Vivekananda, whom I have mentioned already. He made a stunning impression on those who heard him, both by his appearance—beturbaned and robed in orange and crimson—and by what he said. He was immediately lionized by high society in Boston and New York. Philosophers at Harvard were mightily impressed. And it wasn't long until he had gathered a hard core of disciples who supported him and his grandiose dream: the evangelizing of the Western world by Hinduism, and more particularly, by Vedantic (or monistic) Hinduism. Vedanta Societies were established in the large cities of this country and in Europe. But these centers were only a part of his work. More important was *introducing Vedantic ideas into the bloodstream of academic thinking.* Dissemination was the goal. It mattered little to Vivekananda whether credit was given to Hinduism or not, so long as the message of Vedanta reached everyone. On many occasions he said: Knock on every door. Tell everyone he is Divine.

Today parts of his message are carried in paperbacks that you can find in any bookstore—books by Aldous Huxley, Christopher Isherwood, Somerset Maugham, Teilhard de Chardin, and even Thomas Merton.

Thomas Merton, of course, constitutes a special threat to Christians, because he presents himself as a contemplative Christian monk, and his work has already affected the vitals of Roman Catholicism, its monasticism. Shortly before his death, Father Merton wrote an appreciative introduction to a new translation of the *Bhagavad Gita,* which is the spiritual manual or "Bible" of all Hindus, and one of the foundation blocks of monism or Advaita Vedanta. The *Gita,* it must be remembered, opposes almost every important teaching of Christianity. His book on the *Zen Masters,* published posthumously, is also noteworthy, because the entire work is based on a treacherous mistake: the assumption that all the so-called "mystical experiences" in every religion are true. He should have known better. The warnings against this are loud and clear, both in Holy Scripture and in the Holy Fathers.

Today I know of one Catholic monastery in California where cloistered monks are experimenting with Hindu religious practices. They were trained by an Indian who became a Catholic priest. Unless the ground had been prepared, I think this sort of thing couldn't be happening. But, after all, this was the purpose of Vivekananda's coming to the West: to prepare the ground.

Vivekananda's message of Vedanta is simple enough. It looks like more than it is because of its trappings: some dazzling Sanskrit jargon, and a very intricate philosophical structure. The message is essentially this: All religions are true, but Vedanta is the ultimate truth. Differences are only a matter of "levels of truth." In Vivekananda's words: "Man is not travelling from error to truth, but climbing up from truth to truth, from truth that is lower to truth that is higher. The matter of today is the spirit of the future. The worm of today—the God of tomorrow." The Vedanta rests on this: that man is God. So it is for man to work out his own salvation. Vivekananda put it this way: "Who can help the Infinite? Even the hand that comes to you through the darkness will have to be your own."

Vivekananda was canny enough to know that straight Vedanta would be too much for Christians to follow, right off the bat. But "levels of truth" provided a nice bridge to perfect ecumenism—where there is no conflict because everyone is right. In the Swami's words: "If one religion be true, then all the others also must be true. Thus the Hindu faith is yours as much as mine. We Hindus do not merely tolerate, we unite ourselves with every religion, praying in the mosque of the Mohammedan, worshipping before the fire of the Zoroastrian, and kneeling to the Cross of the Christian. We know that all religions alike, from the lowest fetishism to the highest absolutism, are but so many attempts of the human soul to grasp and realize the Infinite. So we gather all these flowers and, binding them together with the cords of love, make them into a wonderful bouquet of worship."

Still, all religions were only steps to the ultimate religion, which was Advaita Vedanta. He had a special contempt for Christianity, which at best was a "low truth"—a dualistic truth. In private conversation he said that only a coward would turn the other cheek. But whatever he said about other religions, he always returned to the necessity of Advaita Vedanta. "Art, science, and religion," he said, "are but three different ways of expressing a single truth. But in order to understand this we must have the theory of Advaita."

The appeal to today's youth is unmistakable. Vedanta declares the perfect freedom of every soul to be itself. It denies all distinction between sacred and secular: they are only different ways of expressing the single truth. And the sole purpose of religion is to provide for the needs of different temperaments: a god and a practice to suit everyone. In a word, religion is "doing your own thing."

All this may sound far-fetched, but Vivekananda did an effective job. Now I'll show how successful he was in introducing these Hindu ideas into Roman Catholicism, where his success has been the most striking.

Swami Vivekananda first came to America to represent Hinduism at the 1893 Parliament of Religions. 1968 was the 75th anniversary of this event, and at that time a Symposium of Religions was held under the auspices of the Vivekananda Vedanta Society of Chicago. Roman Catholicism was represented by a Dominican theologian from De Paul University, Father Robert Campbell. Swami Bhashyananda opened the meeting with the reading of good-will messages from three very important people. The second was from an American Cardinal.

Father Campbell began the afternoon session with a talk on the conflict of the traditionalist versus the modernist in modern Catholicism. He said: "In my own university, surveys taken of Catholic student attitudes show a great swing towards the liberal views within the last five or six years. I know that the great Swami Vivekananda would himself be in favor of most of the trends in the direction of liberal Christianity." What Father Campbell apparently didn't know was that the modernistic doctrines he described were *not Christian at all;* they were pure and simple Vedanta.

So there will be no question of misinterpretation, I shall quote the Father's words on the modernists' interpretation of five issues, just as they appeared in three international journals: the *Prabuddha Bharata* published in Calcutta, the *Vedanta Kesheri* published in Madras, and *Vedanta and the West,* published in London.

On doctrines: "Truth is a relative thing, these doctrines and dogmas (i.e., the nature of God, how man should live, and the after-life) are not fixed things, they change, and we are coming to the point where we deny some things that we formerly affirmed as sacred truths."

On God: "Jesus is divine, true, but any one of us can be divine. As a matter of fact, on many points, I think you will find the liberal Christian outlook is moving in the direction of the East in much of its philosophy—both in its concept of an impersonal God and in the concept that we are all divine."

On Original Sin: "This concept is very offensive to liberal Christianity, which holds that man is perfectible by training and proper education."

On the world: "… The liberal affirms that it can be improved and that we should devote ourselves to building a more humane society instead of pining to go to heaven."

On other religions: "The liberal group says: 'Don't worry about the old-fashioned things such as seeking converts, etc., but let us develop better relations with other religions.'"

So says Father Campbell for the modernistic Catholics. The modernist has been led like a child by the generous offer of higher truth, deeper philosophy and greater sublimity—which can be had by merely *subordinating the living Christ to modern man.*

Here, then, we see the spectacular success of Hinduism, or Swami Vivekananda, or the power behind Vivekananda. It's made a clean sweep of Roman Catholicism. Her watchdogs have taken the thief as the friend of the master, and the house is made desolate before their eyes. The thief said: "Let us have interfaith understanding," and he was through the gate. And the expedient was so simple. The Christian Hindus (the Swamis) had only to recite the *Vedanta philosophy using Christian terms.* But the Hindu Christians (the modernist Catholics), had to extrapolate their religion to include Hinduism. Then necessarily, truth became error, and error, truth. Alas, some would now drag the Orthodox Church into this desolate house. But let the modernists remember the words of Isaiah: *Woe unto them that call evil good and good evil; that put darkness for light, and light for darkness; that put bitter for sweet and sweet for bitter! Woe unto them that are wise in their own eyes, and prudent in their own sight!* (Is. 5:20–21).

5. *The Goal of Hinduism: The Universal Religion*

I was amazed to see the inroads that Hinduism had made during my absence from Christianity. It may seem odd that I discovered these changes all at once. This was because my guru held dominion over my every action, and all this time I was, quite literally, "cloistered," even in the world. The Swami's severe injunctions kept me from reading any Christian books or speaking with Christians. For all their pretentious talk that all religions are true, the Swamis know that Christ is their nemesis. So for twenty years I was totally immersed in the study of oriental philosophy and in the practice of its disciplines. I was ordered by my guru to get a degree in philosophy and anthropology, but these were only avocations that filled time between the important parts of my life: time with Swami and time with the teachings and practices of Vedanta.

Swami Vivekananda's mission has been fulfilled in many particulars, but one piece is yet to be accomplished. This is the establishing of a Universal Religion. In this rests the ultimate victory of the Devil. Because the Universal Religion may not contain any "individualistic, sectarian" ideas, it will have nothing in common with Christianity, except in its semantics. The World and the Flesh may be fires in the stove and the chimney, but the Universal Religion will be a total conflagration of Christianity. The point of all this is that the Jesuit priest Teilhard de Chardin has already laid the foundation for a "New Christianity," and *it is precisely to Swami Vivekananda's specifications for this Universal Religion.*

Teilhard de Chardin is an anomaly because, unlike traditional Roman theologians, he is highly appreciated by scholarly clergy who, in charity, I believe don't have any idea what he is talking about, because Teilhard's ideas are to a great extent plagiarisms from Vedanta and Tantra gummed together with Christian-sounding jargon and heavily painted with evolutionism.

Let me quote one example from him: "The world I live in becomes divine. Yet these flames do not consume me, nor do these waters dissolve me; for, unlike the false forms of monism that impel us through passivity towards unconsciousness, the pan-Christianism I am finding places union at the term of an arduous process of differentiation. I shall attain the spirit only by releasing completely and exhaustively all the powers of matter.... I recognize that, following the example of the incarnate God revealed to me by the Catholic faith, I can be saved only by becoming one with the universe." This is outright Hinduism. It has a little bit of everything in it—a recognizable verse from an Upanishad and pieces from several of the philosophical systems along with their practices.

In a press conference given by Father Arrupe, General of the Society of Jesus, in June of 1965, Teilhard de Chardin was defended on the grounds that "he was not a professional theologian and philosopher, so that it was possible for him to be unaware of all the philosophical and theological implications attached to some of his intuitions." Then Father Arrupe praised him: "Pere Teilhard is one of the great masters of contemporary thought, and his success is not to be wondered at. He carried through, in fact, a great attempt to reconcile the world of science with the world of faith." The upshot of this reconciliation is a new religion. And in Teilhard's words: "The new religion will be exactly the same as our old Christianity but with a new life drawn from the legitimate evolution of its dogmas as they come in contact with new ideas." With this bit of background let us look at Vivekananda's Universal Religion and Teilhard's "New Christianity."

The Universal Religion as proposed by Vivekananda must have five characteristics. First, it must be scientific. It will be built on spiritual laws. Hence, it will be a true and scientific religion. In effect, both Vivekananda and Teilhard use theoretical scientism as an article of their faith.

Second, its foundation is evolution. In Teilhard's words: "A hitherto unknown form of religion—one that no one could yet have imagined or described, for lack of a universe large enough and organic enough to contain it—is burgeoning in men's hearts, from a seed sown by the idea of evolution." And again: "Original sin ... binds us hand and foot and drains the blood from us" because "as it is now expressed, it represents a survival of static concepts that are an anachronism in our evolutionist system of thought." Such a pseudo-religious concept of "evolution," which was consciously rejected by Christian thought, has been basic to Hindu thought for millennia; every Hindu religious practice assumes it.*

Third, the Universal Religion will not be built around any particular personality, but will be founded on "eternal principles." Teilhard is well on his way towards the impersonal God when he writes: "Christ is becoming more and more indispensable to me ... but at the same time the figure of the

---

* *Editor's note to the fifth edition:* For an exposition of Vivekananda's evolutionary views, see "Swami Vivekananda on Darwin, Evolution, and the Perfect Man," *What Is Enlightenment?* Spring/Summer 2002, pp. 58–63, 150–51. The guru Sri Aurobindo (1872–1950) was another major proponent of modern evolutionism according to Hindu metaphysics; see his book *The Life Divine,* Lotus Press, Twin Lakes, Wisconsin, 1985.

historical Christ is becoming less and less substantial and distinct to me." "… My view of him is continually carrying me further and higher along the axis of (I hope!) orthodoxy." Sad to say, this non-historical "Christ" spirit is Hindu orthodoxy, not Christian.

Fourth, the main purpose of the Universal Religion will be to satisfy the spiritual needs of men and women of diverse types. Individualistic, sectarian religions cannot offer this. Teilhard believed that Christianity did not fit everybody's religious aspirations. He records his discontent in these words: "Christianity is still to some extent a refuge, but it does not embrace, or satisfy or even lead the 'modern soul' any longer."

Fifth and final, within the Universal Religion (or New Christianity) we are all wending our way to the same destination. For Teilhard de Chardin it is the Omega Point, which belongs to something that is beyond representation. For Vivekananda it is the Om, the sacred syllable of the Hindus: "All humanity, converging at the foot of that sacred place where is set the symbol that is no symbol, the name that is beyond all sound."

Where will it end, this deformation of Christianity and triumph of Hinduism? Will we have the Om, or will we have the Omega?

III

A Fakir's "Miracle"

AND THE PRAYER OF JESUS

By Archimandrite Nicholas Drobyazgin

The author of this testimony, a new martyr of the Communist Yoke, enjoyed a brilliant worldly career as a naval commander, being also deeply involved in occultism as editor of the occult journal Rebus. *Being saved from almost certain death at sea by a miracle of St. Seraphim, he made a pilgrimage to Sarov and then renounced his worldly career and occult ties to become a monk. After being ordained priest, he served as a missionary in China, India and Tibet, as the priest of various embassy churches, and as abbot of several monasteries. After 1914 he lived at the Kiev Caves Lavra, where he discoursed to the young people who visited him concerning the influence of occultism on contemporary events in Russia. In the autumn of 1924, one month after he had been visited by a certain Tuholx, the author of the book* Black Magic, *he was murdered in his cell "by persons unknown," with obvious Bolshevik connivance, stabbed by a dagger with a special handle apparently of occult significance.*

The incident here described, revealing the nature of one of the mediumistic "gifts" which are common in Eastern religions,

The Fakir's "Miracle"

took place not long before 1900, and was recorded about 1922 by Dr. A.P. Timofievich, lately of Novo-Diveyevo Convent, New York. (Russian text in Orthodox Life, *1956, no. 1.)*

O N A WONDROUS early tropical morning our ship was cleaving the waters of the Indian Ocean, nearing the island of Ceylon [now Sri Lanka—ed.]. The lively faces of the passengers, for the most part Englishmen with their families who were travelling to their posts or on business in their Indian colony, looked avidly in the distance, seeking out with their eyes the enchanted isle, which for practically all of them had been bound up since childhood with so much that was interesting and mysterious in the tales and descriptions of travellers.

The island was still scarcely visible when already a fine, intoxicating fragrance from the trees growing on it more and more enveloped the ship with each passing breeze. Finally a kind of blue cloud lay on the horizon, ever increasing in size as the ship speedily approached. Already one could notice the buildings spread out along the shore, buried in the verdure of majestic palms, and the many-colored crowd of the local inhabitants who were awaiting the ship's arrival. The passengers, who had quickly become acquainted with each other on the trip, were laughing and conversing animatedly with each other on the deck, admiring the wondrous scene of the fairy-tale isle as it unfolded before their eyes. The ship swung slowly around, preparing to moor at the dock of the port city of Colombo.

Here the ship stopped to take on coal, and the passengers had sufficient time to go ashore. The day was so hot that many passengers decided not to leave the ship until evening, when a pleasant coolness replaced the heat of the day. A small group of eight people, to which I joined myself, was led by Colonel

Elliott, who had been in Colombo before and knew the city and its environs well. He made an alluring proposition. "Ladies and gentlemen! Wouldn't you like to go a few miles out of town and pay a visit to one of the local magician-fakirs? Perhaps we shall see something interesting." All accepted the colonel's proposition with enthusiasm.

It was already evening when we left behind the noisy streets of the city and rolled along a marvelous jungle road which was twinkling with the sparks of millions of fireflies. Finally, the road suddenly widened and in front of us there was a small clearing surrounded on all sides by jungle. At the edge of the clearing under a big tree there was a kind of hut, next to which a small bonfire was smoldering and a thin, emaciated old man with a turban on his head sat cross-legged and with his unmoving gaze directed at the fire. Despite our noisy arrival, the old man continued to sit completely immovable, not paying us the slightest attention. Somewhere from out of the darkness a youth appeared and, going up to the colonel, quietly asked him something. In a short while he brought out several stools and our group arranged itself in a semi-circle not far from the bonfire. A light and fragrant smoke arose. The old man sat in the same pose, apparently noticing no one and nothing. The half-moon which arose dispelled to some extent the darkness of the night, and in its ghostly light all objects took on fantastic outlines. Involuntarily everyone became quiet and waited to see what would happen.

"Look! Look there, on the tree!" Miss Mary cried in an excited whisper. We all turned our heads in the direction indicated. And indeed, the whole surface of the immense crown of the tree under which the fakir was sitting was as it were gently flowing in the soft illumination of the moon, and the tree itself began gradually to melt and lose its contours;

literally, some unseen hand had thrown over it an airy covering which became more and more concentrated with every moment. Soon the undulating surface of the sea presented itself with complete clarity before our astonished gaze. With a light rumble one wave followed another, making foaming white-caps; light clouds were floating in a sky which had become blue. Stunned, we could not tear ourselves away from this striking picture.

And then in the distance there appeared a white ship. Thick smoke poured out of its two large smokestacks. It quickly approached us, cleaving the water. To our great amazement we recognized it as our own ship, the one on which we had come to Colombo! A whisper passed through our ranks when we read on the stern, traced out in gold letters, the name of our ship, *Luisa.* But what astounded us most of all was what we saw on the ship—ourselves! Don't forget that at the time when all this happened cinematography hadn't even been thought of and it was impossible even to conceive of something like this. Each of us saw ourselves on the ship's deck amongst people who were laughing and talking to each other. But what was especially astonishing: I saw not only myself, but at the same time the whole deck of the ship down to the smallest details, as if in a bird's-eye view—which of course simply could not be in actuality. At one and the same time I saw myself among the passengers, and the sailors working at the other end of the ship, and the captain in his cabin, and even our monkey "Nelly," a favorite of all, eating bananas on the main mast. All my companions at the same time, each in his own way, were greatly excited at what they were seeing, expressing their emotions with soft cries and excited whispers.

I had completely forgotten that I was a priest-monk and, it would seem, had no business at all participating in such a spectacle. The spell was so powerful that both the mind and the heart were silent. My heart began to beat painfully in alarm. Suddenly I was beside myself. A fear took hold of my whole being.

My lips began to move and say: "Lord Jesus Christ, Son of God, have mercy on me, a sinner!" Immediately I felt relieved. It was just as if some mysterious chains which had bound me began to fall away. The prayer became more concentrated, and with it my peace of soul returned. I continued to look at the tree, and suddenly, as if pursued by the wind, the picture became clouded and was dispersed. I saw nothing more except the big tree, illuminated by the light of the moon, and likewise the fakir sitting in silence by the bonfire, while my companions continued to express what they were experiencing while gazing at the picture, which for them had not been broken off.

But then something apparently happened to the fakir also. He reeled to the side. The youth ran up to him in alarm. The séance was suddenly broken up.

Deeply moved by everything they had experienced, the spectators stood up, animatedly sharing their impressions and not understanding at all why the whole thing had been cut off so sharply and unexpectedly. The youth explained it as owing to the exhaustion of the fakir, who was sitting as before, his head down, and paying not the slightest attention to those present.

Having generously rewarded the fakir through the youth for the opportunity to be participants of such an astonishing spectacle, our group quickly got together for the trip back. While starting out, I involuntarily turned back once more in order to imprint in my memory the whole scene, and suddenly—I shuddered from an unpleasant feeling. My gaze met the gaze of the fakir, which was full of hatred. It was but for a single instant, and then he again assumed his habitual position; but this glance once and for all opened my eyes to the realization of *whose* power it was that had produced this "miracle."

Eastern "spirituality" is by no means limited to such mediumistic "tricks" as this fakir practiced; we shall see some of its more sincere aspects in the next chapter. Still, all the power *that is given to the practitioners of Eastern religions comes from the same phenomenon of mediumism, whose central characteristic is a passiveness before "spiritual" reality that enables one to enter into contact with the "gods" of the non-Christian religions. This phenomenon may be seen in Eastern "meditation" (even when it may be given the name of "Christian"), and perhaps even in those strange "gifts" which in our days of spiritual decline are mislabeled "charismatic"...*

IV

Eastern Meditation Invades Christianity

A S AN ANSWER to the question of the possibility of a "dialogue" of Orthodox Christianity with the various non-Christian religions, the reader has been presented the testimony of three Orthodox Christians who confirm, on the basis of Orthodox doctrine and their own experience, what the Orthodox Church has always taught: that Orthodox Christians do not at all have the "same God" as the so-called "monotheists" who deny the Holy Trinity; that the gods of the pagans are in fact demons; and that the experiences and powers which the pagan "gods" can and do provide are satanic in nature. All this in no way contradicts the words of St. Peter, that *God is no respecter of persons: but in every nation he that feareth Him and worketh righteousness is acceptable to Him* (Acts 10:34–35); or the words of St. Paul, that *God in times past suffered all nations to walk in their own ways. Nevertheless He left not Himself without witness, in that He did good, and gave us rain from heaven, and fruitful seasons, filling our hearts with food and gladness* (Acts 14:17). Those who live in the bondage of satan, the *prince of this world* (John 12:31), in darkness which is unenlightened by the Christian Gospel—are judged in the light of that natural testimony of God which every man may have, despite this bondage.

For the Christian, however, who has been given God's Revelation, no "dialogue" is possible with those outside the Faith. *Be ye not unequally yoked with unbelievers: for what fellowship hath righteousness with unrighteousness? and what communion hath light with darkness? and what concord hath Christ with Belial? or what part hath he that believeth with an infidel?... Wherefore come out from among them, and be ye separate, saith the Lord* (II Cor. 6:14–17). The Christian calling is rather to bring the light of Orthodox Christianity to them, even as St. Peter did to the God-fearing household of Cornelius the Centurion (Acts 10:34–48), in order to enlighten their darkness and join them to the chosen flock of Christ's Church.

All of this is obvious enough to Orthodox Christians who are aware of and faithful to the Truth of God's Revelation in the Church of Christ. But many who consider themselves Christians have very little awareness of the radical difference between Christianity and all other religions; and some who may have this awareness have very little discernment in the area of "spiritual experiences"—a discernment that has been practiced and handed down in Orthodox Patristic writings and Lives of Saints for nearly 2,000 years.

In the absence of such awareness and discernment, the increasing presence of Eastern religious movements in the West, especially in the past decade or two, has caused great confusion in the minds of many would-be Christians. The case of Thomas Merton comes immediately to mind: a sincere convert to Roman Catholicism and Catholic monasticism some forty years ago (long before the radical reforms of Vatican II), he ended his days proclaiming the equality of Christian religious experiences and the experience of Zen Buddhism and other pagan religions. Something has "entered the air" in these past two decades or so that has eroded whatever remained of a sound Christian outlook in Protestantism and Roman Catholicism and now is attacking the Church itself, Holy Orthodoxy. The "dialogue with non-Christian religions" is a result rather than a cause of this new "spirit."

In this chapter we shall examine some of the Eastern religious movements which have been influential in the 1970s, with special emphasis on the attempts to develop a syncretism of Christianity and Eastern religions, particularly in the realm of "spiritual practices." Such attempts more often than not cite the *Philokalia* and the Eastern Orthodox tradition of contemplative prayer as being more akin to Eastern spiritual practices than anything that exists in the West; it is time enough, then, to point out clearly the great abyss that exists between Christian and non-Christian "spiritual experience," and why the religious philosophy that underlies this new syncretism is false and dangerous.

1. "Christian Yoga"

Hindu Yoga has been known in the West for many decades, and especially in America it has given rise to innumerable cults and also to a popular form of physical therapy which is supposedly non-religious in its aims. Nearly twenty years ago a French Benedictine monk wrote of his experiences in making Yoga a "Christian" discipline; the description that follows is taken from his book.*

---

* J. M. Dechanet, *Christian Yoga,* Harper & Row, New York, 1972; first English translation, 1960.

Hindu Yoga is a discipline that presupposes a rather abstemious, disciplined life, and is composed of breath control and certain physical postures which produce a state of relaxation in which one meditates, usually with the help of a mantra or sacred utterance which aids concentration. The essence of Yoga is not the discipline itself, but the meditation which is its end. The author is correct when he writes: "The aims of Hindu Yoga are spiritual. It is tantamount to treason to forget this and retain only the purely physical side of this ancient discipline, to see in it no more than a means towards bodily health or beauty" (p. 54). To this it should be added that the person who uses Yoga only for physical well-being is already disposing himself towards certain spiritual attitudes and even experiences of which he is undoubtedly unaware; of this more will be said below.

The same author then continues: "The art of the yogi is to establish himself in a complete silence, to empty himself of all thoughts and illusions, to discard and forget everything but this one idea: man's true self is divine; it is God, and the rest is silence" (p. 63).

This idea, of course, is not Christian but pagan, but the aim of "Christian Yoga" is to use the technique of Yoga for a different spiritual end, for a "Christian" meditation. The object of the Yoga technique, in this view, is to make one relaxed, content, unthinking, and passive or receptive to spiritual ideas and experiences. "As soon as you have taken up the posture, you will feel your body relaxing and a feeling of general well-being will establish itself in you" (p. 158). The exercises produce an "extraordinary sense of calm" (p. 6). "To begin with, one gets the feeling of a general unwinding, of a well-being taking hold, of a euphoria that will, and in fact does, last. If one's nerves have been tense and overstrung, the exercises calm them, and fatigue disappears in a little time" (p. 49). "The goal of all his [the yogi's] efforts is to silence the thinking self in him by shutting his eyes to every kind of enticement" (p. 55). The euphoria which Yoga brings "could well be called a 'state of health' that allows us to do more and do it better on the human plane to begin with, and on the Christian religious, spiritual plane afterwards. The most apt word to describe it is contentedness, a contentedness that inhabits body and soul and predisposes us ... toward the spiritual life" (p. 31). One's whole personality can be changed by it: "Hatha Yoga influences character to the good. One man, after some weeks of practice, admits he no longer knows himself, and everyone notices a change in his bearing and reaction. He is gentler and more understanding. He faces experience calmly. He is content.... His whole personality has been altered and he himself feels it steadying and opening out; from this there arises an almost permanent condition of euphoria, of 'contentedness'" (p. 50).

But all of this is only a preparation for a "spiritual" aim, which begins to make itself felt in a very short time: "By becoming contemplative in a matter of weeks, my prayer had been given a particular and novel cast" (p. 7). Becoming extraordinarily calm, the author notices "the ease I felt in entering into prayer, in concentrating on a subject" (p. 6). One becomes "more receptive to impulses and promptings from heaven" (p. 13). "The practice of Yoga makes for increased suppleness and receptivity, and thus for openness to those personal exchanges between God and the soul that mark the way of the mystical life" (p. 31). Even for the "apprentice yogi" prayer becomes "sweet" and "embraces the whole of man" (p. 183). One is relaxed and "ready to tremble at the touch of the Holy Ghost, to receive and welcome what God in his Goodness thinks fit to let us experience" (p. 71). "We shall be making our being ready to be taken, to be seized—and this is surely one of the forms, in fact the highest of Christian contemplation" (p. 72). "Every day the exercises, and indeed the whole ascetic discipline of my Yoga, make it easier for the grace of Christ to flow in me. I feel my hunger for God growing, and my thirst for righteousness, and my desire to be a Christian in the full strength of the word" (p. 11).

Anyone who understands the nature of *prelest* or spiritual deception (see below, pp. 143–44, 149, 162) will recognize in this description of "Christian Yoga" precisely the characteristics of those who have gone spiritually astray, whether into pagan religious experiences or sectarian "Christian" experiences. The same striving for "holy and divine feelings," the same openness and willingness to be "seized" by a spirit, the same seeking not for God but for "spiritual consolations," the same self-intoxication which is mistaken for a "state of grace," the same incredible ease with which one becomes "contemplative" or "mystical," the same "mystical revelations" and pseudo-spiritual states. These are the common characteristics of all who are in this particular state of spiritual deception. But the author of *Christian Yoga,* being a Benedictine monk, adds some particular "meditations" which reveal him as fully in the spirit of the Roman Catholic "meditation" of recent centuries, with its free play of fantasies on Christian themes. Thus, for example, having meditated on a theme of the Christmas Eve mass, he begins to *see* the Child in the arms of His Mother: "I gaze; nothing more. Pictures, ideas (associations of ideas: Saviour-King-Light-Halo-Shepherd-Child-Light again) come one after the other, march past.... All these pieces of a sacred puzzle taken together arouse one idea in me ... a silent vision of the whole mystery of Christmas" (pp. 161–62). Anyone with the slightest knowledge of Orthodox spiritual discipline will see that this pitiable "Christian yogi" has fallen handily into a trap set by one of the lesser demons that lie in wait for the seeker of "spiritual experiences": he has not even seen an "angel of light," but has only given way to his own "religious fancies," the product of a heart and mind totally unprepared for spiritual warfare and the deceptions of the demons. Such "meditation" is being practiced today in a number of Roman Catholic convents and monasteries.

The fact that the book concludes with an article by the French translator of the *Philokalia,* together with excerpts from the *Philokalia,* only reveals the abyss that separates these dilettantes from the true spirituality of Orthodoxy, which is totally inaccessible to the modern "wise men" who no longer understand its language. A sufficient indication of the author's incompetence in understanding the *Philokalia* is the fact that he gives the name "prayer of the heart" (which in Orthodox tradition is the highest mental prayer, acquired by very few only after many years of ascetic struggle and being humbled by a true God-bearing Elder) to the easy trick of reciting syllables in rhythm with the heartbeat (p. 196).

We shall comment more fully below on the dangers of this "Christian Yoga" when noting what it possesses in common with other forms of "Eastern meditation" which are being offered to Christians today.

2. "Christian Zen"

An eastern religious practice on a more popular level is offered in the book of an Irish Catholic priest, William Johnston: *Christian Zen.** The author starts from basically the same place as the author of *Christian Yoga:* a feeling of dissatisfaction with

---

* Harper & Row, New York, 1971.

Western Christianity, a desire to give it a dimension of contemplation or meditation. "Many people, discontented with old forms of prayer, discontented with the old devotions that once served so well, are looking for something that will satisfy the aspirations of the modern heart" (p. 9). "Contact with Zen ... has opened up new vistas, teaching me that there are possibilities in Christianity I never dreamed of." One may "practice Zen as a way of deepening and broadening his Christian faith" (p. 2).

The technique of Japanese Zen is very similar to that of Indian Yoga—from which it is ultimately derived—although it is rather simpler. There is the same basic posture (but not the variety of postures of Yoga), breathing technique, the repetition of a sacred name if desired, as well as other techniques peculiar to Zen. The aim of these techniques is the same as that of Yoga: to abolish rational thinking and attain a state of calm, silent meditation. The sitting position "impedes discursive reasoning and thinking" and enables one to go "down to the center of one's being in imageless and silent contemplation" (p. 5) to "a deep and beautiful realm of psychic life" (p. 17), to "deep interior silence" (p. 16). The experience thus attained is somewhat similar to that achieved by taking drugs, for "people who have used drugs understand a little about Zen, since they have been awakened to the realization that there is a depth in the mind worth exploring" (p. 35). And yet this experience opens up "a new approach to Christ, an approach that is less dualistic and more Oriental" (p. 48). Even absolute beginners in Zen can attain "a sense of union and an atmosphere of supernatural presence" (p. 31), a savoring of "mystical silence" (p. 30); through Zen, the state of contemplation hitherto restricted to a few "mystics" can be "broadened out," and "all may have vision, all may reach *samadhi*" (enlightenment) (p. 46).

The author of *Christian Zen* speaks of the renewal of Christianity; but he admits that the experience he thinks can bring it about may be had by anyone, Christian or non-Christian. "I believe that there is a basic enlightenment which is neither Christian nor Buddhist nor anything else. It is just human" (p. 97). Indeed, at a convention on meditation at a Zen temple near Kyoto "the surprising thing about the meeting was lack of any common faith. No one seemed the slightest bit interested in what anyone else believed or disbelieved, and no one, as far as I recall, even mentioned the name of God" (p. 69). This agnostic character of meditation has a great advantage for "missionary" purposes, for "in this way meditation can be taught to people who have little faith—to those who are troubled in conscience or fear that God is dead. Such people can always sit and breathe. For them meditation becomes a search, and I have found ... that people who begin to search in this way eventually find God. Not the anthropomorphic God they have rejected, but the great being in whom we live, move, and are" (p. 70).

The author's description of the Zen "enlightenment" experience reveals its basic identity with the "cosmic" experience provided by shamanism and many pagan religions. "I myself believe that within us are locked up torrents and torrents of joy that can be released by meditation—sometimes they will burst through with incredible force, flooding the personality with an extraordinary happiness that comes from one knows not where" (p. 88). Interestingly, the author, on returning to America after twenty years in Japan, found this experience to be very close to the Pentecostal experience, and he himself received the "Baptism of the Spirit" at a "charismatic" meeting (p. 100). The author concluded: "Returning to the Pentecostal meeting, it seems to me that the imposition of hands, the prayers of the people, the charity of the community—these can be forces that release the psychic power that brings enlightenment to the person who has been consistently practicing *zazen*" (pp. 92–93). We shall examine in the seventh chapter of this book the nature of the Pentecostal or "charismatic" experience.

Little need be said in criticism of these views; they are basically the same as those of the author of *Christian Yoga,* only less esoteric and more popular. Anyone who believes that the agnostic, pagan experience of Zen can be used for a "contemplative renewal within Christianity" (p. 4) surely knows nothing whatever of the great contemplative tradition of Orthodoxy, which presupposes burning faith, true belief, and intense ascetic struggle; and yet the same author does not hesitate to drag the *Philokalia* and the "great Orthodox schools" into his narrative, stating that they also lead to the condition of "contemplative silence and peace" and are an example of "Zen within the Christian tradition" (p. 39); and he advocates the use of the Prayer of Jesus during Zen meditation for those who wish this (p. 28). Such ignorance is positively dangerous, especially when the possessor of it invites the students at his lectures, as an experiment in "mysticism," to "sit in *zazen* for forty minutes each evening" (p. 30). How many sincere, misguided false prophets there are in the world today, each thinking he is bringing benefit to his fellow men, instead of an invitation to psychic and spiritual disaster! Of this we shall speak more in the conclusion below.

3. *Transcendental Meditation*

The technique of Eastern meditation known as "Transcendental Meditation" (or "TM" for short) has attained such popularity in a few years, especially in America, and is advocated in such an outrageously flippant tone, that any serious student of contemporary religious currents will be inclined at first to dismiss it as merely an over-inflated product of American advertising and showmanship. But this would be a mistake, for in its serious claims it does not differ markedly from Yoga and Zen, and a close look at its techniques reveals it as perhaps more authentically "Eastern" than either of the somewhat artificial syncretisms, "Christian Yoga" and "Christian Zen."

According to one standard account of this movement,* "Transcendental Meditation" was brought to America (where it has had its most spectacular success) by a rather "unorthodox" Indian Yogi, Maharishi Mahesh Yogi, and began to grow noticeably about 1961. In 1967 it received widespread publicity when the popular singers known as the "Beatles" were converted to it and gave up drugs; but they soon abandoned the movement (although they continued to meditate), and the Maharishi hit his low point the next year when his American tour, together with another convert singing group called the "Beach Boys," was abandoned as a financial failure. The movement itself, however, continued to grow: By 1971 there were some 100,000 meditators following it, with 2,000 specially trained instructors, making it already by far the largest movement of "Eastern spirituality" in America. In 1975 the movement reached its peak, with about 40,000 trainees a month and upwards of 600,000 followers in all. During these years it was widely used in the Army, public schools, prisons, hospitals, and by church groups, including parishes of the Greek Archdiocese in America, as a supposedly neutral form of "mental

---

* All citations in this section are from Jhan Robbins and David Fisher, *Tranquility without Pills (All about Transcendental Meditation)*, Peter H. Wyden, Inc., New York, 1972.

therapy" which is compatible with any kind of religious belief or practice. The "TM" course is one especially tailored to the American way of life and has been sympathetically called "a course in how to succeed spiritually without really trying" (p. 17); the Maharishi himself calls it a technique which is "just like brushing your teeth" (p. 104). The Maharishi has been strongly criticized by other Hindu Yogis for cheapening the long tradition of Yoga in India by making this esoteric practice available to the masses for money. (The charge in 1975 was $125 for the course, $65 for college students, and progressively less for high school, junior high school, and very young children.)

In its aims, presuppositions, and results, "TM" does not differ markedly from "Christian Yoga" or "Christian Zen"; it differs from them chiefly in the simplicity of its techniques and of its whole philosophy, and in the ease with which its results are obtained. Like them, "TM does not require any belief, understanding, moral code, or even agreement with the ideas and philosophy" (p. 104); it is a technique pure and simple, which "is based on the natural tendency of the mind to move toward greater happiness and pleasure.... During transcendental meditation your mind is expected to follow whatever is most natural and most pleasant" (p. 13). "Transcendental meditation is a practice first and a theory afterwards. It is essential at the beginning that an individual does not think intellectually at all" (p. 22).

The technique which the Maharishi has devised is invariably the same at all "TM" centers throughout the world: After two introductory lectures, one pays the fee and then comes for "initiation," bringing with him a seemingly strange collection of articles, always the same: three pieces of sweet fruit, at least six fresh flowers, and a clean handkerchief (p. 39).

These are placed in a basket and taken to the small "initiation room," where they are placed on a table before a portrait of the Maharishi's guru, from whom he received his initiation into yoga; on the same table a candle and incense are burning. The disciple is alone in the room with his teacher, who is himself required to have received initiation and to have been instructed by the Maharishi personally. The ceremony before the portrait lasts for half an hour and is composed of soft singing in Sanskrit (with meaning unknown to the initiate) and a chanting of the names of past "masters" of Yoga; at the end of the ceremony the initiate is given a "mantra," a secret Sanskrit word which he is to repeat ceaselessly during meditation, and which no one is to know except his teacher (p. 42). The English translation of this ceremony is never revealed to initiates; it is available only to teachers and initiators themselves. It is contained in an unpublished handbook called "The Holy Tradition," and its text has now been printed by the "Spiritual Counterfeits Project" in Berkeley as a separate pamphlet. This ceremony is nothing but a traditional Hindu ceremony of worship of the gods *(puja),* including the deified guru of the Maharishi (Shri Guru Dev) and the whole line of "Masters" through which he himself received his initiation. The ceremony ends with a series of twenty-two "offerings" made to the Maharishi's guru, each ending with the words "To Shri Guru Dev I bow down." The initiator himself bows down before a portrait of Guru Dev at the end of the ceremony and invites the initiate to do likewise; only then is the latter initiated. (The bowing is not absolutely required of the initiate, but the offerings are.)

Thus the modern agnostic, usually quite unawares, has been introduced to the realm of Hindu religious practices; quite easily he has been made to do something to which his own Christian ancestors, perhaps, had preferred torture and cruel death: he has offered sacrifice to pagan gods. On the spiritual plane it may be this sin, rather than the psychic technique itself, that chiefly explains the spectacular success of "TM."

Once he has been initiated, the student of "TM" meditates twice daily for twenty minutes each time (precisely the same amount recommended by the author of *Christian Yoga),* letting the mind wander freely, and repeating the mantra as often as he thinks of it; frequently, one's experiences are checked by his teacher. Quite soon, even on the first attempt, one begins to enter a new level of consciousness, which is neither sleep nor wakefulness: the state of "transcendental meditation." "Transcendental meditation produces a state of consciousness unlike anything we've known before, and closest to that state of Zen developed after many years of intense study" (p. 115). "In contrast to the years that must be spent to master other religious disciples and Yoga, which offer the same results that TM proponents claim, teachers say TM can be taught in a matter of minutes" (pp. 110–11). Some who have experienced it describe it as a "state of fulfillment" similar to some drug experiences (p. 85), but the Maharishi himself describes it in traditional Hindu terms: "This state lies beyond all seeing, hearing, touching, smelling, and tasting—beyond all thinking and feeling. This state of the unmanifested, absolute, pure consciousness of Being is the ultimate state of life" (p. 23). "When an individual has developed the ability to bring this deep state to the conscious level on a permanent basis, he is said to have reached cosmic consciousness, the goal of all meditators" (p. 25). In the advanced stages of "TM" the basic Yoga positions are taught, but they are not necessary to the success of the basic technique; nor is any ascetic preparation required. Once one has attained the "transcendental state of being," all that is required of one is twenty minutes of meditation twice daily, since this form of meditation is not at all a separate way of life, as in India, but rather a discipline for those who lead an active life. The Maharishi's distinction lies in having brought this state of consciousness to everyone, not just a chosen few.

There are numerous success stories for "TM," which claims to be effective in almost all cases: drug habits are overcome, families are reunited, one becomes healthy and happy; the teachers of TM are constantly smiling, bubbling over with happiness. Generally, TM does not replace other religions, but *strengthens* belief in almost anything; "Christians," whether Protestant or Catholic, also find that it makes their belief and practice more meaningful and deeper (p. 105).

The swift and easy success of "TM," while it is symptomatic of the waning influence of Christianity on contemporary mankind, has also led to its early decline. Perhaps more than any other movement of "Eastern spirituality," it has had the character of a "fad," and the Maharishi's announced aim to "initiate" the whole of humanity is evidently doomed to failure. After the peak year of 1975, enrollment in "TM" courses has steadily declined, so much so that in 1977 the organization announced the opening of a whole new series of "advanced" courses, obviously devised in order to regain public interest and enthusiasm. These courses are intended to lead initiates to the "siddhis" or "supernatural powers" of Hinduism: walking through walls, becoming invisible, levitating and flying through the air, and the like. The courses have generally been greeted with cynicism, even though a "TM" brochure features a photograph of a "levitating" meditator (see *Time* Magazine, August 8, 1977, p. 75). Whether or not the courses (which cost up to $3,000) will produce the claimed results—which are in the province of the traditional "fakirs" of India (see above, pp. 30–35)—"TM" itself stands revealed as a passing phase of the occult interest in the second half of the 20th century. Already many examples have been publicized of "TM" teachers and disciples alike who have been afflicted with the common maladies of those who dabble in the occult: mental and emotional illness, suicide, attempted murder, demonic possession.

In 1978 a United States Federal Court came to the decision that "TM" is indeed religious in nature and may not be taught in public schools.* This decision will undoubtedly further limit the influence of "TM," which, however, will probably continue to exist as one of the many forms of meditation which many see as compatible with Christianity—another sad sign of the times.

---

* See *TM in Court:* The complete text of the Federal Court's opinion in the case of Malnak v. Maharishi Mahesh Yogi; Spiritual Counterfeits Project, P. O. Box 4308, Berkeley, Calif. 94704.

V

The "New Religious Consciousness"

THE SPIRIT OF THE EASTERN CULTS
IN THE 1970s

THE THREE KINDS of "Christian meditation" described above are only the beginning; in general, it may be said that the influence of Eastern religious ideas and practices upon the once-Christian West has reached astonishing proportions in the decade of the 1970s. In particular America, which barely two decades ago was still religiously "provincial" (save in a few large cities), its spiritual horizon largely limited to Protestantism and Roman Catholicism—has seen a dazzling proliferation of Eastern (and pseudo-Eastern) religious cults and movements.

The history of this proliferation can be traced from the restless disillusionment of the post-World War II generation, which first manifested itself in the 1950s in the empty protest and moral libertinism of the "beat generation," whose interest in Eastern religions was at first rather academic and mainly a sign of dissatisfaction with "Christianity." There followed a second generation, that of the "hippies" of the 1960s with its "rock" music and psychedelic drugs and search for "increased awareness" at any cost; now young Americans plunged whole-heartedly into political protest movements (notably against the war in Vietnam) on the one hand, and the fervent practice of Eastern religions on the other. Indian gurus, Tibetan lamas, Japanese Zen masters, and other Eastern "sages" came to the West and found a host of ready disciples who made them successful beyond the dreams of the westernized swamis of preceding generations; and young people travelled to the ends of the world, even to the heights of the Himalayas, to find the wisdom or the teacher or the drug that would bring them the "peace" and "freedom" they sought.

In the 1970s a third generation has succeeded the "hippies." Outwardly quieter, with fewer "demonstrations" and generally less flamboyant behavior, this generation has gone more deeply into Eastern religions, whose influence now has become much more pervasive than ever before. For many of this newer generation the religious "search" has ended: they have found an Eastern religion to their liking and are now seriously occupied in practicing it. A number of Eastern religious movements have already become "native" to the West, especially in America: there are now Buddhist monasteries composed entirely of Western converts, and for the first time there have appeared American and other Western gurus and Zen masters.

Let us look at just a few pictures—descriptions of actual events in the early and mid-1970s—which illustrate the dominance of Eastern ideas and practices among many young Americans (who are only the "avant-garde" of the youth of the whole world). The first two pictures show a more superficial involvement with Eastern religions, and are perhaps only a leftover from the generation of the 1960s; the last two reveal the deeper involvement characteristic of the 1970s.

1. Hare Krishnas in San Francisco

"On a street bordering Golden Gate Park in the Haight-Ashbury section of San Francisco stood the Krishna Consciousness temple.... Above the entrance to the temple were the two-foot-high wooden letters 'Hare Krishna.' The large storefront windows were covered with red and orange-patterned blankets.

"The sounds of chanting and music filled the street. Inside there were dozens of brightly colored paintings on the wall, thick red rugs on the floor, and a smoky haze in the air. This smoke was incense, an element of the ceremony in progress. The people in the room were softly chanting barely audible Sanskrit words. The room was nearly full, with about fifty people who all appeared to be young sitting on the floor. Assembled in front were about twenty persons wearing long, loose-fitting orange and saffron robes, with white paint on their noses. Many of the men had shaved their heads except for a ponytail. The women with them also had white paint on their noses and small red marks on their foreheads. The other young persons in the room appeared no different from other denizens of the Haight-Ashbury, costumed in headbands, long hair, beards, and an assortment of rings, bells, and beads, and they were also enthusiastically participating in the ceremony. The ten or so persons sitting in the rear appeared to be first-time visitors.

"The chanting ceremony (mantra) increased in tempo and in volume. Two girls in long saffron robes were now dancing to the chant. The leader of the chant began to cry the words (of the chant in Sanskrit).... The entire group repeated the words, and attempted to maintain the leader's intonation and rhythm. Many of the participants played musical instruments. The leader was beating a hand drum in time with his chanting. The two swaying, dancing girls were playing finger cymbals. One young man was blowing a sea shell; another was beating on a tambourine.... On the walls of the temple were over a dozen paintings of scenes from the *Bhagavad-Gita.*

"The music and the chanting grew very loud and fast. The drum was ceaselessly pounding. Many of the devotees started personal shouts, hands up-stretched, amidst the general chant. The leader knelt in front of a picture of the group's 'spiritual master' on a small shrine near the front of the room. The chanting culminated in a loud crescendo and the room became silent. The celebrants knelt with their heads to the floor as the leader said a short prayer in Sanskrit. Then he shouted five times, 'All glories to the assembled devotees,' which the others repeated before they sat up."*

This is one of the typical worship services of the "Krishna Consciousness" movement, which was founded in America in 1966 by an Indian ex-businessman, A.C. Bhaktivedanta, in order to bring the Hindu discipline of bhakti yoga to the disoriented and searching young people of the West. The earlier phase of interest in Eastern religions (in the 1950s and early 1960s) had emphasized intellectual investigation without much personal involvement; this newer phase demands wholehearted participation. Bhakti yoga means uniting oneself to one's chosen "god" by love and worshipping him, and changing one's whole life in order to make this one's central occupation. Through the non-rational means of worship (chanting, music, dance, devotion) the mind is "expanded" and "Krishna consciousness" is attained, which—if enough people will do

---

* Charles Glock and Robert Bellah, *The New Religious Consciousness,* University of California Press, Berkeley, 1976, pp. 31–32.

it—is supposed to end the troubles of our disordered age and usher in a new age of peace, love, and unity.

The bright robes of the "Krishnas" became a familiar sight in San Francisco, especially on the day every year when the immense idol of their "god" was wheeled through Golden Gate Park to the ocean, attended by all the signs of Hindu devotion—a typical scene of pagan India, but something new for "Christian" America. From San Francisco the movement has spread to the rest of America and to Western Europe; by 1974 there were fifty-four Krishna temples throughout the world, many of them near colleges and universities (members of the movement are almost all very young.)

The recent death of the founder of the movement has raised questions about its future; and indeed its membership, although very visible, has been rather small in number. As a "sign of the times," however, the meaning of the movement is clear, and should be very disturbing to Christians: many young people today are looking for a "god" to worship, and the most blatant form of paganism is not too much for them to accept.

2. Guru Maharaj-ji at the Houston Astrodome

By the fall of 1973 a number of Eastern gurus of the newer school, led by Maharishi Mahesh Yogi with his "TM," had come to the West and gathered a following, only to fade from the public eye after a brief reign in the glare of publicity. Guru Maharaj-ji was the most spectacular and, one might say, outrageous of these gurus. Fifteen years old, he had already been proclaimed to be "God," his family (mother and three brothers) was the "Holy Family," and his organization (the "Divine Light Mission") had communities (ashrams) all over America. His 80,000 followers ("premies"), like the followers of Krishna, were expected to give up worldly pleasures and meditate in order to attain an "expanded" consciousness which made them perfectly peaceful, happy, and "blissed out"—a state of mind in which everything seems beautiful and perfect just the way it is. In a special initiation at which they "receive the knowledge," disciples are shown an intense light and three other signs within themselves, which later they were able to meditate on by themselves (*The New Religious Consciousness,* p. 54). In addition to this "knowledge," disciples are united in believing that Maharaj-ji is the "Lord of the Universe" who has come to inaugurate a new age of peace for mankind.

For three days in November 1973, the "Divine Light Mission" rented the Houston Astrodome (an immense sports arena entirely covered by a dome) in order to stage "the most holy and significant event in the history of mankind." "Premies" from all over the world were to gather to worship their "god" and begin the conversion of America (through the mass media, whose representatives were carefully invited) to the same worship, thus beginning the new age of mankind. Appropriately, the event was called "Millennium '73."

Typical of Maharaj-ji's convinced disciples was Rennie Davis, leftist demonstrator of the 1960s and one of the "Chicago Seven" accused of inciting riots at the 1968 Democratic National Convention. He spent the summer of 1973 giving press conferences and speeches to whomever would listen, telling America: "He is the greatest event in history and we sleep through it.… I feel like shouting in the streets. If we knew who he was, we would crawl across America on our hands and knees to rest our heads at his feet."*

---

* Robert Greenfield, *The Spiritual Supermarket,* Saturday Review Press, New York, 1975, p. 43.

Indeed, the worship of Maharaj-ji is expressed in a full prostration before him with one's head to the ground, together with a Sanskrit phrase of adoration. A tremendous ovation greeted his appearance at "Millennium '73," he sat atop a tall throne, crowned by an immense golden "crown of Krishna," as the Astrodome scoreboard flashed the word "G-O-D." Young American "premies" wept for joy, others danced on the stage, the band played "The Lord of the Universe"—adapted from an old Protestant hymn (*The Spiritual Supermarket,* pp. 80, 94).

All this, let us say again—in *"Christian" America.* This is already something beyond mere worship of pagan "gods." Until a very few years ago such worship of a living man would have been inconceivable in any "Christian" country; now it has become an ordinary thing for many thousands of religious "seekers" in the West. Here we have already had a preview of the worship of antichrist at the end of the age—the one who will *sit in the temple of God, setting himself forth as God* (II Thess. 2:4).

"Millennium '73" seems to have been the peak of Maharaj-ji's influence. As it was, only 15,000 followers attended it (much less than expected), and there were no "miracles" or special signs to indicate the "new age" had actually begun. A movement so dependent on media publicity and so much bound up with the popular taste of a particular generation (the music at "Millennium '73" was composed mostly of the popular songs of the "counterculture" of the 1960s) can expect to go out of fashion rather quickly; and the recent marriage of Maharaj-ji to his secretary has further weakened his popularity as a "god."

Other of the "spiritual" movements of our times seem to be less subject to the whims of popular fashion and more indicative of the depth of the influence which Eastern religions are now attaining in the West.

3. Tantric Yoga in the Mountains of New Mexico

In a grassy meadow at the 7,500-foot elevation in the Jemez Mountains of northern New Mexico, a thousand young Americans (most of them between the ages of 20 and 25) gathered for ten days of spiritual exercises at the time of the summer solstice in June 1973. They arise at four a.m. every day and assemble before sunrise (wrapped in blankets against the morning frost) to sit on the ground in rows in front of an outdoor stage. Together, they begin the day with a mantra in Punjabi (a Sanskritic language) in order to "tune in" to the spiritual practices that are to follow.

First there are several hours of kundalini yoga—a series of strenuous physical exercises, chanting, and meditation aimed at acquiring conscious control of body and mind processes and preparing one for "God realization." Then there is the ceremony of the raising of two flags: the American flag and the "flag of the Aquarian nation"—this "nation" being the peaceful people of the "Aquarian Age" or millennium for which this cult is preparing—accompanied by the singing of "God Bless America" and a prayer for the American nation. After a vegetarian meal (typical of almost all the new cults) and lectures on spiritual and practical subjects, all prepare for a long session of tantric yoga.

Tantric yoga has been little heard of and almost never practiced in the West up to now. All authorities agree that it is an extremely dangerous exercise, practiced always by male and female together, that evokes a very powerful psychic energy, requiring close supervision and control. Supposedly, there is only one master of tantric yoga living on the earth at any one time;

the exercises at "Solstice" in New Mexico were led by the "Great Tantric" of our days, Yogi Bhajan.

All, dressed identically in white, sit down in long, straight lines, men opposite women, packed shoulder-to-shoulder down the lines and back-to-back with the next line. About ten double lines stretch out from the stage, each seventy-five feet long; assistants make sure the lines are perfectly straight to assure the proper "flow" of the yogic "magnetic field."

The chanting of mantras begins, with special chants invoking a departed guru who is Yogi Bhajan's "special protector." The Yogi himself, an impressive man—six feet four inches tall with a great black beard, dressed in white robe and turban—appears and begins to speak of his dream for "a new beautiful creative nation" of America which can be built by the spiritual preparation of people today; the tantric exercises, which are a key in this preparation, transform people from their usual "individual consciousness" to "group consciousness" and finally to "universal consciousness."

The exercises begin. They are extremely difficult, involving strong physical effort and pain and evoking strong emotions of fear, anger, love, etc. Everyone must do exactly the same thing at the same time; difficult positions are held motionlessly for long periods; complicated mantras and exercises must be executed in precise coordination with one's partner and with everyone in one's own row; each separate exercise may take from thirty-one to sixty-one minutes. Individual awareness disappears in the intense group activity, and strong after-effects are felt—physical exhaustion and sometimes temporary paralysis, emotional exhaustion or elation. Further, since no one at "Solstice" is allowed to converse with anyone else, there is no opportunity to make rational sense of the experience by sharing it with others; the aim is to effect a radical change in oneself.

Following afternoon classes in such subjects are Oriental arts of self-defense, practical medicine and nutrition, and the running of an ashram, there is an evening session (after another meal) of "spiritual singing": Sanskrit mantras are sung to current folk and "rock" music, "rock festival" and "joyful worship" in a foreign tongue are joined together—part of Yogi Bhajan's effort to make his religion "native American" (*The New Religious Consciousness,* pp. 8–18).

The religion described above is a modern adaption of the Sikh religion of northern India, joined to several practices of yoga. Called the "3HO" (Healthy-Happy-Holy Organization), it was founded in 1969 in Los Angeles by Yogi Bhajan, who originally came to America to take up a teaching position and only incidentally became a religious leader when he discovered that his courses in yoga appealed to the "hippies" of southern California. Combining the "spiritual" search of the "hippies" with his own knowledge of Indian religions, he formed an "American" religion that differs from most Eastern religions by its emphasis on a this-worldly practical life (like the Sikhs in India, who are mostly a merchant class); marriage and a stable home life, responsible employment, and social service are required of all members.

Since its foundation in 1969, "3HO" has expanded to over 100 ashrams (communities which serve as gathering-places for non-resident participants) in American cities, as well as a few in Europe and Japan. Although externally it is quite distinct from the other new Eastern cults (full members of the cult formally become Sikhs and thereafter wear the characteristic Sikh turban and white clothing), "3HO" is one with them in appealing to ex-"hippies," making an "expanded" (or "universal" or "transcendental") consciousness its central aim, and in seeing itself as a spiritual "avant-garde" that will bring about a new millennial age (which most groups see in astrological terms as the "Aquarian Age").

As a cult that advocates a relatively normal life in society, "3HO" is still just as much a "sign of the times" as the Hindu cults that promote an obvious "escapism"; it is preparing for a "healthy, happy and holy" America *totally without reference to Christ*. When convinced and "happy" Americans speak calmly about God and their religious duties without mention of Christ, one can no longer doubt that the "post-Christian" age has come in earnest.

4. Zen Training in Northern California

In the forested mountains of northern California, in the shadow of immense Mount Shasta—a "holy" mountain to the original Indian inhabitants, and long a center of occult activities and settlements, which are now once again on the increase—there has been since 1970 a Zen Buddhist monastery. Long before 1970 there had been Zen temples in the larger cities of the West Coast where Japanese had settled, and there had been attempts to start Zen monasteries in California; but "Shasta Abbey," as it is called, is the first successful *American* Zen monastery. (In Zen Buddhism a "monastery" is primarily a training school for Zen "priests," both male and female.)

In Shasta Abbey the atmosphere is very orderly and businesslike. Visitors (who are allowed to take guided tours at restricted times, but may not fraternize with the residents) find the monks or trainees in traditional black robes and with shaved heads; everyone seems to know exactly what he is doing, and a clear sense of seriousness and dedication is present.

The training itself is a strict five-year (or more) program which allows graduates to become "priests" and teachers of Zen and to conduct Buddhist ceremonies. As at secular schools, trainees pay a fee for room and board ($175 a month, payable in advance for each month—already a means of weeding out unserious candidates!), but the life itself is that of "monks" rather than students. Strict rules govern dress and behavior, vegetarian meals are eaten in silence communally, no visitors or idle conversations are allowed; life centers about the meditation hall, where trainees eat and sleep in addition to meditating, and no non-Zen religious practices are allowed. The life is a very intense and concentrated one, and every event of daily life (even washing and toilet) has its Buddhist prayer, which is recited silently.

Although the Abbey belongs to a "reformed" Soto Zen sect—to emphasize its independence from Japan and its adaptation to American conditions of life—rites and ceremonies are in the Japanese Zen tradition. There is the ceremony of becoming a Buddhist, equinox rites celebrating the "transformation of the individual," the ceremonial "feeding of hungry ghosts" (remembrance of the dead), the "Founder's Day" ceremony of expressing gratitude to the transmitters of Zen down to the present master, the festival of Buddha's enlightenment, and others. Homage is paid by bowing down before images of Buddha, but the primary emphasis of the teaching is on the "Buddha-nature" within one.

The Zen Master at Shasta Abbey is a Westerner and a woman (Buddhist practice permitting this): Jiyu Kennett, an Englishwoman born of Buddhist parents in 1924, who received Buddhist training in several traditions in the Far East and "ordination" at a Soto Zen monastery in Japan. She came to America in 1969 and founded the monastery the next year with a few young followers; since then the community has grown rapidly, attracting mostly young men (and women) in their twenties.

The reason for the success of this monastery—apart from the natural appeal of Zen to a generation sick of rationalism and mere outward learning—seems to lie in the mystique of "authentic transmission" of the Zen experience and tradition, which the "Abbess" provides through her training and certification in Japan; her personal qualities as a foreigner and a born Buddhist who is still in close touch with the contemporary mind (with a very "American" practicality), seem to seal her influence with the young American convert generation of Buddhists.

The aim of Zen training at Shasta Abbey is to fill all of life with "pure Zen." Daily meditation (at times for as much as eight or ten hours in one day) is the center of a concentrated, intense religious life that leads, supposedly, to "lasting peace and harmony of body and mind." Emphasis is on "spiritual growth," and the publications of the Abbey—a bi-monthly journal and several books by the Abbess—reveal a high degree of awareness of spiritual posing and fakery. The Abbey is opposed to the adoption of Japanese national (as opposed to Buddhist) customs; warns of the dangers of "guru-hopping" and falsely worshipping the Zen Master; forbids astrology, fortune-telling (even the *I Ching*), astral travelling and all other psychic and occult activities; mocks the academic and intellectual (as opposed to experiential) approach to Zen; and emphasizes hard work and rigorous training, with the banishing of all illusions and fantasies about oneself and "spiritual life." Discussions on "spiritual" matters by young Zen "priests" (as recorded in the Abbey's *Journal*) sound, in their sober and knowledgeable tone, remarkably like discussions among serious young Orthodox converts and monks. In intellectual formation and outlook, these young Buddhists seem quite close to many of our Orthodox converts. The young Orthodox Christian of today might well say: "There, but for the grace of God, I myself might be," so convincingly authentic is the spiritual outlook of this Zen monastery, which offers almost everything the young religious seeker of today might desire—except, of course, Christ the true God and the eternal salvation which He alone can give.

The monastery teaches a Buddhism that is not "a cold and distant discipline," but is filled with "love and compassion." Contrary to the usual expositions of Buddhism, the Abbess emphasizes that the center of Buddhist faith is *not* ultimate "nothingness," but a living "god" (which she claims to be the esoteric Buddhist teaching): "The secret of Zen ... is to *know* for certain, for *oneself,* that the Cosmic Buddha exists. A true master is he or she who does not waver in his certainty of, and love for, the Cosmic Buddha.... I was overjoyed when I finally knew for certain that He existed; the love and gratitude in me knew no bounds. Nor have I ever felt such love as came forth from Him; I so want everyone else to feel it too."*

There are presently some seventy priest-trainees at Shasta Abbey and its "branch priories," chiefly in California. The monastery is now in a state of rapid expansion, both on its own grounds and in its "mission" to the American people; there is a growing movement of lay Buddhists who make the Abbey their religious center and often come there, together with psychologists and other interested persons, on meditation retreats of varying lengths. With their publications, counseling and instruction in California cities, a projected children's school and

---

* *The Journal of Shasta Abbey,* Jan.–Feb. 1978, p. 6.

65

a home for the elderly—Shasta Abbey is indeed progressing in its aim of "growing Zen Buddhism in the West."

Towards Christianity the Abbess and her disciples have a condescending attitude; they respect the *Philokalia* and other Orthodox spiritual texts, recognizing Orthodoxy as the closest to them among "Christian" bodies, but regard themselves as being "beyond such things as theologies, doctrinal disputes and 'isms," which they regard as not belonging to "True Religion" (*Journal,* Jan.–Feb. 1978, p. 54).

Zen has, in fact, no theological foundation, relying entirely on "experience" and thus falling into the "pragmatic fallacy" that has already been noted earlier in this book, in the chapter on Hinduism: "If it works, it must be true and good." Zen, without any theology, is no more able than Hinduism to distinguish between good and evil spiritual experiences; it can only state what *seems* to be good because it brings "peace" and "harmony," as judged by the natural powers of the mind and not by any revelation—everything else it rejects as more or less illusory. Zen appeals to the subtle pride—so widespread today—of those who think they can save themselves, and thus have no need of any Saviour outside themselves.

Of all of today's Eastern religious currents, Zen is probably the most sophisticated intellectually and the most sober spiritually. With its teaching of compassion and a loving "Cosmic Buddha," it is perhaps as high a religious ideal as the human mind can attain—without Christ. Its tragedy is precisely that it has no Christ in it, and thus no salvation, and its very sophistication and sobriety effectively prevent its followers from seeking salvation in Christ. In its quiet, compassionate way it is perhaps the saddest of all the reminders of the "post-Christian" times in which we live. Non-Christian "spirituality" is no longer a foreign importation in the West; it has become a native American religion putting down deep roots into the consciousness of the West. Let us be warned from this: the religion of the future will not be a mere cult or sect, but a powerful and profound religious orientation which will be absolutely convincing to the mind and heart of modern man.

5. The New "Spirituality" vs. Christianity

Other examples of the new Eastern cults in the West could be multiplied; each year finds new ones, or new transformations of old ones. In addition to the overtly religious cults, the last decade especially has seen an increase of secular "consciousness cults," as one popular newsmagazine calls them (*U.S. News and World Report,* Feb. 16, 1976, p. 40). These "mind-therapy" groups include the "Erhard Seminars Training" established in 1971, "Rolfing," "Silva Mind Control," and various forms of "encounter" and "biofeedback," all of which offer a "release of tensions" and a "tapping of the hidden capabilities" of man, expressed in a more or less plausible 20th-century "scientific" jargon. One is reminded also of other "consciousness" movements that have become less fashionable today, from "Christian Science" to "Science of Mind" to "Scientology."

All these movements are incompatible with Christianity. Orthodox Christians must be told absolutely to *stay away from them.*

Why do we speak so categorically?

1. These movements have no foundations in Christian tradition or practice, but are purely the product of Eastern pagan religions or of modern spiritism, more or less diluted and often presented as "non-religious." They not only teach wrongly, not in accordance with Christian doctrine, about

67

spiritual life; they also lead one, whether through pagan religious experiences or psychic experiments, into a wrong spiritual path whose end is spiritual and psychic disaster, and ultimately the loss of one's soul eternally.

2. Specifically, the experience of "spiritual quietness" which is given by various kinds of meditation, whether without specific religious content (as is claimed by "TM," some forms of Yoga and Zen, and the secular cults) or with pagan religious content (as in Hare Krishna, the "Divine Light Mission," "3HO," etc.), is an entrance to the "cosmic" spiritual realm where the deeper side of the human personality enters into contact with actual spiritual beings. These beings, in man's fallen state, are first of all the *demons* or fallen spirits who are closest to man.* Zen Buddhist meditators themselves, despite all their cautions about spiritual "experiences," describe their encounters with these spirits (mixed with human fantasies), all the while emphasizing that they are not "clinging" to them.**

3. The "initiation" into experiences of the psychic realm which the "consciousness cults" provide involves one in something beyond the conscious control of the human will; thus, once having been "initiated," it is often a very difficult thing to untangle oneself from undesirable psychic experiences. In this way, the "new religious consciousness" becomes an enemy of Christianity that is much more powerful and dangerous than any of the heresies of the past. When *experience* is emphasized above doctrine, the normal Christian safeguards which protect

---

* See Bishop Ignatius Brianchaninov's exposition of the Orthodox teaching on the spiritual and sensuous perception of spirits and the opening of man's "doors of perception," in *The Orthodox Word,* no. 82, 1978.
** See Jiyu Kennett, *How to Grow a Lotus Blossom,* Shasta Abbey, 1977—a Zen Master's description of her near-death visions.

one against the attacks of fallen spirits are removed or neutralized, and the passiveness and "openness" which characterize the new cults literally open one up to be used by demons. Studies of the experiences of many of the "consciousness cults" show that there is a regular progression in them from experiences which at first are "good" or "neutral" to experiences which become strange and frightening and in the end clearly demonic. Even the purely physical sides of psychic disciplines like Yoga are dangerous, because they are derived from and dispose one towards the psychic attitudes and experiences which are the original purpose of Yoga practice.

The seductive power of the "new religious consciousness" is so great today that it can take possession of one even while he believes that he is remaining a Christian. This is true not only of those who indulge in the superficial syncretisms or combinations of Christianity and Eastern religions which have been mentioned above; it is true also of an increasing number of people who regard themselves as fervent Christians. The profound ignorance of true Christian spiritual experience in our times is producing a false Christian "spirituality" whose nature is closely kin to the "new religious consciousness."

In Chapter VII we will take a long and careful look at the most widespread current of "Christian spirituality" today. In it we will see the frightening prospect of a "new religious consciousness" taking possession of well-meaning Christians, even Orthodox Christians—to such an extent that we cannot help but think of the spirituality of the contemporary world in the apocalyptic terms of the "strong delusion" that will deceive almost all of mankind before the end of the age. To this subject we shall return at the end of this book.

VI

"Signs from Heaven"

AN ORTHODOX CHRISTIAN UNDERSTANDING
OF UNIDENTIFIED FLYING OBJECTS (UFOs)

THE post-World War II decades that have witnessed the astonishing increase of Eastern religious cults and influence in the West have also seen the beginning and spread of a parallel phenomenon which, although at first sight it seems totally unrelated to religion, on closer examination turns out to be just as much a sign of the "post-Christian" age and the "new religious consciousness" as the Eastern cults. This phenomenon is that of the "unidentified flying objects" which have supposedly been seen in almost every part of the world since the first "flying saucer" was spotted in 1947.

Human credulity and superstition—which are no less present today than at any time in human history—have caused this phenomenon to be connected to some degree with the "crack-pot fringe" of the cult world; but there has also been a sufficiently serious and responsible interest in it to produce several government investigations and a number of books by reputable scientists. These investigations have come to no positive result in identifying the objects as physical reality. However, the newest hypotheses made by several scientific investigators in order to explain the phenomena actually seem to come closer to a satisfactory explanation than other theories that have been proposed in the past; but at the same time, these newest hypotheses bring one to the "edge of reality" (as one of the new scientific books on them is called), to the boundaries of psychic and spiritual reality which these investigators are not equipped to handle. The richness of Scriptural and Patristic knowledge precisely of this latter reality places the Orthodox Christian observer in a uniquely advantageous position from which to evaluate these new hypotheses and the "UFO" phenomena in general.

The Orthodox Christian observer, however, is less interested in the phenomena themselves than he is in the *mentality* associated with them: how are people commonly interpreting UFOs, and why? Among the first to approach the UFO question in this manner, in a serious study, was the renowned Swiss psychologist C. G. Jung. In his book of 1959, *Flying Saucers: A Modern Myth of Things Seen in the Skies,* he approached the phenomena as primarily something psychological and religious in meaning; and although he himself did not attempt to identify them as "objective reality," he nonetheless did grasp the realm of human knowledge to which they actually belong. Today's investigators, while starting from the "objective" and not the psychological side of the question, have also found it necessary to put forth "psychic" hypotheses to explain the phenomena.

In approaching the religious and psychological side of UFO phenomena, it is important for us, first of all, to understand the background in terms of which "flying saucers" have generally been interpreted (by those who believe in their existence) from the time of their first appearance in the 1940s. *What were men prepared to see in the sky?* The answer to this question may be found in a brief look at the literature of popular "science fiction."

1. The Spirit of Science Fiction

Historians of science fiction usually trace the origins of this literary form back to the early 19th century. Some prefer to see its beginning in the short stories of Edgar Allen Poe, which combined a persuasive realism in style with a subject-matter always tinged with the "mysterious" and occult. Others see the first science fiction writer in Poe's English contemporary, Mary Wollstonecraft Shelley (wife of the famous poet); her *Frankenstein, or the Modern Prometheus,* combines fantastical science with occultism in a way characteristic of many science-fiction stories since then.

The typical science-fiction story, however, was to come with the late 19th and early 20th centuries, from Jules Verne and H.G. Wells to our own days. From a largely second-rate form of literature in the American periodical "pulps" of the 1930s and 1940s, science fiction has come of age and become a respectable international literary form in recent decades. In addition, a number of extremely popular motion pictures have shown how much the spirit of science fiction has captivated the popular imagination. The cheaper and more sensational science-fiction movies of the 1950s have given way in the last decade or so to fashionable "idea" movies like *2001: A Space Odyssey, Star Wars,* and *Close Encounters of the Third Kind,* not to mention one of the most popular and long-lived American television series, "Star Trek."

The spirit of science fiction is derived from an underlying philosophy or ideology, more often implied than expressed in so many words, which is shared by virtually all those who create in science-fiction forms. This philosophy may be summed up in the following main points:

1. Religion, in the traditional sense, is absent, or else present in a very incidental or artificial way. The literary form itself is obviously a product of the "post-Christian age" (evident already in the stories of Poe and Shelley). The science-fiction universe is a totally secular one, although often with "mystical" overtones of an occult or Eastern kind. "God," if mentioned at all, is a vague and impersonal power, not a personal being (for example, the "Force" of *Star Wars,* a cosmic energy that has its evil as well as good side). The increasing fascination of contemporary man with science-fiction themes is a direct reflection of the loss of traditional religious values.

2. The center of the science-fiction universe (in place of the absent God) is *man* — not usually man as he is now, but man as he will "become" in the future, in accordance with the modern mythology of evolution. Although the heroes of science-fiction stories are usually recognizable humans, the story interest often centers about their encounters with various kinds of "supermen" from "highly evolved" races of the future (or sometimes, the past), or from distant galaxies. The idea of the possibility of "highly evolved" intelligent life on other planets has become so much a part of the contemporary mentality that even respectable scientific (and semi-scientific) speculations assume it as a matter of course. Thus, one popular series of books (Erich von Daniken, *Chariots of the Gods?, Gods from Outer Space),* finds supposed evidence of the presence of "extraterrestrial" beings or "gods" in ancient history, who are supposedly responsible for the sudden appearance of intelligence in man, difficult to account for by the usual evolutionary theory. Serious scientists in the Soviet Union speculate that the destruction of Sodom and Gomorrah was due to a nuclear explosion,

that "extraterrestrial" beings visited earth centuries ago, that Jesus Christ may have been a "cosmonaut," and that today "we may be on the threshold of a 'second coming' of intelligent beings from outer space."* Equally serious scientists in the West think the existence of "extraterrestrial intelligences" likely enough that for at least eighteen years they have been trying to establish contact with them by means of radio telescopes, and currently there are at least six searches being conducted by astronomers around the world for intelligent radio signals from space. Contemporary Protestant and Roman Catholic "theologians"—who have become accustomed to follow wherever "science" seems to be leading—speculate in turn in the new realm of "exotheology" (the "theology of outer space") concerning what nature the "extraterrestrial" races might have.** It can hardly be denied that the myth behind science fiction has a powerful fascination even among many learned men of our day.

The future "evolved" beings in science fiction literature are invariably seen as having "outgrown" the limitations of present-day humanity, in particular the limitations of "personality." Like the "God" of science fiction, "man" also has become strangely impersonal. In Arthur C. Clarke's *Childhood's End,* the new race of humans has the appearance of children but faces devoid of personality; they are about to be guided into yet higher "evolutionary" transformations, on the way to becoming absorbed in the impersonal "Overmind." In general the literature of science fiction—in direct contrast to Christi-

---

* Sheila Ostrander and Lynn Schroeder, *Psychic Discoveries Behind the Iron Curtain,* Bantam Books, 1977, pp. 98–99. See articles in Russian of Dr. Vyacheslav Zaitsev, "Visitors from Outer Space," in *Sputnik,* January 1967, and "Temples and Spaceships," *Sputnik,* January 1968.
** See *Time* magazine, April 24, 1978.

anity, but exactly in accordance with some schools of Eastern thought—sees "evolutionary advancement" and "spirituality" in terms of increased impersonality.

3. The future world and humanity are seen by science fiction ostensibly in terms of "projections" from present-day scientific discoveries; in actuality, however, these "projections" correspond quite remarkably to the everyday reality of occult and overtly demonic experience throughout the ages. Among the characteristics of the "highly evolved" creatures of the future are: communication by mental telepathy, ability to fly, materialize and dematerialize, transform the appearances of things or create illusionary scenes and creatures by "pure thought," travel at speeds far beyond any modern technology, to take possession of the bodies of earthmen; and the expounding of a "spiritual" philosophy which is "beyond all religions" and holds promise of a state where "advanced intelligences" will no longer be dependent on matter. All these are the standard practices and claims of sorcerers and demons. A recent history of science fiction notes that "a persistent aspect of the vision of science fiction is the desire to transcend normal experience ... through the presentation of characters and events that transgress the conditions of space and time as we know them."* The scripts of "Star Trek" and other science-fiction stories, with their futuristic "scientific" devices, read in parts like excerpts from the lives of ancient Orthodox Saints, where the actions of sorcerers are described at a time when sorcery was still a strong part of pagan life. Science fiction in general is usually not very scientific at all, and not really very "futuristic" either; if anything, it is a retreat to the "mystical" origins of

---

* Robert Scholes and Eric S. Rabkin, *Science Fiction: History, Science, Vision,* Oxford University Press, 1977, p. 175.

modern science—the science before the age of the 17th and 18th-century "Enlightenment" which was much closer to occultism. The same history of science fiction remarks that "the roots of science fiction, like the roots of science itself, are in magic and mythology."* Present-day research and experiments in "parapsychology" point also to a future connection of "science" with occultism—a development with which science-fiction literature is in full harmony.

Science fiction in the Soviet Union (where it is just as popular as in the West, although its development has been a little different) has exactly the same themes as Western science fiction. In general, "metaphysical" themes in Soviet science fiction (which labors under the watchful eye of "materialist" censors) come from the influence of Western writers or from direct Hindu influence, as in the case of the writer Ivan Efremov. The reader of Soviet science fiction, according to one critic, "emerges with a vague ability to distinguish the critical demarcations between Science and Magic, between scientist and sorcerer, between future and fantasy." Science fiction both East and West, says the same writer, like other aspects of contemporary culture, "all confirm the fact that the higher stage of humanism is occultism."**

4. Almost by its very nature as "futuristic," science fiction tends to be utopian; few novels or stories actually describe a future perfect society, but most of them deal with the "evolution" of today's society into something higher, or the encounter with an advanced civilization on another planet, with the hope or capability of overcoming today's problems and mankind's limi-

---

* Scholes and Rabkin, p. 183.
** G.V. Grebens, *Ivan Efremov's Theory of Soviet Science Fiction,* Vantage Press, New York, 1978, pp. 108, 110.

tations in general. In Efremov's and other Soviet science fiction, Communism itself becomes "cosmic" and "begins to acquire nonmaterialistic qualities," and "the post-industrial civilization will be Hindu-like."* The "advanced beings" of outer space are often endowed with "saviour"-like qualities, and the landings of spacecraft on earth often herald "apocalyptic" events—usually the arrival of benevolent beings to guide men in their "evolutionary advancement."

In a word, the science-fiction literature of the 20th century is itself a clear sign of the loss of Christian values and the Christian interpretation of the world; it has become a powerful vehicle for the dissemination of a non-Christian philosophy of life and history, largely under open or concealed occult and Eastern influence; and in a crucial time of crisis and transition in human civilization it has been a prime force in creating the hope for and actual expectation of "visitors from outer space" who will solve mankind's problems and conduct man to a new "cosmic" age of its history. While appearing to be scientific and non-religious, science-fiction literature is in actuality a leading propagator (in a secular form) of the "new religious consciousness" which is sweeping mankind as Christianity retreats.

All of this is a necessary background for discussing the actual manifestations of "Unidentified Flying Objects," which strangely correspond to the pseudo-religious expectations which have been aroused in "post-Christian" man.

2. UFO Sightings and the Scientific Investigation of Them

Although fiction, one might say, has in a way prepared men for the appearance of UFOs, our understanding of their

---

* Ibid., pp. 109–10.

"objective" reality obviously cannot be derived from literature or human expectations and fantasies. Before we can understand what they might be, we must know something of the nature and reliability of the observations which have been made of them. Is there really something "out there" in the sky, or is the phenomenon entirely a matter of misperception on the one hand, and psychological and pseudo-religious wish fulfillment on the other?

A reliable outline of UFO phenomena has been given by Dr. Jacques Vallee, a French scientist now living in California who has advanced degrees in astrophysics and computer science and has been involved in the scientific analysis of UFO reports for a number of years. His testimony is all the more valuable to us in that he has studied closely UFO sightings outside of the United States, especially in France, and is thus able to give a fair international picture of their distribution.

Dr. Vallee finds* that although strange flying objects have been observed at various times in past centuries, their "modern history" as a mass phenomenon begins in the years during and just after World War II. American interest began with the sightings in 1947, but there were a number of sightings before that in Europe. In World War II many pilots reported strange lights which seemed to be under intelligent control** and in 1946, particularly in July, there were a whole series of sightings in Sweden and other northern European countries.*** Sightings in this "Scandinavian wave" were interpreted first as "meteors," then as "rockets" (or "ghost rock-

---

* *UFOs in Space: Anatomy of a Phenomenon,* Ballantine Books, New York, 1977 (first published by Henry Regnery Company, 1965); page numbers as indicated in parentheses in text above.
** Ibid., p. 47.
*** Ibid., pp. 47–53.

ets") or "bombs," and finally as some "new type of aircraft" capable of extraordinary movements in the sky but leaving no trace on the ground even when they seemed to land. The European press was full of reports of this wave of sightings, and everyone in Sweden was talking of them; some thousands of sightings were reported, but not once was the hypothesis of "extraterrestrial" or "interplanetary" origin suggested. Dr. Vallee concludes that the "wave" was caused by actually existing but unidentified objects and not by any previously existing "UFO rumor" or expectation of "visitors from outer space."* In this and succeeding "saucer waves" he finds a total absence of any correlation between widespread interest in science fiction and peaks of UFO activity; earlier, also, there had been no "saucer wave" at the time of the American panic over Orson Welles' 1938 radio adaptation of H. G. Wells' *War of the Worlds.* He concludes that "the birth, growth and expansion of a UFO wave is an objective phenomenon independent of the conscious or unconscious influence of the witnesses, and their reactions to it."**

The first publicized sighting in the United States occurred in June 1947, when Kenneth Arnold, a salesman flying his own plane, saw nine disc-like objects, looking something like "saucers," flying near Mt. Rainier in Washington state. The newspapers picked up the story, and the "flying saucer" era began. Interestingly, however, this was not actually the first American sighting at all; other unpublicized sightings had been made in the months before this. There was also a UFO wave (with fifty reports) in Hungary early in June. Therefore, the 1947 sightings cannot all be set down to hysteria over the

---

* Ibid., p. 53.
** Ibid., p. 31.

Arnold incident. There were a number of other sightings in the American wave of 1947, chiefly in June, July, and August. Although some newspapers speculated on "interplanetary visitors," these sightings were taken seriously by scientists, who assumed they were the result of advanced human technology, most likely American, or perhaps Russian (pp. 54–57).

A second wave occurred in July 1948, with sightings in America and France. In the United States there was a spectacular night sighting made by the pilots of an Eastern Airlines DC-3 plane of a torpedo-shaped craft with two rows of "portholes," surrounded by a blue glow and with a tail of orange flames, which maneuvered to avoid collision and disappeared. In August of the same year there were many sightings in Saigon and other parts of Southeast Asia of a "long fish-like object" (pp. 57–59).

1949 saw reports of strange discs and spheres in Sweden and more UFOs in America, including two observations by trained astronomical observers (pp. 60–62). Small UFO waves, as well as isolated sightings, continued in 1950 and 1951, especially in the United States, but also in Europe (pp. 62–65).

In 1952 the first real international UFO wave occurred, with many sightings in the United States, France, and North Africa. At the peak of the wave, two sensational sightings were made above the Capitol and the White House in Washington, D.C. (an area under constant control by radar). In September there was a wave encompassing Denmark, Sweden, and northern Germany and Poland. At the same time in France the first UFO "landing" was reported, together with a description of "little men" (pp. 65–69).

In 1953 there were no waves, but there were a number of individual sightings. The most remarkable one occurred in Bismarck, North Dakota, where four objects hovered and maneuvered over an air filter station for three hours at night; an official report of this event consisted of several hundred pages, with accounts from many witnesses, mainly pilots and military personnel (pp. 69–70).

1954 saw the largest international wave yet. France was literally inundated with sightings, with dozens of reports every day in September, October, and November. In the French wave the problems facing a serious scientific investigation of UFO phenomena are well demonstrated: "The phenomenon was so intense, the impact on public opinion so deep, the newspapers' reaction so emotional that scientific reflexes were saturated long before a serious investigation could be organized. As a result, no scientist could risk his reputation by studying openly a phenomenon so emotionally distorted; French scientists remained silent until the wave passed and died" (p. 71).

During the French wave, the typical characteristics of later UFO encounters were often present: UFO "landings" (with at least some circumstantial evidence of them), beams of light issuing from the UFO to the witness, stoppage of motors in the vicinity of sightings, strange small beings in "diving suits," serious psychic and physical harm to witnesses.

Since 1954 many sightings have been made every year in various countries, with major international waves in 1965, 1967, and 1972–1973; sightings have been especially numerous and profound in their effects in South American countries.

The best-known government investigation of UFOs was that undertaken by the United States Air Force shortly after the first American sightings in 1947; this investigation, known from 1951 on as "Project Blue Book," lasted until 1969, when it was abandoned on the recommendation of the "Condon Report" of 1968—the work of a scientific committee led by a noted physicist of the University of Colorado. Close observers both of "Blue Book" and the "Condon Committee," however, have noted that neither of them took UFO phenomena seriously and that their main occupation was more the "public relations" task of explaining away mystifying aerial phenomena in order to calm public fears about them. Some "Flying Saucer" groups claimed that the United States government was using these investigations as a "cover-up" of its own knowledge of the "real nature" of UFOs; but all evidence points to the fact that the investigations themselves were simply careless because the phenomena were not taken seriously—especially after some of the stranger UFO stories had begun to make the subject distasteful to scientists. The first director of "Blue Book," Captain Edward Ruppelt, admitted that "had the Air Force tried to throw up a screen of confusion, they couldn't have done a better job.... The problem was tackled with organized confusion.... Everything was being evaluated on the premise that UFOs couldn't exist."* The Condon Report contains some classic "explanations" of UFOs; one, for example, states that "this unusual sighting should therefore be assigned to the category of some almost certainly natural phenomenon which is so rare that it apparently has never been reported before or since." The chief scientific consultant of "Blue Book" for most of its twenty-two years, Northwestern University astronomer J. Allen Hynek, openly calls the whole thing "a pseudo-scientific project."**

In its twenty-two years of investigations, such as they were, "Project Blue Book" collected over 12,000 cases of puzzling aerial phenomena, 25% of which remained "unidenti-

---

* Ruppelt, *Report on Unidentified Flying Objects,* Ace Books, New York, 1956, pp. 80, 83.
** Hynek, *The UFO Experience: A Scientific Inquiry,* Ballantine Books, New York, 1977, pp. 215, 219.

fied" even after its often strained "explanations." Many thousands of other cases have been and are being collected and investigated by private organizations in the United States and in other countries, although almost all government organizations refrain from comment on them. In the Soviet Union the subject was first given public mention (which means government approval) in 1967, when Dr. Felix U. Ziegel of the Moscow Institute of Aviation, in an article in the Soviet magazine *Smena,* stated that "Soviet radar has picked up unidentified flying objects for twenty years."* At the same time there was a Soviet scientific conference "On Space Civilizations," led by the Armenian astronomer Victor Ambartsumyam, which urged a preliminary study of the scientific and technical problems of communicating with such "civilizations," whose existence is taken for granted.** The next year, however, the subject of UFOs became once more forbidden in the Soviet Union, and since then Soviet scientists have told of their researches and hypotheses only unofficially to Western scientists.

In the United States, the subject of UFOs remains somewhat "off-limits" for military and scientific men, but in recent years an increasing number especially among younger scientists have begun to take the subject seriously and come together to discuss it and suggest means of researching it. Drs. Hynek and Vallee speak of an "invisible college" of scientists who are now

---

* "UFOs, What Are They?" in *Smena,* Apr. 7, 1967. See also his article "Unidentified Flying Objects" in *Soviet Life,* February 1968; Ostrander and Schroeder, *Psychic Discoveries Behind the Iron Curtain,* pp. 94–103.
** Felix Ziegel, "On Possible Exchange of Information with Extra-Terrestrial Civilizations," paper presented at the All-Union Engineering Institute in Moscow, March 13, 1967; *Psychic Discoveries,* p. 96.

actively interested in UFO phenomena, although most of them do not wish their names publicly associated with the subject.

There are, of course, those who continue to deny the phenomenon altogether, explaining it as misperceptions of natural objects, balloons, airplanes, etc., not to mention hoaxes and psychological "projections." One of these, Philip Klass, takes delight in "debunking" UFOs, investigating some of the sightings and finding them to be either natural phenomena or frauds. His study has convinced him that "the idea of wondrous spaceships from a distant civilization really is a fairy story that is tailored to the adult mentality."* Such hard-headed investigators, however, usually restrict themselves to cases where *actual physical proof* of a UFO has been left (the so-called "Close Encounters of the Second Kind," as we shall see below); and even staunch defenders of their reality are forced to admit that there is very little of this even in the most convincing UFO sightings. The one thing that has persuaded a number of scientists in recent years to take the phenomena seriously is not the physical proof of them, but the fact that *many serious and reliable people have seen something which cannot be explained and which often has a powerful effect upon them.* Dr. Hynek writes of his investigation: "Invariably I have had the feeling that I was talking to someone who was describing a very *real event.* To him or her it represented an outstanding experience, vivid and not at all dreamlike, an event for which the observer was usually totally unprepared—something soon recognized as being beyond comprehension" (*The UFO Experience,* p. 14).

This combination of the often intense reality of the experience of encountering a UFO (especially in the "Close Encounters"), and the almost total lack of physical evidence of

---

* Philip J. Klass, *UFOs Explained,* Random House, New York, 1974, p. 360.

84

it—makes the investigation of UFOs by nature not chiefly an examination of physical phenomena but more an investigation of the human reports of it, their credibility, consistency, etc. Already this places the investigation somewhat in the realm of psychology, and is enough to tell us that the approach solely in search of "physical proof" is an inadequate one. However, Mr. Klass' opinion that the "wondrous spaceships" are a "fairy story for adults" is perhaps also not far from the truth. One thing is the observations made of UFOs, and quite another is the *interpretation* which people give their (or others') observations—the former could be real, and the latter a "fairy story" or a myth of our times.

Dr. Hynek has done much to remove some of the common misconceptions about UFO sightings. Thus, he makes it clear that most UFO sightings are not reported by cultists, unstable or uneducated people. The few reports made by such people are usually easily identified as unreliable and not further investigated. But the most coherent and articulate reports come from normal, responsible people (often with scientific training), who are genuinely surprised or shocked by their experience and simply don't know how to explain it (*The UFO Experience,* pp. 10–11); the stronger the experience and the closer the UFO is seen, the less willing the witnesses are to report it at all. UFO records are a collection of "incredible tales told by credible persons," as one Air Force general has remarked. There can be no reasonable doubt that there is *something* behind the many thousands of serious UFO reports.

3. The Six Kinds of UFO Encounters

Dr. Hynek, who has studied the question more thoroughly than any other distinguished scientist, has conveniently divided UFO phenomena into six general categories.* The first, "Nocturnal Lights," is the one most commonly reported and the least strange of all. Most of such reports are easily explained as heavenly bodies, meteors, etc., and are not considered UFOs. Truly puzzling Nocturnal Lights (those that remain "unidentified"), which seem to display intelligent action but are not explainable as ordinary aircraft, are often seen by multiple witnesses, including police officers, airplane pilots, and airport tower operators.

The second category of UFOs is "Daylight Discs," whose behavior is close to that of Nocturnal Lights. These are the original "flying saucers," and in fact almost all of the unidentified sightings in this category are of discs which vary in shape from circular to cigar-shaped. They are often metallic in appearance, and are reported as capable of extremely rapid starts and stops and high speed, as well as maneuvers (such as sudden reversals of direction and motionless hovering) that are beyond the capacity of any present aircraft. There are many purported photographs of such discs, but none of them is very convincing owing to the distance involved and the possibility of trick photography. Like Nocturnal Lights, UFOs in this category are almost always reported as being totally noiseless, and sometimes two or more of them are seen.

The third category is that of "Radar-Visual" reports— that is, radar sightings that are confirmed by independent visual observation (radar by itself being subject to various kinds of misperceptions). Most of these cases occur at night, and the best cases involved simultaneous sightings by airplanes (sometimes purposely dispatched to follow the UFO) at fairly close

---

* *The Hynek UFO Report,* Dell Publishing Co., New York, 1977, chs. 4–9; *The UFO Experience,* chs. 5–10.

range; in these cases the UFO always outmaneuvers the airplane, sometimes following it, and finally disappears in a burst of speed (up to 4000 miles and more per hour). Sometimes, as in categories 1 and 2 also, the object seems to divide and become two or more distinct objects; and sometimes clear visual sightings of such objects by pilots in the air are not picked up by radar at all. Sightings in this category, just as in the first two, last from between a few minutes to several hours.

A number of cases in the first three categories are well documented, with numerous reliable, experienced, and independent witnesses. Still, any *one* case, as Dr. Hynek notes, might be caused by some extremely unusual set of circumstances and not by some new and totally unknown phenomenon. But when many well-documented cases, all similar to each other, accumulate, the chances that they are all unusual misperceptions of familiar objects becomes very small (*The UFO Experience,* p. 92). This is why serious UFO investigators are now concentrating on the collection of a number of well-documented cases, and the comparison of numbers of reliable testimonies already begins to show definite patterns of UFO activity.

The emotional response of those who have witnessed UFOs of the first three categories is one of simple perplexity and puzzlement; they have seen something whose behavior seems totally unexplainable, and they are left with a tantalizing desire to see it "just a little closer." Only in a few cases—generally involving pilots who have tried to pursue the unidentified objects—has something like real fear been experienced at the encounters with something that seems intelligently directed and possessing a technology in advance of anything known today. In cases involving "Close Encounters," on the other hand, the human response becomes much deeper and the "psychic" side of the phenomena more pronounced.

"Close Encounters of the First Kind" (CE–1) are sightings of a luminous object at close range (about 500 feet or less), the light being sometimes very bright and casting luminescence on the ground below. When the shape of the object is described, it is generally stated to be oval, sometimes with a dome on top, and the lights are often described as rotating, usually in a counterclockwise direction. The objects often hover close to the ground, without sound or (occasionally) with a humming sound, sometimes moving close to the ground over considerable distances, and eventually taking off extremely rapidly, soundlessly, and usually straight up. There are numerous multiple-witness accounts of such "Close Encounters"; these accounts are invariably quite similar to each other, as though it is indeed one and the same object (or similar objects) that is being observed in all well-documented cases. Typically, these cases occur at night in sparsely settled areas, and there are a small number of witnesses for each sighting (an average of three to four in the cases examined by Dr. Hynek).

"Close Encounters of the First Kind" are always awesome and often frightening, but leave no visible marks; witnesses are usually so overwhelmed by the experience that they neglect to take photographs of the object even when a camera is nearby. Typical of the effect on witnesses is this comment in a 1955 UFO report: "I can assure you, once anyone has seen an object such as this so closely and for a period of even one minute, it would be etched in their memory for all time" (*The Hynek UFO Report,* p. 145). The experience is so unusual that witnesses are often not believed when they report it—a fact that causes many to report it only confidentially, after many years, or not at all. The experience is intensely real to those who experience it—but largely unbelievable to others.

A typical "Close Encounter of the First Kind" involved two Portage County, Ohio, deputy sheriffs in 1966. About 5:00 a.m. on the morning of April 16, after stopping to investigate a parked car on a country road, they saw an object "as big as a house" ascending to tree-top level (about 100 feet). As it approached the deputies it became increasingly bright, illuminating the area all around, then stopped and hovered over them with a humming sound. When it moved away they pursued it for some seventy miles into Pennsylvania, at speeds of up to 105 miles per hour. Two other police officers saw the object clearly at a higher elevation before it went straight up and disappeared about dawn. Congressional pressure forced "Project Blue Book" to investigate this case; it was "explained" as an "observation of Venus," and the officers who saw it were subjected to considerable ridicule in the press, leading to the breakup of one officer's family and the ruin of his health and career (*The UFO Experience*, pp. 114–24). Personal tragedies of this kind among people who have "Close Encounters" with UFOs are so common that they should definitely be included in the "typical characteristics" of this phenomenon.

"Close Encounters of the Second Kind" (CE–II) are essentially similar to CE–I experiences, with the one difference that they leave some striking physical and/or psychological effect of their presence. These effects include marks on the ground, the scorching or blighting of plants and trees, interference with electrical circuits causing radio static and the stoppage of automobile engines, discomfort to animals as evidenced by strange behavior, and effects on humans which include temporary paralysis or numbness, a feeling of heat, nausea, or other discomfort, temporary weightlessness (sometimes causing levitation), sudden healing of sores and pains, and various psychological and physical after-effects, including strange marks on the body. This kind of UFO encounter gives the greatest possibility for scientific investigation, since in addition to human testimony there is physical evidence that can be examined; but little investigation has actually been undertaken, both because most scientists are afraid to get involved in the whole question of UFOs, and because the evidence itself is usually inconclusive or partially subjective. One catalog has been compiled of over 800 cases of this type in twenty-four countries (*The Hynek UFO Report,* p. 30). No actual "piece" of a UFO has ever been authenticated, however, and the markings left on the ground are often as baffling as the sightings themselves. The most frequent marking left on the ground after a sighting (the UFO itself having been seen either on the ground or just above it) is a burned, dehydrated, or depressed area in the shape of a ring, usually twenty to thirty feet in diameter and one to three feet thick. These "rings" persist for weeks or months and the interior of the ring (and sometimes the whole circle) is reported to be barren for a season or two after the sighting. A few chemical analyses of the soil in such rings have produced no definite conclusions as to the possible origin of this condition.

"Close Encounters of the Second Kind" often happen to persons during the night in isolated sections of road. In many similar cases a glowing object lands in a field nearby or on the road in front of an automobile or truck, the engine and headlights on the automobile fail, and the occupants become terrified until the UFO leaves, often shooting suddenly straight up without a sound; the engine of the vehicle then can operate again, and often comes on by itself.

The strangest of all UFO reports are those that deal with "Close Encounters of the Third Kind" (CE–III)—that is,

UFO experiences involving "animated beings" ("occupants" or "humanoids"). The first thought of many people when hearing of such reports is to picture "little green men" and dismiss the whole phenomenon as unbelievable—a hoax or hallucination. However, the success of the recent American science-fiction film, named precisely for this category of UFO phenomena, *Close Encounters of the Third Kind* (for which Dr. Hynek served as technical consultant), together with evidence of the Gallup Poll in 1974 that 54% of those who are aware of UFOs believe that they are real, and 46% of all those interviewed believe in intelligent life on other planets* (the percentage today would certainly be greater)—point to the rapidly increasing acceptance by contemporary men of the possibility of actual encounters with "non-human" intelligences. Science fiction has given the images, "evolution" has produced the philosophy, and the technology of the "space age" has supplied the plausibility for such encounters.

Astonishingly, these encounters seem actually to be occurring today, as attested by the evidence of many believable witnesses. Of crucial importance, therefore, is the *interpretation* that must be made of these occurrences; is the reality behind them an actual contact with "visitors from outer space," or is this only an explanation provided by the "spirit of the times" for a contact of a different kind altogether? As we shall see below, today's scientific investigators of UFOs have already asked these questions.

Dr. Hynek admits his own repugnance to face the possibility of CE–III experiences: "To be frank, I would gladly omit

---

* J. Allen Hynek and Jacques Vallee, *The Edge of Reality: A Progress Report on Unidentified Flying Objects,* Henry Regnery Co., Chicago, 1975, pp. 289–90.

this part if I could without offense to scientific integrity" (*The UFO Experience,* p. 158). However, since his aim is scientific objectivity, he finds it impossible to ignore the well-documented cases, from believable witnesses, of this strange phenomenon. Of nearly 1,250 "Close Encounters" reported in a catalog by Dr. Jacques Vallee, 750 report the landing of a craft, and more than 300 of these report "humanoids" in or about the craft; one-third of all these are multiple-witness cases (*Ibid.,* p. 161).

In one "humanoid" case, which occurred in November 1961, in one of the northern plains' states in the U.S.A., four men were returning from a hunting trip late at night, when one of the men noticed a flaming object coming down, as if it were an airplane crashing about a half mile up the road from them. When they reached the site of the "crash," all four men saw a silo-shaped craft in a field, sticking in the ground at an angle, with four seemingly human figures standing around it (this was at a distance of about 150 yards). They flashed a light on one of the figures who was about 4½ feet high and wearing what looked like white coveralls; he made a gesture to the men to stay back. After some hesitation (still thinking it was a plane crash), they went to a nearby town for a police officer, and when they returned they saw only some small red lights, something like automobile lights. They drove into the field with the officer and followed the lights, only to discover that they suddenly disappeared, leaving no tracks whatsoever, despite the muddiness of the field. After the puzzled police officer left, the men again saw the "silo" coming down out of the sky with a reddish glow. Instantly after the object "landed," two figures were visible next to it; a shot was fired (although none of the men admitted to firing it) and one of the figures was "hit" in the shoulder with a thud, and spun around and down to his knees. In panic the men ran to their car and raced off, agreeing among themselves not to mention the incident to anyone. They returned home with a strange feeling that there was some period of time "lost" during the night. The next day one of the men was visited at his work by several well-groomed "official-looking" men, who asked him questions about the incident (but without mentioning the shooting) and then took him in their car to his home, where they questioned him about his clothes and boots and then left, telling him not to say anything about the incident to anyone. The hunter assumed these men were United States Air Force investigators trying to conceal some new "secret device," but the men never identified themselves and never contacted him again. All four men were extremely shaken up by the incident, and after six years one of them felt compelled to tell the whole story to a U.S. Treasury agent (*Edge of Reality,* pp. 129–41).

The main incidents in this story are typical of many "Close Encounters of the Third Kind." A little different case of this sort is the famous UFO "landing" at Kelly, a small town near Hopkinsville, Kentucky, which was investigated extensively by the police, Air Force, and independent researchers. In the evening and night of August 21, 1955, seven adults and four children in one farm household had a prolonged encounter with "humanoids." The incident began at seven o'clock, when the teenaged son of the family saw a flying object "land" behind the farmhouse. No one believed him, but an hour later a "little man" emitting a "strange glow" came walking toward the house with its hands raised. Two of the men in the house, out of fear, shot at the creature when it was twenty feet away; it somersaulted and disappeared in the dark. Soon another similar creature appeared at a window; they again fired at it, and again it disappeared. Going outside, the men shot at another creature with a claw-like hand which they saw on the roof; still another on a tree nearby floated to the ground when it was shot. Other creatures also were seen and hit (or perhaps the same creatures reappearing), but the men saw the bullets seem to ricochet off from them and have no real effect; the sound was like shooting into a bucket. After firing four boxes of shells with no effect, all eleven people, thoroughly terrified, drove to the Hopkinsville police station. The police arrived at the farmhouse after midnight and made a thorough search of the premises, finding a few unusual markings and seeing several strange "meteors" that came in the direction of the farmhouse, but discovering no "creatures." After the police left, the creatures reappeared, causing more consternation in the household.

The "humanoids" in this case were described as being about 3 to 4 feet tall, with huge hands and eyes (without pupils or eyelids), large pointed ears, and arms that hung to the ground. They seemed to have no clothing but to be "nickel-plated." They approached the house always from the darkest side and did not approach when outside lights were turned on.*

Dr. Hynek sharply distinguishes between "Close Encounters of the Third Kind" and "contactee" cases. "Contactees" have repeated encounters with UFO beings, often bringing pseudo-religious messages from them about "highly evolved" beings on other planets who are about to come to bring "peace on earth," and are often connected with UFO religious cults. Ordinary CE–III experiences, on the other hand, are in general very similar to other "Close Encounters"; they occur to people of similar occupations and reliability, are just as unexpected, and produce

---

* Vallee, *UFOs in Space,* pp. 187–91; Hynek, *The UFO Experience,* pp. 172–77.

the same kind of shock at the sight of something so unbelievable. The "occupants" who are seen (usually from a little distance) are often reported as picking up samples of earth and rocks, showing a seeming interest in human installations and vehicles, or "repairing" their own craft. The "humanoids" are described as having large heads with largely non-human features (no eyes or large eyes widely spaced, small or no nose, a bare slit for a mouth), spindly legs, no neck; some are reported to be of human size, others about 3 feet high, as in the Kelly-Hopkinsville incident. Recently a new catalog of over 1,000 CE–III cases has been compiled (Hynek, *The UFO Experience*, p. 31).

There have been a number of cases, seriously reported by seemingly reliable people, of "abductions" by UFO occupants, usually for purposes of "testing." Almost all evidence of these cases (if we exclude "contactees") has been obtained by regressive hypnosis; the experience is so traumatic to the witnesses that the conscious mind does not remember it, and it is only some time later that such people agree to be hypnotized in order to explain some mysterious "time loss" in connection with their "Close Encounter" experience—the first part of which they do remember.

One of the best-known "abduction" cases occurred at about midnight on September 19, 1961, near Whitfield, New Hampshire. It was made the subject of a book by John Fuller (*The Interrupted Journey*), which was printed in a condensed form in *Look* magazine. On this night Barney and Betty Hill were returning from a vacation trip when they saw a descending UFO which landed right in front of their car on a side road. Some "humanoids" approached them, and the next thing they remembered, it was two hours later and they were thirty-five miles farther down the road. This amnesia bothered them, leading to physical and mental disorders, and they finally went to a psychiatrist. Under hypnosis they both independently related what had happened during the missing time. Both stated that they had been taken aboard the "craft" by the "humanoids" and given physical examinations, with samples taken of fingernails and skin. They were released after being given the hypnotic suggestion that they would remember nothing of the experience. Under hypnosis they related the experience with great emotional disturbance (*The UFO Experience,* pp. 178–84).

In a similar case, at 2:30 a.m. on December 3, 1967, a policeman in Ashland, Nebraska, saw an object with a row of flickering lights in the road, which took off into the air when he approached it. He reported a "flying saucer" to his superiors and went home with a strong headache, a buzzing noise in his ears, and a red welt below the left ear. Later, it was discovered that there had been a period of twenty minutes that night of which he remembered nothing; under hypnosis he revealed that he had followed the UFO, which again landed. The occupants flashed a bright light at him, and then took him aboard their "craft," where he saw control panels and computer-like machines. (An engineer in France had seen something similar when he was "abducted" for eighteen days.) The "humanoids," wearing coveralls with a winged-serpent emblem, told the policeman that they came from a nearby galaxy, had bases in the United States, and operated their craft by "reverse electromagnetism"; they contact people by chance and "want to puzzle them." They released the man, telling him "not to speak wisely about this night" (*The Invisible College,* pp. 57–59).

At first sight, such incidents seem simply unbelievable, like some strange cases of hallucination or disordered imagination. But there have been too many of them now to dismiss them quite so easily. As reports of encounters with actual physical aircraft, to be sure, they are not very convincing. Further, psychiatrists themselves caution that the results of "regressive hypnosis" are very uncertain; the person being hypnotized is often not capable of distinguishing between actual experiences and "suggestions" planted in his mind, whether by the hypnotist or by someone else at the time of the supposed "Close Encounter." But even if these experiences are not fully "real" (as objective phenomena in space and time), the very fact that so many of them have been "implanted" in human minds in recent years is already significant enough. Without doubt there is *something* behind the "abduction" experiences also, and recently UFO investigators have begun to look in a different direction for an explanation of them.

Such experiences, and especially the "Close Encounters" of the 1970s, are noticeably bound up with "paranormal" or occult phenomena. People sometimes have strange dreams just before seeing UFOs, or hear knocks on the door when no one is there, or have strange visitors afterwards; some witnesses receive telepathic messages from UFO occupants. UFOs now sometimes simply materialize and dematerialize instead of coming and going at great speeds; sometimes "miraculous healings" occur in their presence or when one is exposed to their light.* But "Close Encounters" with UFOs have also resulted in leukemia and radiation sickness; often there are tragic psychological effects: personality deterioration, insanity, suicide.**

The increase of the "psychic component" in UFO sightings has led researchers to seek similarities between UFO expe-

---

* Jacques Vallee, *The Invisible College,* E.P. Dutton, Inc., New York, 1975, pp. 17, 21.
** John A. Keel, *UFOs: Operation Trojan Horse,* G. P. Putnam's Sons, New York, 1970, p. 303.

riences and occult phenomena, and to seek the key to understanding UFOs in the psychic effects they produce (*The Invisible College,* p. 29). Many researchers note the similarity between UFO phenomena and 19th-century spiritism, which also combined psychic phenomena with strange physical effects, but with a more primitive "technology." In general, the 1970s have seen a narrowing of the gap between the "normal" UFO phenomena of the past and the UFO cults, in accordance with the increased receptivity of mankind in this decade to occult practices.

4. Explanation of the UFO Phenomena

Dr. Jacques Vallee's newest book on UFOs, *The Invisible College,* reveals what reputable scientific researchers are now thinking about them. He believes that we are now "very close" to understanding what they are. He notes that the idea of "extraterrestrial" intelligent life has in a few years become astonishingly fashionable, among scientists as well as fortune tellers, as a result of "a great thirst for contact with superior minds that will provide guidance for our poor, harassed, hectic planet" (p. 195). He significantly sees that the idea of visitors from outer space has become the great myth or "wonderful untruth" of our times: *"It has become very important for large numbers of people to expect visitors from outer space"* (p. 207, emphasis in the original).

Yet he finds it naive to believe in this myth: "This explanation is too simple-minded to account for the diversity of the reported behavior of the occupants and their perceived interaction with human beings" (p. 27). Dr. Hynek has noted that in order to explain the various effects produced by UFOs, we must assume that they are "a phenomenon that undoubtedly has physical effects but also has the attributes of the psychic world" (*The Edge of Reality,* p. 259). Dr. Vallee believes that "they are constructed *both as physical craft* (a fact which has long appeared to me undeniable) *and as psychic devices,* whose exact properties remain to be defined" (*The Invisible College,* p. 202, emphasis in the original). Actually, the theory that UFOs are not physical craft at all, but some kind of "paraphysical" or psychic phenomenon, was suggested by a number of researchers in the early 1950s; but this opinion was largely submerged later, on the one hand by the cultists, with their insistence on the "extraterrestrial" origin of UFOs, and on the other hand by the official government explanations, which corresponded to the widespread popular view that the whole phenomenon was imaginary (Keel, *UFOs: Operation Trojan Horse,* pp. 38-41). Only lately have serious investigators begun to agree that UFOs, while having certain "physical" characteristics, cannot at all be explained as somebody's "space ships," but are clearly something of the paraphysical or occult realm.

Why, indeed, are so many UFO "landings" precisely in the middle of roads? Why do such fantastically "advanced" craft so often need "repairs"? Why do the occupants so often need to pick up rocks and sticks (over and over again for twenty-five years!), and to "test" so many people—if they are actually reconnaissance vehicles from another planet, as the "humanoids" usually claim? Dr. Vallee well asks whether the "visitors from outer space" idea might not "serve precisely a diversionary role in masking the real, infinitely more complex nature of the technology that gives rise to the sightings?" (*The Invisible College,* p. 28). He believes "we are not dealing with successive waves of visitations from space. We are dealing with a control system" (p. 195). "What takes place through close

99

encounters with UFOs is control of human beliefs" (p. 3). "With every new wave of UFOs, the social impact becomes greater. More young people become fascinated with space, with psychic phenomena, with new frontiers in consciousness. More books and articles appear, changing our culture" (pp. 197–98). In another book he notes that "it is possible to make large sections of any population believe in the existence of supernatural races, in the possibility of flying machines, in the plurality of inhabited worlds, by exposing them to a few carefully engineered scenes, the details of which are adapted to the culture and superstitions of a particular time and place."*

An important clue to the meaning of these "engineered scenes" may be seen in an observation often made by careful observers of UFO phenomena, especially CE–III and "contactee" cases: that they are profoundly "absurd," or contain at least as much absurdity as rationality (Vallee, *The Invisible College,* p. 196). Individual "Close Encounters" have absurd details, like the four pancakes given by a UFO occupant to a Wisconsin chicken farmer in 1961;** more significantly, the encounters themselves are strangely pointless, without clear purpose or meaning. A Pennsylvania psychiatrist has suggested that the absurdity present in almost all UFO close encounters is actually a *hypnotic technique.* "When the person is disturbed by the absurd or contradictory, and their mind is searching for meaning, they are extremely open to thought transference, to receiving psychic healing, etc." (*The Invisible College,* p. 115). Dr. Vallee compares this technique to the irrational *koans* of Zen

---

* Vallee, *Passport to Magonia,* Henry Regnery Co., Chicago, 1969, pp. 150–51.

** Ibid., pp. 23–25. One of the pancakes was actually analyzed by the Food and Drug Laboratory of the U.S. Department of Health, Education, and Welfare, and was found to be "of terrestrial origin."

Masters (p. 27), and notices the similarity between UFO encounters and occult initiation rituals which "open the mind" to a "new set of symbols" (p. 117). All of this points to what he calls "the next form of religion" (p. 202).

Thus, UFO encounters are but a contemporary form of an occult phenomenon which has existed throughout the centuries. Men have abandoned Christianity and look for "saviours" from outer space, and therefore the phenomenon supplies images of spacecraft and space beings. But what is this phenomenon? Who is doing the "engineering," and to what purpose?

Today's investigators have already supplied the answers to at least the first two questions, although, being without competence in the realm of religious phenomena, they do not fully understand the significance of what they have found. One investigator, Brad Steiger, an Iowa college professor who has written several books on the subject, after a recent detailed study of the Air Force "Blue Book" files, concluded: "We are dealing with a multi-dimensional paraphysical phenomenon, which is largely indigenous to planet earth" (*Canadian UFO Report,* Summer, 1977). Drs. Hynek and Vallee have advanced the hypothesis of "earth-bound aliens" to account for UFO phenomena, and speculate on "interlocking universes" right here on earth from which they might come, much as "poltergeists" produce physical effects while remaining themselves invisible. John Keel, who began his UFO investigation as a skeptic and is himself an agnostic in religion, writes: "The real UFO story ... is one of ghosts and phantoms and strange mental aberrations; of an invisible world which surrounds us and occasionally engulfs us.... It is a world of illusion ... where reality itself is distorted by strange forces which can seemingly manipulate space, time, and physical matter—forces which are almost entirely beyond our powers of comprehension.... The UFO manifestations seem to be, by and large, merely minor variations of the age-old demonological phenomenon" (*UFOs: Operation Trojan Horse,* pp. 46, 299). In a recent bibliography of UFO phenomena prepared by the Library of Congress for the United States Air Force Office of Scientific Research, the introduction states that "Many of the UFO reports now being published in the popular press recount alleged incidents that are strikingly similar to demonic possession and psychic phenomena which have long been known to theologians and parapsychologists."* Most UFO researchers are now turning to the occult realm and to demonology for insight into the phenomena they are studying.

Several recent studies of UFOs, by evangelical Protestants, put all this evidence together and come to the conclusion that UFO phenomena are simply and precisely demonic in origin.** The Orthodox Christian investigator can hardly come to a different conclusion. Some or many of the experiences, it may be, are the result of hoaxes or hallucinations; but it is simply impossible to dismiss *all* of the many thousands of UFO reports in this way. A great number of modern mediums and their spiritistic phenomena are also fraudulent; but mediumistic spiritism itself, when it is genuine, undeniably produces real "paranormal" phenomena under the action of demons. UFO phenomena, having the same source, are no less real.

Case histories of people who have been drawn into contact with UFOs reveal the standard characteristics which go

---

* Lynn G. Catoe, *UFOs and Related Subjects: An Annotated Bibliography,* U.S. Government Printing Office, Washington, D.C., 1969.
** Clifford Wilson and John Weldon, *Close Encounters: A Better Explanation,* Master Books, San Diego, 1978; *Spiritual Counterfeits Project Journal,* Berkeley, Calif., August 1977: "UFOs: Is Science Fiction Coming True?"

with involvement with demons in the occult realm. A police officer in southern California, for example, began to see UFOs in June 1966, and thereafter saw them frequently, almost always at night. After one "landing" he and his wife saw distinct traces of the UFO on the ground. "During these weeks of tantalizing sightings, I became totally obsessed with the UFOs, convinced that something *great* was about to happen. I abandoned my daily Bible reading and turned my back on God as I began reading every UFO book I could lay my hands on.... Many nights I watched in vain, trying to mentally communicate with what I then thought were extraterrestrial beings, almost praying to them to appear and establish some sort of contact with me." Finally he had a "Close Encounter" with a "craft" some eighty feet in diameter, with rotating white, red, and green lights. It sped off and left him still expecting something "great" to happen—but nothing ever did happen; the UFOs ceased appearing, and in his frustration he turned to alcohol, depression, thoughts of suicide, until his conversion to Christ ended this period of his life. People who have actually contacted the UFO beings have much worse experiences; the beings sometimes literally "possess" them and try to kill them when they resist (*UFOs: A Better Explanation,* pp. 298–305). Such cases effectively remind us that, quite apart from the meaning of UFO phenomena as a whole, each UFO "Close Encounter" has the specific purpose of deceiving the individual who is contacted and leading him, if not to further "contacts" and spreading of the UFO "message," then at least to personal spiritual confusion and disorientation.

The most puzzling aspect of UFO phenomena to most researchers—namely, the strange mingling of physical and psychic characteristics in them—is no puzzle at all to readers of Orthodox spiritual books, especially the Lives of Saints. Demons also have "physical bodies," although the "matter" in them is of such subtlety that it cannot be perceived by men unless their spiritual "doors of perception" are opened, whether with God's will (as in the case of holy men) or against it (as in the case of sorcerers and mediums).*

Orthodox literature has many examples of demonic manifestations which fit precisely the UFO pattern: apparitions of "solid" beings and objects (whether demons themselves or their illusionary creations) which suddenly "materialize" and "dematerialize," always with the aim of awing and confusing people and ultimately leading them to perdition. The Lives of the 4th-century St. Anthony the Great** and the 3rd-century St. Cyprian the Former Sorcerer*** are filled with such incidents.

The Life of St. Martin of Tours (†397) by his disciple, Sulpicius Severus, has an interesting example of demonic power in connection with a strange "physical" manifestation which closely parallels today's UFO "Close Encounters." A certain youth named Anatolius became a monk near St. Martin's monastery, but out of false humility he became the victim of demonic deception. He fancied that he conversed with "angels," and in order to persuade others of his sanctity, these "angels" agreed to give him a "shining robe from out of heaven" as a sign of the "Power of God" that dwelt in the youth. One night about midnight there was a tremendous thudding of dancing feet and a murmuring as of many voices in the hermitage, and Anatolius' cell became ablaze with light. Then came silence,

---

* The Orthodox doctrine of demons and angels, their manifestations and the human perception of them, as summarized by the great Orthodox Father of the 19th century, Bishop Ignatius Brianchaninov, is set forth in the book *The Soul After Death,* St. Herman of Alaska Brotherhood, Platina, Calif., 1979.
** Eastern Orthodox Books, Willits, Calif., 1976.
*** *The Orthodox Word,* no. 70, 1976.

and the deceived one emerged from his cell with the "heavenly" garment. "A light was brought and all carefully inspected the garment. It was exceedingly soft, with a surpassing luster, and of a brilliant scarlet, but it was impossible to tell the nature of the material. At the same time, under the most exact scrutiny of eyes and fingers it seemed to be a garment and nothing else." The following morning, Anatolius' spiritual father took him by the hand in order to lead him to St. Martin to discover whether this was actually a trick of the devil. In fear, the deceived one refused to go, "and when he was being forced to go against his will, between the hands of those who were dragging him the garment disappeared." The author of the account (who either witnessed the incident himself or had it from eyewitnesses) concludes that "the devil was unable to keep up his illusions or conceal their nature when they were to be submitted to Martin's eyes." "It was so fully within his power to see the devil that he recognized him under any form, whether he kept to his own character or changed himself into any of the various shapes of 'spiritual wickedness'"—including the forms of pagan gods and the appearance of Christ Himself, with royal robes and crown and enveloped in a bright red light.*

It is clear that the manifestations of today's "flying saucers" are quite within the "technology" of demons; indeed, nothing else can explain them as well. The multifarious demonic deceptions of Orthodox literature have been adapted to the mythology of outer space, nothing more; the Anatolius mentioned above would be known today simply as a "contactee." And the purpose of the "unidentified" object in such accounts is clear: to awe the beholders with a sense of the "mysterious," and to

---

* F. R. Hoare, translator, *The Western Fathers,* Harper Torchbacks, New York, 1965, pp. 36–41.

produce "proof" of the "higher intelligences" ("angels," if the victim believes in them, or "space visitors" for modern men), and thereby to gain trust for the *message* they wish to communicate. We shall look at this message below.

A demonic "kidnapping" quite close to UFO "abductions" is described in the Life of St. Nilus of Sora, the 15th-century founder of Skete life in Russia. Some time after the Saint's death there lived in his monastery a certain priest with his son. Once, when the boy was sent on some errand, "suddenly there came to him a certain strange man who seized him and carried him, as if on the wind, into an impenetrable forest, bringing him into a large room in his dwelling and placing him in the middle of this cabin, in front of the window." When the priest and the monks prayed for St. Nilus' help in finding the lost boy, the Saint "came to the boy's aid and stood before the room where the boy was standing, and when he struck the window-frame with his staff the building was shaken and all the unclean spirits fell to the earth." The Saint told the demon to return the boy to the place from which he had taken him, and then became invisible. Then, after some howling among the demons, "the same strange one seized the boy and brought him to the Skete like the wind ... and placing him on a haystack, he became invisible." After being seen by the monks, "the boy told them everything that happened to him, what he had seen and heard. And from that time this boy became very humble, as if he had been stupefied. The priest out of terror left the Skete with his son."* In a similar demonic "kidnapping" in 19th-century Russia, a young man, after his mother cursed him, became the slave of a demon "grandfather" for

---

* *The Northern Thebaid,* St. Herman of Alaska Brotherhood, Platina, Calif., 1975, pp. 91–92. [Third edition, 2004, pp. 95–96.]

twelve years and was capable of appearing invisibly among men in order to help the demon sow confusion in their midst.*

Such true stories of demonic activity were commonplace in earlier centuries. It is a sign of the spiritual crisis of today that modern men, for all their proud "enlightenment" and "wisdom," are becoming once more aware of such experiences—*but no longer have the Christian framework with which to explain them.* Contemporary UFO researchers, seeking for an explanation of phenomena which have become too noticeable to overlook any longer, have joined today's psychic researchers in an attempt to formulate a "unified field theory" that will encompass psychic as well as physical phenomena. But such researchers only continue the approach of "enlightened" modern men and trust their scientific observations to give answers in a *spiritual* realm that cannot be approached "objectively" at all, but only with faith. The physical world is morally neutral and may be known relatively well by an objective observer; but the invisible spiritual realm comprises beings both good and evil, and the "objective" observer has no means of distinguishing one from the other unless he accepts the revelation which the invisible God has made of them to man. Thus, today's UFO researchers place the Divine inspiration of the Bible on the same level as the satanically inspired automatic writing of spiritism, and they do not distinguish between the actions of angels and those of demons. They know now (after a long period when materialistic prejudices reigned among scientists) that there is a non-physical realm that is real, and they see its effects in UFO phenomena; but as long as they approach this realm "scientifically," they will be just as easily

---

* S. Nilus, *The Power of God and Man's Weakness* (in Russian), St. Sergius' Lavra, 1908; St. Herman Brotherhood, 1976, pp. 279–98.

deceived by the unseen powers as the most naive "contactee." When they try to determine *who* or *what* is behind the UFO phenomena, and what the purpose of the phenomena might be, they are forced to indulge in the wildest speculations. Thus Dr. Vallee confesses himself baffled whether the source of UFO manifestations might be a morally neutral "unattended clockwork," a benevolent "solemn gathering of wise men" (as the "extraterrestrial" myth would have us believe), or "a terrible superhuman monstrosity the very contemplation of which would make a man insane," that is, the activity of demons (*The Invisible College*, p. 206).

A true evaluation of the UFO experience may be made only on the basis of Christian revelation and experience, and is accessible only to the humble Christian believer who trusts these sources. To be sure, it is not given to man entirely to "explain" the invisible world of angels and demons; but enough Christian knowledge has been given us to know how these beings act in our world and how we should respond to their actions, particularly in escaping the nets of the demons. UFO researchers have come to the conclusion that the phenomena they have studied are essentially identical with phenomena that used to be called "demonic"; but only the Christian—the Orthodox Christian, who is enlightened by the Patristic understanding of Scripture and the 2,000-year experience of Saints' encounters with invisible beings—is able to know the full meaning of this conclusion.

5. The Meaning of UFOs

What, then, is the meaning of the UFO phenomena of our time? Why have they appeared just at this time in history? What is their message? To what future do they point?

First, UFO phenomena are but one part of an astonishing outpouring of "paranormal" events—what just a few years ago most people would have considered as "miracles." Dr. Vallee, in *The Invisible College,* expresses the secular appreciation of this fact: "Observations of unusual events suddenly loom into our environment by the thousands" (p. 87), causing "a general shifting of man's belief patterns, his entire relationship to the concept of the invisible" (p. 114). "Something is happening to human consciousness" (p. 34); the same "powerful force [that] has influenced the human race in the past is again influencing it now" (p. 14). In Christian language this means: a new demonic outpouring is being loosed upon mankind. In the Christian apocalyptic view (see the end of this book), we can see that the power which until now has restrained the final and most terrible manifestation of demonic activity on earth has been taken away (II Thess. 2:7), Orthodox Christian government and public order (whose chief representative on earth was the Orthodox emperor) and the Orthodox Christian worldview no longer exist as a whole, and satan has been "loosed out of his prison," where he was kept by the grace of the Church of Christ, in order to "deceive the nations" (Apoc. 20:7–8) and prepare them to worship antichrist at the end of the age. Perhaps never since the beginning of the Christian era have demons appeared so openly and extensively as today. The "visitors from outer space" theory is but one of the many pretexts they are using to gain acceptance for the idea that "higher beings" are now to take charge of the destiny of mankind.*

---

* Many of the reports of "Bigfoot" and other "monsters" show the same occult characteristics as UFO sightings, and often they occur in connection with such sightings.

Second, UFOs are but the newest of the *mediumistic techniques* by which the devil gains initiates into his occult realm. They are a terrible sign that man has become susceptible to demonic influence as never before in the Christian era. In the 19th century it was usually necessary to seek out dark séance rooms in order to enter into contact with demons, but now one need only look into the sky (usually at night, it is true). Mankind has lost what remained of basic Christian understanding up to now, and now passively places itself at the disposal of whatever "powers" may descend from the sky. The new film, *Close Encounters of the Third Kind,* is a shocking revelation of how *superstitious* "post-Christian" man has become—ready in an instant and unquestioningly to believe and follow hardly-disguised demons wherever they might lead.*

Third, the "message" of the UFOs is: prepare for anti-

---

* Two other recently discovered "paranormal" phenomena reveal how boldly the demons are now making use of physical means (in particular, modern technical devices) in order to enter into contact with men. (1) One Latvian researcher (now followed by others) has discovered the phenomenon of mysterious voices which appear unexplainably on tape recorders, even when the recording is done under clinical conditions in a totally soundless atmosphere, with results very similar to those of seances. The presence of a medium or "psychic" in the room seems to help the phenomenon (Konstantin Raudive, *Breakthrough: An Amazing Experiment in Electronic Communication with the Dead,* Taplinger Publishing Co., New York, 1971). (2) Metallic-voiced "space people" for some time have supposedly been using the telephone to communicate with both "contactees" and UFO researchers. The possibility of a hoax in such a phenomenon, of course, is high. But in recent years *the voices of the dead,* convincing to those who are contacted, have been heard in telephone conversations with their loved ones. It can hardly be denied, as the reporter of this phenomenon notes, that "the demons of old are marching among us again"—to a degree unheard of in the past (Keel, *UFOs: Operation Trojan Horse,* p. 306).

christ; the "saviour" of the apostate world is coming to rule it. Perhaps he himself will come in the air, in order to complete his impersonation of Christ (Matt. 24:30; Acts 1:11); perhaps only the "visitors from outer space" will land publicly in order to offer "cosmic" worship of their master; perhaps the "fire from heaven" (Apoc. 13:13) will be only a part of the great demonic spectacles of the last times. At any rate, the message for contemporary mankind is: expect deliverance, not from the Christian revelation and faith in an unseen God, but from vehicles in the sky.

It is one of the signs of the last times that *there shall be terrors and great signs from heaven* (Luke 21:11). Even a hundred years ago Bishop Ignatius Brianchaninov, in his book *On Miracles and Signs* (Yaroslavl, 1870, reprinted by Holy Trinity Monastery, Jordanville, New York, 1960), remarked on "the striving to be encountered in contemporary Christian society to see miracles and even perform miracles.... Such a striving reveals the self-deception, founded on self-esteem and vainglory, that dwells in the soul and possesses it" (p. 32). True wonderworkers have decreased and grown extinct, but people "thirst for miracles more than ever before.... We are gradually coming near to the time when a vast arena is to be opened up for numerous and striking false miracles, to draw to perdition those unfortunate offspring of fleshly wisdom who will be seduced and deceived by these miracles" (pp. 48–49).

Of special interest to UFO investigators, "the miracles of antichrist will be chiefly manifested in the aerial realm, where satan chiefly has his dominion. The signs will act most of all on the sense of sight, charming and deceiving it. St. John the Theologian, beholding in revelation the events that are to precede the end of the world, says that antichrist will perform great signs, and will *even make fire to come down out of heaven upon the earth in the sight of men* (Apoc. 13:13). This is the sign indicated by Scripture as the highest of the signs of antichrist, and the place of this sign is the air; it will be a splendid and terrible spectacle" (p. 13). St. Symeon the New Theologian for this reason remarks that "the struggler of prayer should quite rarely look into the sky out of fear of the evil spirits in the air who cause many and various deceptions in the air" (*Philokalia*, "The Three Forms of Heedfulness"). "Men will not understand that the miracles of antichrist have no good, rational purpose, no definite meaning, that they are foreign to truth, filled with lies, that they are a monstrous, malicious, meaningless play-acting, which increases in order to astonish, to reduce to perplexity and oblivion, to deceive, to seduce, to attract by the fascination of a pompous, empty, stupid effect" (p. 11). "All demonic manifestations have the characteristic that even the slightest heed paid to them is dangerous; from such heedfulness alone, allowed even without any sympathy for the manifestation, one may be sealed with a most harmful impression and subjected to a serious temptation" (p. 50). Thousands of UFO "contactees" and even simple witnesses have experienced the dreadful truth of these words; few have escaped once they become deeply involved.

Even the secular investigators of UFO phenomena have seen fit to warn people against their dangers. John Keel, for example, writes: "Dabbling with UFOs can be as dangerous as dabbling with black magic. The phenomenon preys upon the neurotic, the gullible, and the immature. Paranoid-schizophrenia, demonomania, and even suicide can result—and has resulted in a number of cases. A mild curiosity about UFOs can turn into a destructive obsession. For this reason, I strongly recommend that parents forbid their children from becoming involved. School teachers and other adults should not encourage teenagers to take an interest in this subject" (*UFOs: Operation Trojan Horse,* p. 220).

In a different place Bishop Ignatius Brianchaninov recorded with awe and foreboding the vision of a simple Russian blacksmith in a village near Petersburg at the dawn of our present age of unbelief and revolution (1817). In the middle of the day he suddenly saw a multitude of demons in human form, sitting in the branches of the forest trees, in strange garments and pointed caps, and singing, to the accompaniment of unbelievably weird musical instruments, an eerie and frightful song: "Our years have come, our will be done!"*

We live near the end of this fearful age of demonic triumph and rejoicing, when the eerie "humanoids" (another of the masks of the demons) have become visible to thousands of people and by their absurd encounters take possession of the souls of those men from whom God's grace has departed. The UFO phenomenon is a sign to Orthodox Christians to walk all the more cautiously and soberly on the path to salvation, knowing that we can be tempted and seduced not merely by false religions, but even by seemingly physical objects which just catch the eye. In earlier centuries Christians were very cautious about strange and new phenomena, knowing of the devil's wiles; but after the modern age of "enlightenment" most people have become merely curious about such things and even pursue them, relegating the devil to a half-imaginary realm. Awareness of the nature of UFOs, then, can be a help in awakening Orthodox Christians to a conscious spiritual life and a conscious Orthodox worldview that does not easily follow after the fashionable ideas of the times.

The conscious Orthodox Christian lives in a world that is

---

* S. Nilus, *Svyatynya pod Spudom,* Sergiev Posad, 1911, p. 122.

clearly fallen, both the earth below and the stars above, all being equally far from the lost paradise for which he is striving. He is part of a suffering mankind all descended from the one Adam, the first man, and all alike in need of the redemption offered freely by the Son of God by His saving Sacrifice on the Cross. He knows that man is not to "evolve" into something "higher," nor has he any reason to believe that there are "highly evolved" beings on other planets; but he knows well that there are indeed "advanced intelligences" in the universe besides himself; these are of two kinds, and he strives to live so as to dwell with those who serve God (the angels) and avoid contact with the others who have rejected God and strive in their envy and malice to draw man into their misfortune (the demons). He knows that man, out of self-love and weakness, is easily inclined to follow error and believe in "fairy tales" that promise contact with a "higher state" or "higher beings" without the struggle of Christian life—in fact, precisely as an *escape* from the struggle of Christian life. He distrusts his own ability to see through the deceptions of the demons, and therefore clings all the more firmly to the Scriptural and Patristic guidelines which the Church of Christ provides for his life.

Such a one has the possibility to resist the religion of the future, the religion of antichrist, in whatever form it may present itself; the rest of mankind, save by a miracle of God, is lost.

VII

The "Charismatic Revival"

AS A SIGN OF THE TIMES

Costa Deir took the mike and told us how his heart was burdened for the Greek Orthodox Church. He asked Episcopalian Father Driscoll to pray that the Holy Spirit would sweep that Church as He was sweeping the Catholic Church. While Father Driscoll prayed, Costa Deir wept into the mike. Following the prayer was a long message in tongues and an equally long interpretation saying that the prayers had been heard and the Holy Spirit would blow through and awaken the Greek Orthodox Church.... By this time there was so much weeping and calling out that I backed away from it all emotionally.... Yet I heard myself saying a surprising thing, 'Some day when we read how the Spirit is moving in the Greek Orthodox Church, let us remember that we were here the moment that it began.'*

S IX MONTHS after the event here described occurred at an interdenominational "charismatic" meeting in Seattle, Orthodox Christians did indeed begin to hear that the

---

* Pat King, in *Logos Journal,* Sept.–Oct. 1971, p. 50. This "international charismatic journal" should not be confused with Fr. E. Stephanou's *Logos.*

"charismatic spirit" was moving in the Greek Orthodox Church. Beginning in January 1972, Fr. Eusebius Stephanou's *Logos* began to report on this movement, which had begun earlier in several Greek and Syrian parishes in America and now has spread to a number of others, being actively promoted by Fr. Eusebius. After the reader has read the description of this "spirit" from the words of its leading representatives in the pages that follow, he should not find it difficult to believe that in very fact it was evoked and instilled into the Orthodox world by just such urgent entreaties of "interdenominational Christians." For if one conclusion emerges from this description, it must certainly be that the spectacular present-day "charismatic revival" is not merely a phenomenon of hyper-emotionalism and Protestant revivalism—although these elements are also strongly present—but is actually the work of a "spirit" who can be invoked and who works "miracles." The question we shall attempt to answer in these pages is: *what or who is this spirit?* As Orthodox Christians we know that it is not only God Who works miracles; the devil has his own "miracles," and in fact he can and does imitate virtually every genuine miracle of God. We shall therefore attempt in these pages to be careful to *try the spirits, whether they are of God* (I John 4:1).

We shall begin with a brief historical background, since no one can deny that the "charismatic revival" has come to the Orthodox world from the Protestant and Catholic denominations, which in turn received it from the Pentecostal sects.

1. The 20th-century Pentecostal Movement

The modern Pentecostal Movement, although it did have 19th-century antecedents, dates its origin precisely to 7:00 p.m. on New Year's Eve of the year 1900. For some time before that moment a Methodist minister in Topeka, Kansas, Charles Parham, as an answer to the confessed feebleness of his Christian ministry, had been concentratedly studying the New Testament with a group of his students with the aim of discovering the secret of the *power* of Apostolic Christianity. The students finally deduced that this secret lay in the "speaking in tongues" which, they thought, always accompanied the reception of the Holy Spirit in the Acts of the Apostles. With increasing excitement and tension, Parham and his students resolved to pray until they themselves received the "Baptism of the Holy Spirit" together with speaking in tongues. On December 31, 1900, they prayed from morning to night with no success, until one young girl suggested that one ingredient was missing in this experiment: "laying on of hands." Parham put his hands on the girl's head, and immediately she began to speak in an "unknown tongue." Within three days there were many such "Baptisms," including that of Parham himself and twelve other ministers of various denominations, and all of them were accompanied by speaking in tongues. Soon the revival spread to Texas, and then it had spectacular success at a small Black church in Los Angeles. Since then it has spread throughout the world and claims ten million members.

For half a century the Pentecostal Movement remained sectarian and everywhere it was received with hostility by the established denominations. Then, however, speaking in tongues began gradually to appear in the denominations themselves, although at first it was kept rather quiet, until in 1960 an Episcopalian priest near Los Angeles gave wide publicity to this fact by publicly declaring that he had received the "Baptism of the Holy Spirit" and spoke in tongues. After some initial hostility, the "charismatic revival" gained the official or unofficial approval of all the major denominations and has spread rapidly both in America and abroad. Even the once rigid and exclusivist Roman Catholic Church, once it took up the "charismatic renewal" in earnest in the late 1960s, has been enthusiastically swept up in this movement. In America, the Roman Catholic bishops gave their approval to the movement in 1969, and the few thousand Catholics involved in it then have since increased to untold hundreds of thousands, who gather periodically in local and nationwide "charismatic" conferences whose participants are sometimes numbered in the tens of thousands. The Roman Catholic countries of Europe have also become enthusiastically "charismatic," as witnessed by the "charismatic" conference in the Summer, 1978, in Ireland, attended by thousands of Irish priests. Not long before his death Pope Paul VI met with a delegation of "charismatics" and proclaimed that he too is a pentecostal.

What can be the reason for such a spectacular success of a "Christian" revival in a seemingly "post-Christian" world? Doubtless the answer lies in two factors: first, the receptive ground which consists of those millions of "Christians" who feel that their religion is dry, over-rational, merely external, without fervency or power; and second, the evidently powerful "spirit" that lies behind the phenomena, which is capable, under the proper conditions, of producing a multitude and variety of "charismatic" phenomena, including healing, speaking in tongues, interpretation, prophecy—and, underlying all of these, an overwhelming experience which is called the "Baptism of (or in, or with) the Holy Spirit."

But what precisely *is* this "spirit"? Significantly, this question is seldom if ever even raised by followers of the "charismatic revival"; their own "baptismal" experience is so powerful and has been preceded by such an effective psychological preparation in the form of concentrated prayer and expectation, that there is never any doubt in their minds but that they have received the Holy Spirit and that the phenomena they have experienced and seen are exactly those described in the Acts of the Apostles. Too, the psychological atmosphere of the movement is often so one-sided and tense that it is regarded as the very blasphemy against the Holy Spirit to entertain any doubts in this regard. Of the hundreds of books that have already appeared on the movement, only a very few express any even slight doubts as to its spiritual validity.

In order to obtain a better idea of the distinctive characteristics of the "charismatic revival," let us examine some of the testimonies and practices of its participants, always checking them against the standard of Holy Orthodoxy. These testimonies will be taken, with a few exceptions as noted, from the apologetical books and magazines of the movement, written by people who are *favorable* to it and who obviously publish only that material which seems to support their position. Further, we shall make only minimal use of narrowly Pentecostal sources, confining ourselves chiefly to Protestant, Catholic, and Orthodox participants in the contemporary "charismatic revival."

2. The "Ecumenical" Spirit of the "Charismatic Revival"

Before quoting the "charismatic" testimonies, we should take note of a chief characteristic of the original Pentecostal Movement which is seldom mentioned by "charismatic" writers, and that is that the number and variety of Pentecostal sects is astonishing, each with its own doctrinal emphasis, and many of them having no fellowship with the others. There are "Assemblies of God," "Churches of God," "Pentecostal" and "Holiness" bodies, "Full Gospel" groups, etc., many of them divided into smaller sects. The first thing that one would have to say about the "spirit" that inspires such anarchy is that it certainly is not a spirit of unity, in sharp contrast to the Apostolic church of the first century to which the movement professes to be returning. Nevertheless, there is much talk, especially in the "charismatic revival" within the denominations in the past decade, of the "unity" which it inspires. But what kind of unity is this?—the true unity of the Church which Orthodox Christians of the first and twentieth centuries alike know, or the pseudo-unity of the Ecumenical Movement, which denies that the Church of Christ exists?

The answer to this question is stated quite clearly by perhaps the leading "prophet" of 20th-century Pentecostalism, David Du Plessis, who for the last twenty years has been actively spreading news of the "Baptism of the Holy Spirit" among the denominations of the World Council of Churches, in answer to a "voice" which commanded him to do so in 1951. "The Pentecostal revival within the churches is gathering force and speed. The most remarkable thing is that this revival is found in the so-called liberal societies and much less in the evangelical and not at all in the fundamentalist segments of Protestantism. The last-mentioned are now the most vehement opponents of this glorious revival because it is in the Pentecostal Movement and in the modernist World Council Movements that we find the most powerful manifestations of the Spirit" (Du Plessis, p. 28).*

In the Roman Catholic Church likewise, the "charismatic renewal" is occurring precisely in "liberal" circles, and one of its results is to inspire even more their ecumenism and liturgical experimentation ("guitar masses" and the like); whereas

---

* Most books will be cited in this chapter only by author and page number; full bibliographical information is supplied at the end of the chapter.

traditionalist Catholics are as opposed to the movement as are fundamentalist Protestants. Without any doubt the orientation of the "charismatic revival" is strongly ecumenist. A "charismatic" Lutheran pastor, Clarence Finsaas, writes: "Many are surprised that the Holy Spirit can move also in the various traditions of the historic Church ... whether the church doctrine has a background of Calvinism or Arminianism, this matters little, proving God is bigger than our creeds and that no denomination has a monopoly on Him" (Christenson, p. 99). An Episcopalian pastor, speaking of the "charismatic revival," reports that "ecumenically it is leading to a remarkable joining together of Christians of different traditions, mainly at the local church level" (Harper, p. 17). The California "charismatic" periodical *Inter-Church Renewal* is full of "unity" demonstrations such as this one: "The darkness of the ages was dispelled and a Roman Catholic nun and a Protestant could love each other with a strange new kind of love," which proves that "old denominational barriers are crumbling. Superficial doctrinal differences are being put aside for all believers to come into the unity of the Holy Spirit." The Orthodox priest Fr. Eusebius Stephanou believes that "this outpouring of the Holy Spirit is transcending denominational lines.... The Spirit of God is moving ... both inside and outside the Orthodox Church" (*Logos,* Jan. 1972, p. 12).

Here the Orthodox Christian who is alert to "try the spirits" finds himself on familiar ground, sown with the usual ecumenist cliches. And above all let us note that this new "outpouring of the Holy Spirit," exactly like the Ecumenical Movement itself, arises *outside the Orthodox Church;* those few Orthodox parishes that are now taking it up are obviously following a fashion of the times that matured completely outside the bounds of the Church of Christ.

But what is it that those outside the Church of Christ are capable of teaching Orthodox Christians? It is certainly true (no conscious Orthodox person will deny it) that Orthodox Christians are sometimes put to shame by the fervor and zeal of some Roman Catholics and Protestants for church attendance, missionary activities, praying together, reading the Scripture, and the like. Fervent non-Orthodox persons can shame the Orthodox, even in the error of their beliefs, when they make more effort to please God than many Orthodox people do while possessing the whole fullness of apostolic Christianity. The Orthodox would do well to learn from them and wake up to the spiritual riches in their own Church which they fail to see out of spiritual sloth or bad habits. All this relates to the *human* side of faith, to the human efforts which can be expended in religious activities whether one's belief is right or wrong.

The "charismatic" movement, however, claims to be in contact with *God,* to have found a means for receiving the *Holy Spirit,* the outpouring of God's grace. And yet it is precisely the *Church,* and nothing else, that our Lord Jesus Christ established as the means of communicating grace to men. Are we to believe that the Church is now to be superseded by some "new revelation" capable of transmitting grace outside the Church, among any group of people who may happen to believe in Christ but who have no knowledge or experience of the Mysteries (Sacraments) which Christ instituted and no contact with the Apostles and their successors whom He appointed to administer the Mysteries? No: it is as certain today as it was in the first century that *the gifts of the Holy Spirit are not revealed in those outside the Church.* The great Orthodox Father of the 19th century, Bishop Theophan the Recluse, writes that the gift of the Holy Spirit is given "precisely through the Sacrament of Chrismation, which was introduced by the Apostles in place of the laying on of hands" (which is the form the Sacrament takes in the Acts of the Apostles). "We all—who have been baptized and chrismated—have the gift of the Holy Spirit ... even though it is not active in everyone." The Orthodox Church provides the means for making this gift active, and "there is no other path.... Without the Sacrament of Chrismation, just as earlier without the laying on of hands of the Apostles, the Holy Spirit has never descended and never will descend.*

In a word, the orientation of the "charismatic revival" may be described as one of a new and deeper or "spiritual" ecumenism: each Christian "renewed" in his own tradition, but at the same time strangely united (for it is *the same experience*) with others equally "renewed" in their own traditions, all of which contain various degrees of heresy and impiety! This relativism leads also to openness to completely new religious practices, as when an Orthodox priest allows laymen to "lay hands" on him in front of the Royal Doors of an Orthodox church (*Logos,* April 1972, p. 4). The end of all this is the super-ecumenist vision of the leading Pentecostal "prophet," who says that many Pentecostals "began to visualize the possibility of the Movement becoming the Church of Christ in the clos-

---

* Bishop Theophan the Recluse, *What Is the Spiritual Life,* Jordanville, New York, 1962, pp 247–48 (in Russian). [Second English edition: *The Spiritual Life,* St. Paisius Serbian Orthodox Monastery, Safford, Arizona, 2003, p. 270.] Fr. Eusebius Stephanou (*Logos,* Jan. 1972, p. 13) attempts to justify the present-day "reception of the Holy Spirit" outside the Church by citing the account of the household of Cornelius the Centurion (Acts 10), which received the Holy Spirit *before* Baptism. But the difference in the two cases is crucial: the reception of the Holy Spirit by Cornelius and his household was the sign that they should be joined to the Church by Baptism, whereas contemporary Pentecostals by *their* experience are only confirmed in their delusion that there *is* no one saving Church of Christ.

ing days of time. However, this situation has completely changed during the past ten years. Many of my brethren are now convinced that the Lord Jesus Christ, the head of the Church, will pour out His Spirit upon all flesh and that the historic churches will be revived or renewed and then in this renewal be united by the Holy Spirit" (Du Plessis, p. 33). Clearly, there is no room in the "charismatic revival" for those who believe that the Orthodox Church is the Church of Christ. It is no wonder that even some Orthodox Pentecostals admit that in the beginning they were "suspicious of the Orthodoxy" of this movement (*Logos,* April 1972, p. 9).

But now let us begin to look beyond the ecumenistic theories and practices of Pentecostalism to that which really inspires and gives strength to the "charismatic revival": the actual experience of the *power* of the "spirit."

3. *"Speaking in Tongues"*

If we look carefully at the writings of the "charismatic revival," we shall find that this movement closely resembles many sectarian movements of the past in basing itself primarily or even entirely on one rather bizarre doctrinal emphasis or religious practice. The only difference is that the emphasis now is placed on a specific point which no sectarians in the past regarded as so central: speaking in tongues.

According to the constitution of various Pentecostal sects, "The Baptism of believers in the Holy Ghost is witnessed by the initial physical sign of speaking with other tongues" (Sherrill, p. 79). And not only is this the *first* sign of conversion to a Pentecostal sect or orientation: according to the best Pentecostal authorities, this practice must be continued or the "spirit" may be lost. Writes David Du Plessis: "The practice of praying in tongues should continue and increase in the lives of those who are baptized in the Spirit, otherwise they may find that the other manifestations of the Spirit come seldom or stop altogether" (Du Plessis, p. 89). Many testify, as does one Protestant, that tongues "have now become an essential accompaniment of my devotional life" (Lillie, p. 50). And a Roman Catholic book on the subject, more cautiously, says that of the "gifts of the Holy Spirit" tongues "is often but not always the first received. For many it is thus a threshold through which one passes into the realm of the gifts and fruits of the Holy Spirit" (Ranaghan, p. 19).

Here already one may note an overemphasis that is certainly not present in the New Testament, where speaking in tongues has a decidedly minor significance, serving as a sign of the descent of the Holy Spirit on the Day of Pentecost (Acts 2) and on two other occasions (Acts 10 and 19). After the first or perhaps the second century there is no record of it in any Orthodox source, and it is not recorded as occurring even among the great Fathers of the Egyptian desert, who were so filled with the Spirit of God that they performed numerous astonishing miracles, including raising the dead. The Orthodox attitude to genuine speaking in tongues, then, may be summed up in the words of Blessed Augustine (Homilies on John, VI:10): "In the earliest times *the Holy Spirit fell upon them that believed, and they spake with tongues* which they had not learned, *as the Spirit gave them utterance.* These were signs adapted to the time. For it was fitting that there be this sign of the Holy Spirit in all tongues to show that the Gospel of God was to run through all tongues over the whole earth. That was done for a sign, and it passed away." And as if to answer contemporary Pentecostals with their strange emphasis on this point, Augustine continues: "Is it now expected that they upon whom hands are laid, should speak with tongues? Or when we imposed our hand upon these children, did each of you wait to see whether they would speak with tongues? And when he saw that they did not speak with tongues, was any of you so perverse of heart as to say, 'These have not received the Holy Spirit'?"

Modern Pentecostals, to justify their use of tongues, refer most of all to St. Paul's First Epistle to the Corinthians (chs. 12–14). But St. Paul wrote this passage precisely because "tongues" had become a source of disorder in the Church of Corinth; and even while he does not forbid them, he decidedly minimizes their significance. This passage, therefore, far from encouraging any modern revival of "tongues," should on the contrary discourage it—especially when one discovers (as Pentecostals themselves admit) that there are *other* sources of speaking in tongues besides the Holy Spirit! As Orthodox Christians we already know that speaking in tongues as a true *gift of the Holy Spirit* cannot appear among those outside the Church of Christ; but let us look more closely at this modern phenomenon and see if it possesses characteristics that might reveal from what source it *does* come.

If we are already made suspicious by the exaggerated importance accorded to "tongues" by modern Pentecostals, we should be completely awakened about them when we examine the circumstances in which they occur.

Far from being given freely and spontaneously, without man's interference—as are the true gifts of the Holy Spirit—speaking in tongues can be caused to occur quite predictably by a regular technique of concentrated group "prayer" accompanied by psychologically suggestive Protestant hymns ("He comes! He comes!"), culminating in a "laying on of hands," and sometimes involving such purely physical efforts as repeating a given phrase over and over again (Koch, p. 24), or just making sounds with the mouth. One person admits that, like many others, after speaking in tongues, "I often did mouth nonsense syllables in an effort to start the flow of prayer-in-tongues" (Sherrill, p. 127); and such efforts, far from being discouraged, are actually advocated by Pentecostals. "Making sounds with the mouth is not 'speaking-in-tongues,' but it may signify an honest act of faith, which the Holy Spirit will honor by giving that person the power to speak in another language" (Harper, p. 11). Another Protestant pastor says: "The initial hurdle to speaking in tongues, it seems, is simply the realization that *you* must 'speak forth'.... The first syllables and words may sound strange to your ear. They may be halting and inarticulate. You may have the thought that you are just making it up. But as you *continue to speak in faith* ... the Spirit will shape for you a language of prayer and praise" (Christenson, p. 130). A Jesuit "theologian" tells how he put such advice into practice: "After breakfast I felt almost physically drawn to the chapel where I sat down to pray. Following Jim's description of his own reception of the gift of tongues, I began to say quietly to myself "la, la, la, la." To my immense consternation there ensued a rapid movement of tongue and lips accompanied by a tremendous feeling of inner devotion" (Gelpi, p. 1).

Can any sober Orthodox Christian possibly confuse these dangerous psychic games with the *gifts of the Holy Spirit?!* There is clearly nothing whatever Christian, nothing spiritual here in the least. This is the realm, rather, of psychic mechanisms which can be set in operation by means of definite psychological or physical techniques, and "speaking in tongues" would seem to occupy a key role as a kind of "trigger" in this realm. In any case, it certainly bears no resemblance whatever to the *spiritual* gift described in the New Testament, and if anything is much closer to *shamanistic* "speaking in tongues" as practiced in primitive religions, where the shaman or witch doctor has a regular technique for going into a trance and then giving a message to or from a "god" in a tongue he has not learned.* In the pages that follow we shall encounter "charismatic" experiences so weird that the comparison with shamanism will not seem terribly far-fetched, especially if we understand that primitive shamanism is but a particular expression of a "religious" phenomenon which, far from being foreign to the modern West, actually plays a significant role in the lives of some contemporary "Christians": *mediumism.*

4. "Christian" Mediumism

One careful and objective study of "speaking in tongues" has been made by the German Lutheran pastor, Dr. Kurt Koch *(The Strife of Tongues).* After examining hundreds of examples of this "gift" as manifested in the past few years, he came to the conclusion, on Scriptural grounds, that only four of these cases *might* be the same as the gift described in the Acts of the Apostles; but he was not sure of any of them. The Orthodox Christian, having the full Patristic tradition of the Church of Christ behind him, would be more strict in his judgment than Dr. Koch. As against these few possibly positive cases, however, Dr. Koch found a number of cases of undoubted demonic possession—for "speaking in tongues" is in fact a common "gift" of the possessed. But it is in Dr. Koch's final conclusion that we find what is perhaps the clue to the whole movement. He concludes that the "tongues" movement is not at all a "revival," for there is in it little repentance or conviction of sin, but chiefly the search for power and experi-

---

* See Burdick, pp. 66–67.

ence; the phenomenon of tongues is not the gift described in the Acts, nor is it (in most cases) actual demonic possession; rather, "it becomes more and more clear that perhaps over 95% of the whole tongues movement is *mediumistic* in character" (Koch, p. 35).

What is a "medium"? A medium is a person with a certain psychic sensitivity which enables him to be the vehicle or means for the manifestation of unseen forces or beings (where actual beings are involved, as Starets Ambrose of Optina has clearly stated,* these are always the fallen spirits whose realm this is, and not the "spirits of the dead" imagined by spiritists). Almost all non-Christian religions make large use of mediumistic gifts, such as clairvoyance, hypnosis, "miraculous" healing, the appearance and disappearance of objects as well as their movement from place to place, etc.

It should be noted that several similar gifts have also been possessed by Orthodox Saints—but there is an immense difference between the true Christian gift and its mediumistic imitation. The true Christian gift of healing, for example, is given by God directly in answer to fervent prayer, and especially at the prayer of a man who is particularly pleasing to God, a righteous man or saint (James 5:16), and also through contact in faith with objects that have been sanctified by God (holy water, relics of saints, etc.; see Acts 19:12; II Kings 13:21). But mediumistic healing, like any other mediumistic gift, is accomplished by means of certain definite techniques and psychic states which can be cultivated and brought into use by practice, and which have no relation whatever either to sanctity or to the action of God. The mediumistic ability may be acquired either by inheritance or by transference through contact with

---

* V. P. Bykov, *Tikhie Priyuty,* Moscow, 1913, pp. 168–70.

someone who has the gift, or even through the reading of occult books.*

Many mediums claim that their powers are not at all supernatural, but come from a part of nature about which very little is known. To some extent this is doubtless true; but it is also true that the realm from which these gifts come is the special realm of the fallen spirits, who do not hesitate to use the opportunity afforded by the people who enter this realm to draw them into their own nets, adding their own demonic powers and manifestations in order to lead souls to destruction. And whatever the explanation of various mediumistic phenomena may be, God in His Revelation to mankind has strictly forbidden any contact with this occult realm: *There shall not be found among you any one that useth divination, one that practiseth augury, or an enchanter, or a sorcerer, or a charmer, or a consulter with a familiar spirit, or a necromancer. For whosoever doeth these things is an abomination unto the Lord* (Deut. 18:10–12; see also Lev. 20:6).

In practice it is impossible to combine mediumism with genuine Christianity, the desire for mediumistic phenomena or powers being incompatible with the basic Christian orientation toward the salvation of the soul. This is not to say that there are not "Christians" who are involved in mediumism, often unconsciously (as we shall see); it is only to say that they are not genuine Christians, that their Christianity is only a "new Christianity" such as the one Nicholas Berdyaev preached, which will be discussed again below. Dr. Koch, even from his Protestant background, makes a valid observation when he notes: "A person's *religious* life is not harmed by oc-

---

* See Kurt Koch, *Occult Bondage and Deliverance,* Kregel Publications, Grand Rapids, Michigan, 1970, pp. 168–70.

cultism or spiritism. Indeed spiritism is to a large extent a 'religious' movement. The devil does not take away our 'religiousness'.... [But] there is a great difference between being religious and being born again by the Spirit of God. It is sad to say that our Christian denominations have more 'religious' people in them than true Christians."*

The best-known form of mediumism in the modern West is the spiritistic séance, where contact is made with certain forces that produce observable effects such as knockings, voices, various kinds of communications such as automatic writing and speaking in unknown tongues, the moving of objects, and the apparition of hands and "human" figures that can sometimes be photographed. These effects are produced with the aid of definite attitudes and techniques on the part of those present, concerning which we shall here quote one of the standard textbooks on the subject.**

1. *Passivity:* "A spirit's activity is measured by the degree of passivity or submissiveness which he finds in the sensitive, or medium." "Mediumship ... by diligent cultivation may be attained by anyone who deliberately yields up his body, with his free will, and sensitive and intellectual faculties, to an invading or controlling spirit."

2. *Solidarity in faith:* All present must have a "sympathetic

---

* Kurt Koch, *Between Christ and Satan,* Kregel Publications, 1962, p. 124. This book and Dr. Koch's *Occult Bondage* offer a remarkable confirmation, based on 20th-century experience, of virtually every manifestation of mediumism, magic, sorcery, etc., that is found in the Holy Scriptures and the Orthodox Lives of Saints—the source of all of which, of course, is the devil. On only a few points will the Orthodox reader have to correct his interpretations.
** Simon A. Blackmore, S. J., *Spiritism Facts and Frauds,* Benziger Bros., New York, 1924: Chapter IV, "Mediums," pp. 89–105 *passim.*

attitude of mind in support of the medium"; the spiritistic phenomena are "facilitated by a certain sympathy arising from a harmony of ideas, views and sentiment existing between the experimenters and the medium. When this sympathy and harmony, as well as the personal surrender of the will, are wanting in the members of the 'circle,' the séance proves a failure." Also, "the number of experimenters is of great importance. If larger, they impede the harmony so necessary for success."

3. All present "join hands to form the so-called *magnetic circle.* By this closed circuit, each member contributes the energy of a certain force which is collectively communicated to the medium." However, the "magnetic circle" is required only in less well-developed mediums. Mme. Blavatsky, the founder of modern "theosophy," herself a medium, later laughed at the crude techniques of spiritism when she encountered much more powerful mediums in the East, to which category also belongs the fakir described in Chapter III.

4. "The necessary spiritistic *atmosphere* is commonly induced by artificial means, such as the singing of hymns, the playing of soft music, and even the offering of prayer."

The spiritistic séance, to be sure, is a rather crude form of mediumism—although for that very reason its techniques are all the more evident—and only rarely does it produce spectacular results. There are other more subtle forms, some of them going under the name of "Christian." To realize this one need only look at the techniques of a "faith-healer" such as Oral Roberts (who until joining the Methodist church a few years ago was a minister of the Pentecostal Holiness sect), who causes "miraculous" healings by forming an actual "magnetic circle" composed of people with the proper sympathy, passivity, and harmony of "faith" who put their hands on the television set while he is on the air; the healings can even be brought about by drinking a glass of water that has been placed on the television set and has thus absorbed the flow of mediumistic forces that have been brought into action. But such healings, like those produced by spiritism and witchcraft, can take a heavy toll in later psychic, not to mention spiritual, disorders.*

In this realm one must be very careful, because the devil is constantly aping the works of God, and many people with mediumistic gifts continue to think they are Christians and that their gifts come from the Holy Spirit. But is it possible to say that this is true of the "charismatic revival"—that it is in fact, as some say, primarily a form of mediumism?

In applying the most obvious tests for mediumism to the "charismatic revival," one is struck first of all by the fact that the chief prerequisites for the spiritistic séance described above are all present at "charismatic" prayer meetings, whereas *not one* of these characteristics is present in the same form or degree in the true Christian worship of the Orthodox Church.

1. The "passivity" of the spiritistic séance corresponds to what "charismatic" writers call "a kind of *letting go....* This involves more than the dedication of one's conscious existence through an act of will; it also refers to a large, even hidden area of one's unconscious life.... All that can be done is to offer the self—body, mind, and even the tongue—so that the Spirit of God may have *full possession....* Such persons are ready—the barriers are down and God moves mightily upon and through their whole being" (Williams, pp. 62–63; italics in the original). Such a "spiritual" attitude is not that of Christianity: it is rather the attitude of Zen Buddhism, Eastern "mysticism," hypnosis, and spiritism. Such an exaggerated passivity is entirely foreign to Orthodox spirituality, and is only an open in-

---

* On Oral Roberts, see Kurt Koch, *Occult Bondage,* pp. 52–55.

vitation to the activity of deceiving spirits. One sympathetic observer notes that at Pentecostal meetings people speaking in tongues or interpreting "seem almost to go into a trance" (Sherrill, p. 87). This passivity is so pronounced in some "charismatic" communities that they completely abolish the church organization and any set order of services and do absolutely everything as the "spirit" directs.

2. There is a definite "solidarity in faith"—and not merely solidarity in Christian faith and hope for salvation, but a specific unanimity in the desire for and expectation of "charismatic" *phenomena.* This is true of all "charismatic" prayer meetings; but an even more pronounced solidarity is required for the experience of the "Baptism of the Holy Spirit," which is usually performed in a small separate room in the presence of only a few who have already had the experience. The presence of even one person who has negative thoughts about the experience is often sufficient to cause the "Baptism" not to occur—exactly in the way that the misgivings and the prayer of the Orthodox priest described above (pp. 68–69) was enough to break up the impressive illusion produced by the Ceylonese fakir.

3. The spiritistic "magnetic circle" corresponds to the Pentecostal "laying on of hands," which is always done by those who themselves have already experienced the "Baptism" with speaking in tongues, and who serve, in the words of Pentecostals themselves, as "*channels* of the Holy Spirit" (Williams, p. 64)—a word used by spiritists to refer to mediums.

4. The "charismatic," like the spiritistic, "atmosphere" is induced by means of suggestive hymns and prayers, and often also by hand-clapping, all of which give "an effect of mounting excitement, and almost intoxicating quality" (Sherrill, p. 23).

It may still be objected that all those similarities between mediumism and Pentecostalism are only coincidental; and indeed, in order to show whether or not the "charismatic revival" is actually mediumistic, we shall have to determine what kind of "spirit" it is that is communicated through the Pentecostal "channels." A number of testimonies by those who have experienced it—and who believe that it is the Holy Spirit—point clearly to its nature. "The group moved closer around me. It was as if they were forming with their bodies a funnel through which was concentrated the flow of the Spirit that was pulsing through the room. It flowed into me as I sat there" (Sherrill, p. 122). At a Catholic Pentecostal prayer meeting, "upon entering a room one was practically struck dead by the strong visible presence of God" (Ranaghan, p. 79). (Compare the "vibrant" atmosphere at some pagan and Hindu rites; see above, p. 50.) Another man describes his "Baptismal" experience: "I became aware that the Lord was in the room and that He was approaching me. I couldn't see Him, but I felt myself being pushed over on my back. I seemed to float to the floor ..." (*Logos Journal,* Nov.–Dec. 1971, p. 47). Other similar examples will be given below in the discussion of the physical accompaniments of "charismatic" experience. This "pulsing," "visible," "pushing" spirit that "approaches" and "flows" would seem to confirm the mediumistic character of the "charismatic" movement. Certainly the Holy Spirit could never be described in these ways!

And let us recall a strange characteristic of "charismatic" speaking in tongues that we have already mentioned: that it is given not only at the initial experience of the "Baptism of the Holy Spirit," but is supposed to be continued (both in private and public) and become an "essential accompaniment" of religious life, or else the "gifts of the Spirit" may cease. One Presbyterian "charismatic" writer speaks of the specific function of this practice in "preparing" for "charismatic" meetings: "Often it is the case that ... a small group will spend time ahead praying in the Spirit [i.e., in tongues]. In so doing there is greatly multiplied the sense of God's presence and power that carries over into the gathering." And again: "We find that quiet praying in the Spirit during that meeting helps to maintain an openness to God's presence ... [for] after one has become accustomed to praying in tongues aloud ... it soon becomes a possibility for one's breath, moving across vocal chords and tongue, to manifest the Spirit's breathing, and thereby for prayer to go on quietly, yet profoundly, within" (Williams, p. 31). Let us remember also that speaking in tongues can be triggered by such artificial devices as "making sounds with the mouth"—and we come to the inevitable conclusion that "charismatic" speaking in tongues is not a "gift" at all but a *technique,* itself acquired by other techniques and in turn triggering still other "gifts of the Spirit," *if one continues to practice and cultivate it.* Do we not have here a clue to the chief actual accomplishment of the modern Pentecostal Movement—that *it has discovered a new mediumistic technique for entering into and preserving a psychic state wherein miraculous "gifts" become commonplace?* If this is true, then the "charismatic" definition of the "laying on of hands"—"the simple ministry by one or more persons who themselves are channels of the Holy Spirit to others not yet so blessed," in which "the important thing [is] that those who minister have themselves experienced the movement of the Holy Spirit" (Williams, p. 64)—describes precisely *the transference of the mediumistic gift by those who have already acquired it and have themselves become mediums.* The "Baptism of the Holy Spirit" thus becomes *mediumistic initiation.*

Indeed, if the "charismatic revival" is actually a mediumistic movement, much that is unclear about it if it is viewed as a *Christian* movement, becomes clear. The movement arises in

America, which fifty years before had given birth to spiritism in a similar psychological climate: a dead, rationalized Protestant faith is suddenly overwhelmed by actual experience of an invisible "power" that cannot be rationally or scientifically explained. The movement is most successful in those countries which have a substantial history of spiritism or mediumism: America and England, first of all, then Brazil, Japan, the Philippines, black Africa. There is scarcely to be found an example of "speaking in tongues" in any even nominally Christian context for over 1,600 years after the time of St. Paul (and even then it is an isolated and short-lived hysterical phenomenon), precisely until the 20th-century Pentecostal Movement, as the scholarly historian of religious "enthusiasm" has pointed out;* and yet this "gift" is possessed by numerous shamans and witch doctors of primitive religions, as well as by modern spiritistic mediums and the demonically possessed. The "prophecies" and "interpretations" at "charismatic" services, as we shall see, are strangely vague and stereotyped in expression, without specifically Christian or prophetic content. Doctrine is subordinated to practice: the motto of both movements might be, as "charismatic" enthusiasts say over and over again, *"it works"*—the very trap into which, as we have seen, Hinduism leads its victims. There can scarcely be any doubt that the "charismatic revival," as far as its phenomena are concerned, bears a much closer resemblance to spiritism and in general to non-Christian religion, than it does to Orthodox Christianity. But we shall have yet to give many examples to demonstrate just how true this is.

Up to this point we have been quoting, apart from Dr. Koch's statements, only from those favorable to the "charis-

---

* Ronald A. Knox, *Enthusiasm, A Chapter in the History of Religion,* Oxford (Galaxy Book), 1961, pp. 550–51.

matic revival," who only give their testimonies of what they imagine to be the workings of the Holy Spirit. Now let us quote the testimony of several people who have left the "charismatic" movement, or refused to enter it, because they found that the "spirit" that animates it is *not* the Holy Spirit.

1. "In Leicester (England) a young man reported the following. He and his friend had been believers for some years when one day they were invited to the meeting of a tongues-speaking group. The atmosphere of the meeting got a hold on them and afterwards they prayed for the second blessing and the baptism of the Holy Spirit. After intensive prayer it was as if something hot came over them. They felt very excited inside. For a few weeks they reveled in this new experience, but slowly these waves of feeling abated. The man who told me this noticed that he had lost all desire to read the Bible and to pray. He examined his experience in the light of the Scriptures and realized that it was not of God. He repented and denounced it.... His friend on the other hand continued in these 'tongues' and it destroyed him. Today he will not even consider the idea of going on further as a Christian" (Koch, p. 28).

2. Two Protestant ministers went to a "charismatic" prayer meeting at a Presbyterian church in Hollywood. "Both of us agreed beforehand that when the first person started to speak in tongues, we would pray roughly the following, 'Lord, if this gift is from you, bless this brother, but if it is not of you, then stop it and let there be no other praying in tongues in our presence.' ... A young man began the meeting with a short devotion after which it was open for prayer. A woman started to pray fluently in a foreign language without any stammering or hesitation. An interpretation was not given. The Rev. B. and I started to pray quietly as we had agreed earlier. What happened? No one else spoke in tongues, although usually in these

meetings all of them, except for an architect, pray in unknown tongues" (Koch, p. 15). Note here that in the absence of the mediumistic solidarity of faith, the phenomena do not appear.

3. "In San Diego, California, a woman came for counseling. She told me of a bad experience that she had had during a mission held by a member of the tongues movement. She had gone to his meetings in which he had spoken about the necessity of the gift of tongues, and in an after-meeting she had allowed hands to be laid on herself in order to receive the baptism of the Holy Spirit and the gift of speaking in tongues. At that moment she fell down unconscious. On coming round again she found herself lying on the floor with her mouth still opening and shutting itself automatically without a word being uttered. She was terribly frightened. Standing around her were some of the people who were followers of this evangelist and they exclaimed, 'O sister, you have really spoken wonderfully in tongues. Now you have the Holy Spirit.' But the victim of this so-called baptism of the Holy Spirit was cured. She never again returned to this group of tongues-speakers. When she came to me for advice she was still suffering from the bad after-effects of this 'spiritual baptism'" (Koch, p. 26).

4. An Orthodox Christian in California relates a private encounter with a "spirit-filled" minister who has shared the same platform with the leading Catholic, Protestant, and Pentecostal representatives of the "charismatic revival": "For five hours he spoke in tongues and used every artifice (psychological, hypnotic, and 'laying on of hands') to induce those present to receive the 'baptism of the Holy Spirit.' The scene was really terrible. When he laid hands on our friend she made guttural sounds, moaned, wept, and screamed. He was well pleased by this. He said she was suffering for others—interceding for them. When he 'laid hands' on my head there was a presenti-

ment of real evil. His 'tongues' were interspersed with English: 'You have the gift of prophecy, I can feel it.' 'Just open your mouth and it will flow out.' 'You are blocking the Holy Spirit.' By the grace of God I kept my mouth shut, but I am quite certain that if I had spoken, someone else would have 'interpreted.'" (Private communication.)

5. Readers of *The Orthodox Word* will recall the account of the "prayer-vigil" held by the Syrian Antiochian Archdiocese of New York at its convention in Chicago in August 1970, where, after a dramatic and emotional atmosphere had been built up, young people began to "testify" how the "spirit" was moving them. But several people who were present related later that the atmosphere was "dark and ominous," "stifling," "dark and evil," and by a miraculous intercession of St. Herman of Alaska, whose icon was present in the room, the whole meeting was broken up and the evil atmosphere dispelled (*The Orthodox Word,* nos. 33–34, 1970, pp. 196–99).

There are numerous other cases in which people have lost interest in prayer, reading the Scriptures, and Christianity in general, and have even come to believe, as one student did, that "he would not need to read the Bible any more. God the Father would himself appear and speak to him" (Koch, p. 29).

We shall yet have occasion to quote the testimony of many people who do not find anything negative or evil in their "charismatic" experience, and we shall examine the meaning of their testimony. However, without yet reaching a conclusion as to the *precise* nature of the "spirit" that causes "charismatic" phenomena, on the basis of the evidence here gathered we can already agree this far with Dr. Koch: "The tongues movement is the expression of a delirious condition through which a breaking in of demonic powers manifests itself" (Koch, p. 47). That is, the movement, which is certainly "delirious" in giving itself over to the activity of a "spirit" that is not the Holy Spirit, is not demonic in intention or in itself (as contemporary occultism and satanism certainly are), but by its nature it lays itself particularly open to the manifestation of obvious demonic forces, which do in fact sometimes appear.

This book has been read by a number of people who have participated in the "charismatic revival"; many of them have then abandoned this movement, recognizing that the spirit they had experienced in "charismatic" phenomena was *not* the Holy Spirit. To such people, involved in the "charismatic" movement, who are now reading this book, we wish to say: You may well feel that your experience in the "charismatic" movement has been largely something good (even though you may have reservations about some things you have seen or experienced in it); you may well be unable to believe that there is anything demonic in it. In suggesting that the "charismatic" movement is mediumistic in inspiration, we do not mean to deny the *whole* of your experience while involved in it. If you have been awakened to repentance for your sins, to the realization that the Lord Jesus Christ is the Saviour of mankind, to sincere love for God and your neighbor—all of this is indeed good and would not be lost by abandoning the "charismatic" movement. But if you think that your experience of "speaking in tongues," or "prophesying," or whatever else of the "supernatural" that you may have experienced, is from God—then this book is an invitation for you to find out that the realm of true Christian spiritual experience is much deeper than you have felt up to now, that the wiles of the devil are much more subtle than you may have imagined, that the willingness of our fallen human nature to mistake illusion for truth, emotional comfort for spiritual experience, is much greater than you think. The next section of this chapter will discuss this in detail.

As to the precise nature of the "tongues" that are being spoken today, probably no simple answer can be given. We know quite certainly that in Pentecostalism, just as in spiritism, the elements of both fraud and suggestion play no small role, under the sometimes intense pressures applied in "charismatic" circles to force the phenomena to appear. Thus, one member of the largely Pentecostal "Jesus Movement" testifies that when he spoke in tongues "it was just an emotional build-up thing where I mumbled a bunch of words," and another frankly admits, "When I first became a Christian the people that I was with told me that you had to do it. So I prayed that I could do it, and I went as far as copying off them so they would think that I had the gift" (Ortega, p. 49). Some of the supposed "tongues" are thus doubtless not genuine, or at best the product of suggestion under conditions of emotional near-hysteria. However, there are actually documented cases of Pentecostal speaking in an unlearned language (Sherrill, pp. 90–95); there is also the testimony of many concerning the ease and assurance and calmness (without any hysterical conditions at all) with which they can enter into the state of "speaking in tongues"; and there is a distinctly preternatural character in the related phenomenon of "singing in tongues," where the "spirit" also inspires the melody and many join in to produce an effect that is variously described as "eerie but extraordinarily beautiful" (Sherrill, p. 118) and "unimaginable, humanly impossible" (Williams, p. 33). It would therefore seem evident that no merely psychological or emotional explanation can account for much of the phenomena of contemporary "tongues." If it is not due to the working of the Holy Spirit—and by now it is abundantly evident that it could not be so—then today's "speaking in tongues" as an authentic "supernatural" phenomenon can only be the manifestation of a gift of *some other spirit.*

To identify this "spirit" more precisely, and to understand the "charismatic" movement more fully, not only in its phenomena but also in its "spirituality," we shall have to draw more deeply from the sources of Orthodox tradition. And first of all we shall have to return to a teaching of the Orthodox ascetic tradition that has already been discussed in this series of articles, in explanation of the power which Hinduism holds over its devotees: *prelest,* or spiritual deception.

5. Spiritual Deception

The concept of *prelest,* a key one in Orthodox ascetical teaching, is completely absent in the Protestant-Catholic world which produced the "charismatic" movement; and this fact explains why such an obvious deception can gain such a hold over nominally "Christian" circles, and also why a "prophet" like Nicholas Berdyaev who comes from an Orthodox background should regard it as absolutely essential that in the "new age of the Holy Spirit" *"there will be no more of the ascetic worldview."* The reason is obvious: the Orthodox ascetic worldview gives the only means by which men, having received the Holy Spirit at their Baptism and Chrismation, may truly continue to acquire the Holy Spirit in their lives; and it teaches how to distinguish and guard oneself against spiritual deception. The "new spirituality" of which Berdyaev dreamed and which the "charismatic revival" actually practices, has an entirely different foundation and is seen to be a fraud in the light of the Orthodox ascetical teaching. Therefore, there is not room for both conceptions in the same spiritual universe: to accept the "new spirituality" of the "charismatic revival," one must reject Orthodox Christianity; and conversely, to remain an Orthodox Christian, one must reject the "charismatic revival," which is a counterfeit of Orthodoxy.

To make this quite clear, in what follows we shall give the teaching of the Orthodox Church on spiritual deception chiefly as found in the 19th-century summation of this teaching made by Bishop Ignatius Brianchaninov, himself an Orthodox Father of modern times, in volume one of his collected works.

There are two basic forms of *prelest* or spiritual deception. The first and more spectacular form occurs when a person strives for a high spiritual state or spiritual visions without having been purified of passions and relying on his own judgment. To such a one the devil grants great "visions." There are many such examples in the Lives of Saints, one of the primary textbooks of Orthodox ascetical teaching. Thus St. Nicetas, Bishop of Novgorod (Jan. 31), entered on the solitary life unprepared and against the counsel of his abbot, and soon he heard a voice praying with him. Then "the Lord" spoke to him and sent an "angel" to pray in his place and to instruct him to read books instead of praying, and to teach those who came to him. This he did, always seeing the "angel" near him praying, and the people were astonished at his spiritual wisdom and the "gifts of the Holy Spirit" which he seemed to possess, including "prophecies" which were always fulfilled. The deceit was uncovered only when the fathers of the monastery found out about his aversion for the New Testament (although the Old Testament, which he had never read, he could quote by heart), and by their prayers he was brought to repentance, his "miracles" ceased, and later he attained to genuine sanctity. Again, St. Isaac of the Kiev Caves (Feb. 14) saw a great light and "Christ" appeared to him with "angels"; when Isaac, without making the sign of the Cross, bowed down before "Christ," the demons gained power over him and, after dancing wildly with him, left him all but dead. He also later attained genuine sanctity. There are many similar cases when "Christ" and "angels" appeared to ascetics and granted astonishing powers and "gifts of the Holy Spirit," which often led the deluded ascetic finally to insanity or suicide.

But there is another more common, less spectacular form of spiritual deception, which offers to its victims not great visions but just exalted "religious feelings." This occurs, as Bishop Ignatius has written, "when the heart desires and strives for the enjoyment of holy and divine feelings while it is still completely unfit for them. Everyone who does not have a contrite spirit, who recognizes any kind of merit or worth in himself, who does not hold unwaveringly the teaching of the Orthodox Church but on some tradition or other has thought out his own arbitrary judgment or has followed a non-Orthodox teaching—is in this state of deception." The Roman Catholic Church has whole spiritual manuals written by people in this state; such is Thomas à Kempis' *Imitation of Christ.* Bishop Ignatius says of it: "There reigns in this book and breathes from its pages the unction of the evil spirit, flattering the reader, intoxicating him.... The book conducts the reader directly to communion with God, without previous purification by repentance.... From it carnal people enter into rapture from a delight and intoxication attained without difficulty, without self-renunciation, without repentance, without *crucifixion of the flesh with its passions and desires* (Gal. 5:24), with flattery of their fallen state." And the result, as I. M. Kontzevitch, the great transmitter of Patristic teaching, has written,* is that "the ascetic, striving to kindle in his heart love for God while neglecting repentance, exerts himself to attain a feeling of delight,

---

* See *The Orthodox Word,* no. 4, 1965, pp. 155–58.

of ecstasy, and as a result he attains precisely the opposite: 'he enters into communion with satan and becomes infected with hatred for the Holy Spirit' (Bishop Ignatius)."

And this is the actual state in which the followers of the "charismatic revival," even without suspecting it, find themselves. This may be seen most clearly by examining their experiences and views, point by point, against the teaching of the Orthodox Fathers as set forth by Bishop Ignatius.

A. Attitude toward "Spiritual" Experiences

Having little or no foundation in the genuine sources of Christian spiritual experience—the Holy Mysteries of the Church, and the spiritual teaching handed down by the Holy Fathers from Christ and His Apostles—the followers of the "charismatic" movement have no means of distinguishing the grace of God from its counterfeit. All "charismatic" writers show, to a lesser or greater degree, a lack of caution and discrimination toward the experiences they have. Some Catholic Pentecostals, to be sure, "exorcise satan" before asking for "Baptism in the Spirit"; but the efficacy of this act, as will soon be evident from their own testimony, is similar to that of the Jews in the Acts (19:15), to whose "exorcism" the evil spirit replied: *Jesus I know, and Paul I know; but who are you?* St. John Cassian, the great 5th-century Orthodox father of the West, who wrote with great discernment on the working of the Holy Spirit in his Conference on "Divine Gifts," notes that "sometimes the demons [work miracles] in order to lift into pride the man who believes himself to possess the miraculous gift, and so prepare him for a more miraculous fall. They pretend that they are being burnt up and driven out from the bodies where they were dwelling through the holiness of people whom truly they know to be unholy.... In the Gospel we read: *There shall arise false Christs and false prophets...."* *

The 18th-century Swedish "visionary," Emanuel Swedenborg—who was a strange forerunner of today's occult and "spiritual" revival—had extensive experience with spiritual beings, whom he frequently saw and communicated with. He distinguished two kinds of spirits, the "good" and the "evil"; his experience has been recently confirmed by the findings of a clinical psychologist in his work with "hallucinating" patients in a state mental hospital in Ukiah, California. This psychologist took seriously the voices heard by his patients and undertook a series of "dialogues" with them (through the intermediary of the patients themselves). He concluded, like Swedenborg, that there are two very different kinds of "beings" who have entered into contact with the patients: the "higher" and the "lower." In his own words: "Lower-order voices are similar to drunken bums at a bar who like to tease and torment just for the fun of it. They suggest lewd acts and then scold the patient for considering them. They find a weak point of conscience and work on it interminably.... The vocabulary and range of ideas of the lower order is limited, but they have a persistent will to destroy.... They work on every weakness and belief, claim awesome powers, lie, make promises, and then undermine the patient's will.... All of the lower order are irreligious or antireligious.... To one person they appeared as conventional devils and referred to themselves as demons....

"In direct contrast stand the rarer higher-order hallucinations.... This contrast may be illustrated by the experience of one man. He had heard the lower order arguing for a long

---

* Conference XV:2, in Owen Chadwick, *Western Asceticism,* Westminster Press, Philadelphia, Penn., 1958, p. 258.

while about how they would murder him. (But) he also had a light come to him at night, like the sun. He knew it was a different order because the light respected his freedom and would withdraw if it frightened him…. When the man was encouraged to approach his friendly sun he entered a world of powerful numinous experiences…. [Once] a very powerful and impressive Christ-like figure appeared…. Some patients experience both the higher and lower orders at various times and feel caught between a private heaven and hell. Many only know the attacks of the lower order. The higher order claims power over the lower order and, indeed, shows it at times, but not enough to give peace of mind to most patients…. The higher order appeared strangely gifted, sensitive, wise, and religious."*

Any reader of the Orthodox Lives of Saints and other spiritual literature knows that all of these spirits—both "good" and "evil," the "lower" with the "higher"—are equally demons, and that the discernment between true good spirits (angels) and these evil spirits cannot be made on the basis of one's own feelings or impressions. The widespread practice of "exorcism" in "charismatic" circles offers no guarantee whatever that evil spirits are actually being driven out; exorcisms are also very common (and seemingly successful) among primitive shamans,** who also recognize that there are different kinds of spirits—which are all, however, equally demons, whether they seem to flee when exorcised or come when invoked to give shamanistic powers.

* Wilson Van Dusen, *The Presence of Other Worlds,* Harper and Row, New York, 1974, pp. 120–25.
** See I. H. Lewis, *Ecstatic Religion, An Anthropological Study of Spirit Possession and Shamanism,* Penguin Books, Baltimore, 1971, pp. 45, 88, 156, etc., and illustration 9.

No one will deny that the "charismatic" movement on the whole is firmly oriented against contemporary occultism and satanism. But the more subtle of the evil spirits appear as "angels of light" (II Cor. 11:14), and a great gift of discernment, together with a deep distrust of all one's extraordinary "spiritual" experiences, is required if a person is not to be deceived. In the face of the subtle, invisible enemies who wage unseen warfare against the human race, the naively trusting attitude towards their experiences of most people involved in the "charismatic" movement is an open invitation to spiritual deception. One pastor, for example, counsels meditation on Scriptural passages and then writing down any thought "triggered" by the reading: "This is the Holy Spirit's personal message to you" (Christenson, p. 139). But any serious student of Christian spirituality knows that, for example, "at the beginning of the monastic life some of the unclean demons instruct [novices] in the interpretation of the Divine Scriptures ... gradually deceiving them that they may lead them into heresy and blasphemy" (*The Ladder* of St. John, Step 26:152).

Sadly, the attitude of the Orthodox followers of the "charismatic revival" seems no more discerning than that of Catholics and Protestants. They obviously do not know well the Orthodox Fathers or Lives of Saints, and when they do quote a rare Father, it is often out of context (see later concerning St. Seraphim). The "charismatic" appeal is chiefly one to *experience.* One Orthodox priest writes: "Some have dared to label this experience 'prelest'—spiritual pride. No one who has encountered the Lord in this way could fall into this delusion" (*Logos,* April 1972, p. 10). But it is a very rare Orthodox Christian who is capable of distinguishing very subtle forms of spiritual deception (where "pride," for example, may take the form of "humility") solely on the basis of his *feeling* about them without reference to the Patristic tradition; only one who has already fully assimilated the Patristic tradition into his own thought and practice and has attained great sanctity can presume to do this.

How is the Orthodox Christian prepared to withstand deception? He has the whole body of God-inspired Patristic writings which, together with Holy Scripture, present the judgment of Christ's Church for 1900 years with regard to virtually every conceivable spiritual and pseudo-spiritual experience. Later we shall see that this tradition has a very definite judgment precisely on the chief question the "charismatic" movement raises: concerning the possibility of a new and widespread "outpouring of the Holy Spirit" in the last days. But even before consulting the Fathers on specific questions, the Orthodox Christian is protected against deception by the very knowledge that such deception not only exists, but is everywhere, including within himself. Bishop Ignatius writes: "We are all in deception. The knowledge of this is the greatest preventative against deception. It is the greatest deception to acknowledge oneself to be free of deception." He quotes St. Gregory the Sinaite, who warns us: "It is not a little labor to attain the truth precisely and to make oneself pure of everything that opposes grace; because it is usual for the devil to show his deception, especially to beginners, in the form of truth, giving a spiritual appearance to what is evil." And "God is not angry at him who, fearing deception, watches over himself with extreme caution, even if he should not accept something which is sent from God.... On the contrary, God praises such a one for his good sense."

Thus, totally unprepared for spiritual warfare, unaware that there is such a thing as spiritual deception of the most subtle sort (as opposed to obvious forms of occultism), the Catholic or Protestant or uninformed Orthodox Christian goes to a prayer meeting to be "baptized (or filled) with the Holy Spirit." The atmosphere of the meeting is extremely loose, being intentionally left "open" to the activity of some "spirit." Thus do Catholics (who profess to be more cautious than Protestants) describe some of their Pentecostal gatherings: "There seemed to be no barriers, no inhibitions.... They sat cross-legged on the floor. Ladies in slacks. White-robed monk. Cigarette smokers. Coffee drinkers. Praying in free-form.... It occurred to me that these people were having a good time praying! Is that what they meant by the Holy Spirit dwelling amongst them?" And at another Catholic Pentecostal meeting, "except for the fact that no one was drinking, it seemed like a cocktail party" (Ranaghan, pp. 157, 209). At interdenominational "charismatic" meetings the atmosphere is likewise sufficiently informal that no one is surprised when the "spirit" inspires an elderly woman, in the midst of a fit of general weeping, to stand up and "dance a little jig" (Sherrill, p. 118). To the sober Orthodox Christian, the first thing noticeable about such an atmosphere is its total lack of what he knows in his own Divine services as genuine piety and awe, proceeding from the fear of God. And this first impression is only strikingly confirmed by observation of the truly strange effects which the Pentecostal "spirit" produces when it descends into this loose atmosphere. We shall now examine some of these effects, placing them before the judgment of the Holy Fathers of the Church of Christ.

B. Physical Accompaniments of "Charismatic" Experience

One of the commonest responses to the experience of the "Baptism of the Holy Spirit" is *laughter*. One Catholic testifies: "I was so joyful that all I could do was laugh as I lay on the floor" (Ranaghan, p. 28). Another Catholic: "The sense of the presence and love of God was so strong that I can remember sitting in the chapel for a half hour just laughing out of joy over the love of God" (Ranaghan, p. 64). A Protestant testifies that at his "Baptism" "I started laughing.... I just wanted to laugh and laugh the way you do when you feel so good you just can't talk about it. I held my sides and laughed until I doubled over" (Sherrill, p. 113). Another Protestant: "The new tongue I was given was intermingled with waves of mirth in which every fear I had just seemed to roll away. It was a tongue of laughter" (Sherrill, p. 115). An Orthodox priest, Fr. Eusebius Stephanou, writes: "I could not conceal the broad smile on my face that any minute could have broken out into laughter—a laughter of the Holy Spirit stirring in me a refreshing release" (*Logos,* April 1972, p. 4).

Many, many examples could be collected of this truly strange reaction to a "spiritual" experience, and some "charismatic" apologists have a whole philosophy of "spiritual joy" and "God's foolishness" to explain it. But this philosophy is not in the least Christian; such a concept as the "laughter of the Holy Spirit" is unheard of in the whole history of Christian thought and experience. Here perhaps more clearly than anywhere else the "charismatic revival" reveals itself as not at all Christian in religious orientation; this experience is purely worldly and pagan, and where it cannot be explained in terms of emotional hysteria (for Fr. Eusebius, indeed, laughter provided "relief" and "release" from "an intense feeling of self-consciousness and embarrassment" and "emotional devastation"), it can only be due to some degree of "possession" by one or more of the pagan gods, which the Orthodox church calls demons. Here, for example, is a comparable "initiation" experience of a pagan Eskimo shaman: Not finding initiation, "I would sometimes fall to weeping and feel unhappy without knowing why. Then for no reason all would suddenly be changed, and I felt a great, inexplicable joy, a joy so powerful that I could not restrain it, but had to break into song, a mighty song, with room for only one word: joy, joy! And I had to use the full strength of my voice. And then in the midst of such a fit of mysterious and overwhelming delight I became a shaman.... I could see and hear in a totally different way. I had gained my enlightenment ... and it was not only I who could see through the darkness of life, but the same bright light also shone out of me ... and all the spirits of earth and sky and sea now came to me and became my helping spirits" (Lewis, *Ecstatic Religion,* p. 37).

It is not surprising that unsuspecting "Christians," having deliberately laid themselves open to a similar pagan experience, would still interpret it as a "Christian" experience; psychologically they are still Christians, although spiritually they have entered the realm of distinctly non-Christian attitudes and practices. What is the judgment of the Orthodox ascetic tradition concerning such a thing as a *"laughter of the Holy Spirit?"* Sts. Barsanuphius and John, the 6th-century ascetics, give the unequivocal Orthodox answer in reply to an Orthodox monk who was plagued by this problem (Answer 451): "In the fear of God there is no laughter. The Scripture says of the foolish, that *they raise their voice in laughter* (Sirach 21:23); and the word of the foolish is always disturbed and deprived of grace." St. Ephraim the Syrian just as clearly teaches: "Laughter and familiarity are the beginning of a soul's corruption. If you see these in yourself, know that you have come to the depths of evils. Do not cease to pray God that He will deliver you from this death.... Laughter removes from us that blessing which is promised to those who mourn (Matt. 5:4) and destroys what has been built up. Laughter offends the Holy Spirit, gives no benefit to the soul, dishonors the body. Laughter drives out virtues, has no remembrance of death or thought of tortures" (*Philokalia,* Russian edition, Moscow, 1913: vol. 2, p. 448). Is it not evident how far astray ignorance of basic Christianity can lead one?

At least as common as laughter as a response to charismatic "Baptism" is its psychologically close relative, *tears.* These occur to individuals and, quite often, to whole groups at once (in this case quite apart from the experience of "Baptism"), spreading infectiously for no apparent reason at all (see Sherrill, pp. 109, 117). "Charismatic" writers do not find the reason for this in the "conviction of sin" that produces such results at Protestant revivals; they give no reason at all, and there seems to be none, except that this experience simply comes upon one who is exposed to the "charismatic" atmosphere. The Orthodox Fathers, as Bishop Ignatius notes, teach that tears often accompany the second form of spiritual deception. St. John of the Ladder, telling of the many different causes of tears, some good and some bad, warns: "Do not trust your fountains of tears before your soul has been perfectly purified" (Step 7:35); and of one kind of tears he states definitely: "Tears without thought are proper only to an irrational nature and not to a rational one" (7:17).

Besides laughter and tears, and often together with them, there are a number of other physical reactions to the "Baptism of the Holy Spirit," including warmth, many kinds of trembling and contortions, and falling to the floor. All the examples given here, it should be emphasized, are those of ordinary Protestants and Catholics, and not at all those of any Pentecostal extremists, whose experiences are much more spectacular and unrestrained.

"When hands were laid on me, immediately it felt as if my whole chest were trying to rise into my head. My lips started trembling, and my brain started turning flips. Then I started grinning" (Ranaghan, p. 67). Another was "without emotion following the event, but with great warmth of body and a great ease" (Ranaghan, p. 91). Another gives this testimony: "As soon as I knelt down I began to tremble.... All of a sudden I became filled with the Holy Spirit and realized that 'God is real.' I started laughing and crying at the same time. The next thing I knew I was prostrate before the altar and filled with the peace of Christ" (Ranaghan, p. 34). Another says: "As I knelt quietly thanking the Lord, D. lay prostrate and suddenly began to heave by the power of someone unseen. By an insight that must have been divinely inspired ... I knew D. was being moved quite visibly by the Holy Spirit" (Ranaghan, p. 29). Another: "My hands (usually cold because of poor circulation) grew moist and warm. Warmth enveloped me" (Ranaghan, p. 30). Another: "I knew God was working within me. I could feel a distinct tingling in my hands, and immediately I became bathed in a hard sweat" (Ranaghan, p. 102). A member of the "Jesus Movement" says: "I feel something welling up inside me and all of a sudden I'm speaking in tongues" (Ortega, p. 49). One "charismatic" apologist emphasizes that such experiences are typical in the "Baptism of the Holy Spirit," which "has often been marked by a subjective experience which has brought the recipient into a wonderful new sense of nearness to the Lord. This sometimes demands such an expression of worship and adoration as cannot be contained within the usual restrictions imposed by the etiquette of our Western society! At such times, some have been known to shake violently, to lift up their hands to the Lord, to raise the voice above the normal pitch, or even to fall to the floor" (Lillie, p. 17).

One does not know at what to marvel the more: at the total incongruence of such hysterical feelings and experiences with anything at all spiritual or at the incredible light-mindedness that leads such deceived people to ascribe their contortions to the "Holy Spirit," to "divine inspiration," to the "peace of Christ." These are clearly people who, in the spiritual and religious realm, are not only totally inexperienced and without guidance, but are absolutely *illiterate*. The whole history of Orthodox Christianity does not know of any such "ecstatic" experiences produced by the Holy Spirit. It is only foolishness when some "charismatic" apologists presume to compare these childish and hysterical experiences, which are open to absolutely everyone, with the Divine revelations accorded to the greatest Saints, such as to St. Paul on the road to Damascus or to St. John the Evangelist on Patmos. Those Saints fell down before the true God (without contortions, and certainly without laughter), whereas these pseudo-Christians are merely reacting to the presence of an *invading spirit,* and are worshipping only themselves. The Elder Macarius of Optina wrote to a person in a similar state: "Thinking to find the love of God in consoling feelings, you are seeking not God but yourself, that is, your own consolation, while you avoid the path of sorrows, considering yourself supposedly lost without spiritual consolations."* If these "charismatic" experiences are religious experiences at all, then they are *pagan* religious experiences; and in fact they seem to correspond exactly to the mediumistic initiation experience of *spirit-possession,* which is caused by "an inner force welling up inside attempting to take control" (Koch, *Occult Bondage,* p. 44). Of course, not all "Baptisms of the Holy Spirit" are as ecstatic as some of these

---

* *Starets Macarius of Optina,* Harbin, 1940, p. 100 (in Russian). [English edition: *Elder Macarius of Optina,* St. Herman of Alaska Brotherhood, Platina, Calif., 1995, p. 326.]

experiences (although some are even *more* ecstatic); but this too is in accord with spiritistic practice: "When spirits find a medium friendly or well-disposed in submissiveness or passivity of mind, they enter quietly as into their own home; while, on the contrary, when the psychic is less well-disposed from some resistance, or want of passivity of mind, the spirit enters with more or less force, and this is often reflected in the contortions of the face and tremor of the medium's members" (Blackmore, *Spiritism,* p. 97).

This experience of "spirit-possession," however, should not be confused with actual demonic possession, which is the condition when an unclean spirit takes up permanent habitation in someone and produces physical and psychic disorders which do not seem to be indicated in "charismatic" sources. Mediumistic "possession" is temporary and partial, the medium consenting to be *used* for a particular function by the invading spirit. But the "charismatic" texts themselves make it quite clear that what is involved in these experiences—when they are genuine and not merely the product of suggestion—is not merely the development of some mediumistic ability, but actual possession by a spirit. These people would seem to be correct in calling themselves "spirit-filled"—but it is certainly not the *Holy* Spirit with which they are filled!

Bishop Ignatius gives several examples of such physical accompaniments of spiritual deception: one, a monk who trembled and made strange sounds, and identified these signs as the "fruits of prayer"; another, a monk whom the bishop met who as a result of his ecstatic method of prayer felt such heat in his body that he needed no warm clothing in winter, and this heat could even be felt by others. As a general principle, Bishop Ignatius writes, the second kind of spiritual deception is accompanied by "a material, passionate warmth of the blood"; "the behavior of the ascetics of Latinism, embraced by deception, has always been ecstatic, by reason of this extraordinary material, passionate warmth"—the state of such Latin "saints" as Francis of Assisi and Ignatius Loyola. This *material* warmth of the blood, a mark of the spiritually deceived, is to be distinguished from the *spiritual* warmth felt by those such as St. Seraphim of Sarov who genuinely acquired the Holy Spirit. But the Holy Spirit is not acquired from ecstatic "charismatic" experiences, but by the long and arduous path of asceticism, the "path of sorrows" of which the Elder Macarius spoke, within the Church of Christ.

C. "Spiritual Gifts" Accompanying "Charismatic" Experience

The chief claim of the followers of the "charismatic revival" is that they have acquired "spiritual" gifts. One of the first such "gifts" that becomes noticeable in those "baptized with the Holy Spirit" is a new "spiritual" power and boldness. What gives them boldness is the definite experience which no one can doubt that they have had, although one can certainly doubt their interpretation of it. Some typical examples: "I do not have to believe in Pentecost, because I have seen it" (Ranaghan, p. 40). "I began to feel that I knew exactly what to say to others and what they needed to hear.... I found that the Holy Spirit gave me a real boldness to say it and it had a marked effect" (Ranaghan, p. 64). "I was so confident that the Spirit would be true to His word that I prayed without any ifs. I prayed in wills and shalls and in every other kind of declarative statement" (Ranaghan, p. 67). An Orthodox example: "We pray for wisdom and suddenly we are wise in the Lord. We pray for love and true love is felt for all men. We pray for healings, and health has been restored. We pray for miracles and, believing, we have seen miracles happen. We pray for signs, and receive them. We pray in tongues known and tongues unknown" (*Logos,* April 1972, p. 13).

Here, again, a genuine Orthodox characteristic, acquired and tested by long years of ascetic labor and maturing in faith, is supposedly obtained instantly by means of "charismatic" experience. It is true, of course, that the Apostles and Martyrs were given a magnificent boldness by the special grace of God; but it is only ridiculous when every "charismatic Christian," without any notion of what Divine grace is, wishes to compare himself to these great Saints. Being based on an experience of deception, "charismatic" boldness is no more than a feverish, "revivalistic" imitation of true Christian boldness, and it only serves as another identifying mark of "charismatic" deception. Bishop Ignatius writes that a certain "self-confidence and boldness are usually noticeable in people who are in self-deception, supposing that they are holy or are spiritually progressing." "An extraordinary pomposity appears in those afflicted with this deception: they are as it were intoxicated with themselves, by their state of self-deception, seeing in it a state of grace. They are steeped in, overflowing with high-mindedness and pride, while appearing humble to many who judge by appearances without being able to judge by fruits."

Beyond speaking in tongues itself, the most common "supernatural" gift of those "baptized in the Spirit" is the direct reception of "messages from God" in the form of "prophecies" and "interpretations." One Catholic girl says of her "charismatic" friends: "In some of them I witnessed the speaking in tongues, some of which I have been able to interpret. The messages have always been those of great solace and joy from the Lord" (Ranaghan, p. 32). One "interpretation" is summarized thus: "He was speaking words from God, a message of consolation" (Ranaghan, p. 181). The messages are nothing if not bold; at one meeting "still another young woman announced a 'message from God,' speaking in the first person" (Ranaghan, p. 2). A "charismatic" Protestant writes that in such messages "God's Word is directly spoken!... The Word may suddenly be spoken by anyone present, and so, variously a 'Thus says the Lord' breaks forth in the fellowship. It is usually in the first person (though not always), such as 'I am with you to bless you'" (Williams, p. 27).

A few specific texts of "prophecy" and "interpretation" are given in the apologetical books of the "charismatic" movement:

1. "Be like a tree swaying with His will, rooted in His strength, reaching up to His love and light" (Ford, p. 35).

2. "As the Holy Spirit came down upon Mary and Jesus was formed within her, so the Holy Spirit comes upon you and Jesus is in your midst"—given in tongues by a Roman Catholic and "interpreted" by a Protestant (Ford, p. 35).

3. "The feet of Him who walked the streets of Jerusalem are behind you. His gaze is healing to those who draw near but death to those who flee"—this had special meaning for one member of the prayer group (Ford, p. 35).

4. "I reach out my hand to you. You need only take it and I will lead you"—this same message was given a few minutes earlier to a Roman Catholic priest in another room; he wrote it down and entered the prayer room just in time to hear it uttered in exactly the words he had written down (Ranaghan, p. 54).

5. "Do not worry, I am pleased with the stand you have taken. This is difficult for you but will bring much blessing to another"—this brought final reassurance to one person present concerning a recent difficult decision (Sherrill, p. 88).

6. "My wife walked in and began to play the organ. Suddenly, the Spirit of God came upon her and she began to speak in tongues and prophesy, 'My son, I am with you. Because you have been faithful in little things I am going to use you in a greater way. I am leading you by the hand. I am guiding you, be not afraid. You are in the center of My will. Do not look to the right or to the left, but continue therein"—this "prophecy" was accompanied by a "vision" and was directly responsible for the founding of a large and influential Pentecostal organization, the "Full Gospel Business Men's Fellowship International" (*Logos Journal,* Sept.–Oct. 1971, p. 14).

We may well believe, according to the testimony of witnesses who find that such messages apply directly to them, that there is something preternatural about a number of them, that they are not just "made up." But does the *Holy Spirit* use such artificial methods to communicate with men? (The "spirits" at séances certainly do!) Why is the language so monotonous and stereotyped, sometimes worthy of the penny fortune-telling machines in American cafes? Why are the messages so vague and dreamlike, sounding indeed like trance-utterances? Why is their content always one of "consolation," "solace and joy," reassurance, precisely without prophetic or dogmatic character—as if the "spirit," even like the "spirits" at séances, were especially pleased with his non-denominational audience? *Who, after all, is the strangely characterless "I" that speaks?* Are we wrong in applying the words of a *true* Prophet of God to all this?—*Let not your prophets that are in the midst of you, and your diviners, deceive you.... For they prophesy falsely unto you in My name: I have not sent them, saith the Lord* (Jeremiah 29:8–9).

Just as one "baptized in the Spirit" usually carries the ability to speak in tongues over into his private devotions, and in general is aware that "the Lord" is constantly with him, so too, even outside the atmosphere of the prayer meeting he often has private "revelations," including audible voices and tangible "presences." Thus does the "prophet" of the "charismatic revival" describe one of his experiences: "I was awakened from a deep restful sleep by a voice that seemed loud and clear ... distinctly saying: 'God has no grandsons'.... Then it seemed as if there was someone in my room and the presence made me feel good. Suddenly it dawned on me. It must be the Holy Spirit who spoke to me" (Du Plessis, p. 61).

How can one account for such experiences? Bishop Ignatius writes: "One possessed by this kind of spiritual deception *fancies* of himself [the second form of *prelest* is called 'fancy,' *mnenie* in Russian] that he abounds in the gifts of the Holy Spirit. This fancy is composed of false concepts and false feelings, and in this character which it has it belongs fully to the realm of the father and representative of falsehood, the devil. One who, in praying, strives to unveil in the heart the feeling of the new man, yet does not have any possibility to do this, substitutes for this feelings of his own invention, counterfeits, to which the action of fallen spirits does not tarry to join itself. Acknowledging his incorrect feelings, both his own and those from the demons, to be true and grace-given, he receives conceptions which correspond to the feelings."

Precisely such a process has been observed by writers on spiritism. For someone seriously involved in spiritism (and not only mediums themselves), a moment comes when the whole false spirituality that cultivates passivity of mind and openness to the activity of "spirits," manifested even in such seemingly innocent pastimes as the use of a ouija-board, passes over into the actual possession of this person by an invading spirit, after which undeniably "supernatural" phenomena begin to appear.* In the "charismatic revival" this moment of transition is identified as the experience of the "Baptism of the Holy Spirit," which, when it is genuine, is precisely the moment when self-deception becomes demonic deception, and the "charismatic" victim is virtually assured that from then on his deceived "religious feelings" can expect a response from the "Spirit" and he will enter a "life of miracles."

D. The New "Outpouring of the Holy Spirit"

In general, followers of the "charismatic revival" have the feeling of being (as they constantly repeat) "Spirit-filled." "I felt free, clean and a new person and completely filled with the Holy Spirit" (Ranaghan, p. 98). "Because of what was begun in the baptism of the Spirit, I have now begun to see more a vision of what life in the Spirit is like. It is truly a life of miracles ... of being filled over and over with the life-giving love of the Spirit of God" (Ranaghan, p. 65). They invariably characterize their "spiritual" state in similar words; a Catholic priest writes, "Whatever other particular effects may have occurred, peace and joy seem to have been received by all, almost without exception, of those who have been touched by the Spirit" (Ranaghan, p. 185). One inter-denominational "charismatic" group states that the aim of its members is "to show and spread Jesus Christ's Love, Joy and Peace wherever they are" (*Inter-Church Renewal*). In this "spiritual" state (in which, characteristically, both repentance and salvation are seldom mentioned), some rise to great heights. In one Catho-

---

* See Blackmore, *Spiritism*, pp. 144–75, where an example is given of a Catholic priest who was physically pursued by a ouija-board (propelled, of course, by a demon) when he tried to give up using it!

lic the gift of the "Spirit" "has risen within me to long periods (several hours) of near ecstasy in which I'd swear I was experiencing a foretaste of the Kingdom of Heaven" (Ranaghan, p. 103). Spectacular stories are told of deliverance from drug addiction and the like. The Greek priest Fr. Eusebius Stephanou summarizes this "spirituality" by quoting a Roman Catholic priest who states that the "charismatic" movement involves "a new sense of the presence of God, a new awareness of Christ, a greater desire to pray, an ability to praise God, a new desire to read the Scriptures, the Scriptures coming alive as the Word of God, a new eagerness to have others know about Christ, a new compassion for others and a sensitiveness to their needs, a new sense of peace and joy...." And Fr. Eusebius presents the ultimate argument of the whole movement: "The tree is known by its fruits.... Do these fruits demonstrate the presence of the devil or of the sanctifying Spirit of Christ? No Orthodox in his right mind who has seen the fruits of the Spirit with his own eyes can give a mistaken answer to this question" (*Logos,* Jan. 1972, p. 13).

There is no reason to doubt any of this testimony. True, there is also much testimony—we have given a few examples—that contradicts this and states definitely that the "spirit" of the "charismatic revival" is something dark and ominous; but still it cannot be doubted that many followers of the "charismatic revival" actually feel that it is something "Christian" and "spiritual." As long as these people remain outside the Orthodox Church, we might well leave their opinions without comment. But when an Orthodox priest tells us that sectarian phenomena are produced by the Holy Spirit, and he even exhorts us: "Don't be left out. Open your heart to the promptings of the Holy Spirit and be part of the growing charismatic renewal" (*loc. cit.*)—then we have the right and the duty to examine their opinions quite closely, judging them not by the standard of the vague humanist "Christianity" which prevails in the West and is prepared to call anything "Christian" that merely "feels" so, but by the quite different standard of Orthodox Christianity. And by this standard there is not one item in the above list of "spiritual fruits" but that can be, and has been in the sectarian and heretical movements of the past, produced by the devil appearing as an "angel of light," precisely with the aim of leading people away from the Church of Christ into *some other kind of "Christianity."* If the "spirit" of the "charismatic revival" is not the Holy Spirit, then these "spiritual fruits" likewise are not from God.

According to Bishop Ignatius, the deception known as *fancy* "is satisfied with the invention of counterfeit feelings and states of grace, from which there is born a false, wrong conception of the whole spiritual undertaking.... It constantly invents pseudo-spiritual states, an intimate companionship with Jesus, an inward conversation with him, mystical revelations, voices, enjoyments.... From this activity the blood receives a sinful, deceiving movement, which presents itself as a grace-given delight.... It clothes itself in the mask of humility, piety, wisdom." Unlike the more spectacular form of spiritual deception, *fancy,* while "bringing the mind into the most frightful error, does not however lead it to delirium," so that the state may continue for many years or a whole lifetime and not be easily detected. One who falls into this warm, comfortable, fevered state of deception virtually commits spiritual suicide, blinding himself to his own true spiritual state. Writes Bishop Ignatius: "Fancying of himself ... that he is filled with grace, he will never receive grace.... He who ascribes to himself gifts of grace fences off from himself by this 'fancy' the entrance into himself of Divine grace, and opens wide the door to the infection of sin and to demons." *Thou sayest, I am rich, and increased with goods, and have need of nothing; and knowest not that thou art wretched, and miserable, and poor, and blind, and naked* (Apoc. 3:17).

Those infected with the "charismatic" deception are not only themselves "spirit-filled"; they also see around them the beginning of a "new age" of the "out-pouring of the Holy Spirit," believing, as does Fr. Eusebius Stephanou, that "the world is on the threshold of a great spiritual awakening" (*Logos*, Feb. 1972, p. 18); and the words of the Prophet Joel are constantly on their lips: *I will pour out My Spirit upon all flesh* (Joel 2:28). The Orthodox Christian knows that this prophecy refers in general to the last age that began with the coming of our Lord, and more specifically to Pentecost (Acts 2), and to every Orthodox Saint who truly possesses in abundance the gifts of the Holy Spirit—such as St. John of Kronstadt and St. Nectarios of Pentapolis, who have worked thousands of miracles even in this corrupt 20th century. But to today's "charismatics," miraculous gifts are for everyone; almost everyone who wants to can and does speak in tongues, and there are manuals telling you how to do it.

But what do the Holy Fathers of the Orthodox Church teach us? According to Bishop Ignatius, the gifts of the Holy Spirit "exist only in Orthodox Christians who have attained Christian perfection, purified and prepared beforehand by repentance." They "are given to Saints of God solely at God's good will and God's action, and not by the will of men and not by one's own power. They are given unexpectedly, extremely rarely, in cases of extreme need, by God's wondrous providence, and not just at random" (St. Isaac the Syrian). "It should be noted that at the present time spiritual gifts are granted in great moderation, corresponding to the enfeeblement that has enveloped Christianity in general. These gifts serve entirely the needs of salvation. On the contrary, 'fancy' lavishes its gifts in boundless abundance and with the greatest speed."

In a word, the "spirit" that suddenly lavishes its "gifts" upon this adulterous generation which, corrupted and deceived by centuries of false belief and pseudo-piety, seeks only a "sign"—is not the Holy Spirit of God. These people have never known the Holy Spirit and never worshipped Him. True spirituality is so far beyond them that, to the sober observer, they only mock it by their psychic and emotional—and sometimes demonic—phenomena and blasphemous utterances. Of true spiritual feelings, writes Bishop Ignatius, "the fleshly man cannot form any conception: because a conception of feeling is always based on those feelings already known to the heart, while spiritual feelings are entirely foreign to the heart that knows only fleshly and emotional feelings. Such a heart does not so much as know of the *existence* of spiritual feelings."

SOURCES CITED IN THE TEXT OF THIS CHAPTER

Burdick, Donald W. *Tongues—To Speak or not to Speak*. Moody Press, 1969.

Christenson, Larry. *Speaking in Tongues*. Dimension Books, Minneapolis, 1968.

Du Plessis, David J. *The Spirit Bade Me Go*. Logos International, Plainfield, New Jersey, 1970.

Ford, J. Massingberd. *The Pentecostal Experience*. Paulist Press, N. Y., 1970.

Gelpi, Donald L., S. J. *Pentecostalism, A Theological Viewpoint*. Paulist Press, N. Y., 1971.

Harper, Michael. *Life in the Holy Spirit.* Logos Books, Plainfield, N. J., 1966.

Koch, Kurt. *The Strife of Tongues.* Kregel Publications, Grand Rapids, 1969.

Lillie, D. G. *Tongues under Fire.* Fountain Trust, London, 1966.

Ortega, Ruben, compiler. *The Jesus People Speak Out.* David C. Cook Publishing Co., Elgin, Ill., 1972

Ranaghan, Kevin; Ranaghan, Dorothy. *Catholic Pentecostals.* Paulist Press, 1969.

Sherrill, John L. *They Speak with Other Tongues.* Spire Books, Old Tappan, N. J., 1965

Williams, J. Rodman. *The Era of the Spirit.* Logos International, 1971.

VIII

Conclusion:
The Spirit of the Last Times

1. THE "CHARISMATIC REVIVAL" AS A SIGN OF THE TIMES

To the very end of this age there shall not be lacking Prophets of the Lord God, as also servants of satan. But in the last times those who truly will serve God will succeed in hiding themselves from men and will not perform in their midst signs and wonders as at the present time, but they will travel by a path of activity intermixed with humility, and in the Kingdom of Heaven they will be greater than the Fathers who have been glorified by signs. For at that time no one will perform before the eyes of men miracles which would inflame men and inspire them to strive with zeal for ascetic labors.... Many, being possessed by ignorance, will fall into the abyss, going astray in the breadth of the broad and spacious path.

—Prophecy of St. Niphon of Constantia, Cyprus*

---

* Published in Russian with the writings of Sts. Barsanuphius the Great and John, Moscow, 1855, pp. 654–55.

A. A "Pentecost without Christ"

For Orthodox Christians present-day "tongues," like those described in the New Testament, are also a "sign"; but now they are a sign, not of the beginning of the Gospel of salvation for all people, but of its end. The sober Orthodox Christian will not find it difficult to agree with the apologists of the "charismatic revival" that this new "outpouring of the spirit" may mean indeed that "the consummation of the age is at hand" (Fr. Eusebius Stephanou in *Logos*, April 1972, p. 3). *Now the Spirit speaketh expressly, that in the latter times some shall depart from the faith, giving heed to seducing spirits, and doctrines of devils* (I Tim. 4:1). In the last days we shall see *the spirits of devils, working miracles* (Apoc. 16:14).

The Holy Scriptures and Orthodox Fathers clearly tell us that the character of the last times will not at all be one of a great spiritual "revival," of an "outpouring of the Holy Spirit," but rather one of almost universal apostasy, of spiritual deception so subtle that the very elect, if that were possible, will be deceived, of the virtual disappearance of Christianity from the face of the earth. *When the Son of man cometh, shall He find faith on the earth?* (Luke 18:8). It is precisely in the last times that satan is to be loosed (Apoc. 20:3) in order to produce the final and greatest outpouring of evil upon the earth.

The "charismatic revival," the product of a world without sacraments, without grace, a world thirsting for spiritual "signs" without being able to discern the spirits that give the signs, is itself a "sign" of these apostate times. The ecumenical movement itself remains always a movement of "good intentions" and feeble humanitarian "good deeds"; but when it is joined by a movement with "power," indeed *with all power and signs and lying wonders* (II Thess. 2:9), then who will be able to stop it? *The "charismatic revival" comes to the rescue of a floundering ecumenism,* and pushes it on to its goal. And this goal, as we have seen, is not merely "Christian" in nature—the "re-founding of the Church of Christ," to use the blasphemous utterance of Patriarch Athenagoras of Constantinople—that is only the first step to a larger goal which lies entirely outside of Christianity: the establishment of the "spiritual unity" of all religions, of all mankind.

However, the followers of the "charismatic revival" believe their experience is "Christian"; they will have nothing to do with occultism and Eastern religions; and they doubtless reject outright the whole comparison in the preceding pages of the "charismatic revival" with spiritism. Now it is quite true that religiously the "charismatic revival" is on a higher level than spiritism, which is a product of quite gross credulity and superstition; that its techniques are more refined and its phenomena more plentiful and more easily obtained; and that its whole ideology gives the *appearance* of being "Christian"—not Orthodox, but something that is not far from Protestant fundamentalism with an added "ecumenical" coloring.

And yet we have seen that "charismatic" experience, and particularly the central experience of the "Baptism of the Holy Spirit," is largely if not entirely a *pagan* experience, much closer to "spirit-possession" than to anything Christian. We know also that Pentecostalism was born on the fringes of sectarian "Christianity," where very little remains of genuine Christian attitudes and beliefs, and that it was actually "discovered" as the result of a religious *experiment,* in which Christians do not participate. But it was not until quite recently that it was possible to find a clear testimony of the non-Christian character of "charismatic" experience *in the words of a "charismatic" apologist.* This apologist informs us that the experience of the "Baptism in the Holy Spirit" can indeed be had *without Christ.*

This writer tells the story of a person who had received the "Baptism" with speaking in tongues and was encouraging everyone to seek it. Yet he admitted that repentance had not been part of his experience and that not only had he not been delivered from sinful habits, but even had no particular desire to be delivered from them. The writer concludes: "A pentecost without repentance—a pentecost without Christ—that is what some are experiencing today.... They have heard of tongues, they wish to identify with a status experience, so they seek someone to lay on hands for a quick, cheap, easy impartation which bypasses Christ and His Cross." Nonetheless, this writer admits that speaking in tongues is undeniably "the initial consequence or confirmation" of the "Baptism in the Holy Spirit" (Harry Lunn, in *Logos Journal,* Nov.–Dec. 1971, pp. 44, 47).

Those who bring Christian ideas to the experience *assume* that the "Baptism in the Holy Spirit" is a Christian experience. But if it can be given to those who merely seek a cheap, easy status experience—then there is no necessary connection whatever between this experience and Christ. The very possibility of an experience of a "Pentecost without Christ" means that the experience in itself *is not Christian at all;* "Christians," often sincere and well-meaning, *are reading into the experience a Christian content which in itself it does not have.*

Do we not have here the common denominator of "spiritual experience" which is needed for a new world religion? Is this not perhaps *the key to the "spiritual unity" of mankind which the ecumenical movement has sought in vain?*

B. The "New Christianity"

There may be those who will doubt that the "charismatic revival" is a form of mediumism; that is only a secondary question of the means or technique by which the "spirit" of the "charismatic revival" is communicated. But that this "spirit" has nothing to do with Orthodox Christianity is abundantly clear. And in fact this "spirit" follows almost to the letter the "prophecies" of Nicholas Berdyaev concerning a "New Christianity." It completely leaves behind the "monastic ascetic spirit of historical Orthodoxy," which most effectively exposes its falsity. It is not satisfied with the "conservative Christianity which directs the spiritual forces of man only towards contrition and salvation," but rather, apparently believing like Berdyaev that such a Christianity is still "incomplete," adds a second level of "spiritual" phenomena, not one of which is specifically Christian in character (although one is free to *interpret* them as "Christian"), which are open to people of every denomination with or without repentance, and which are completely unrelated to salvation. It looks to "a new era in Christianity, a new and deep spirituality, which means a new outpouring of the Holy Spirit"—in complete contradiction of Orthodox tradition and prophecy.

This is truly a "New Christianity"—but the specifically "new" ingredient in this "Christianity" is nothing original or "advanced," but merely a modern form of the devil's age-old religion of *shamanistic paganism.* The Orthodox "charismatic" periodical *The Logos* recommends Nicholas Berdyaev as a "prophet" precisely because he was "the greatest theologian of spiritual creativeness" (*Logos,* March 1972, p. 8). And indeed, it is precisely the shamans of every primitive tribe who know how to get in contact with and utilize the primordial *"creative"* *powers* of the universe—those "spirits of earth and sky and sea" which the Church of Christ recognizes as *demons,* and in serving which it is indeed possible to attain to a "creative" ecstasy and joy (the "Nietzschean enthusiasm and ecstasy" to which Berdyaev felt so close) which are unknown to the weary and half-hearted "Christians" who fall for the "charismatic" deception. But there is no Christ here. God has *forbidden* contact with this "creative," occult realm into which "Christians" have stumbled through ignorance and self-deception. The "charismatic revival" will have no need to enter a "dialogue with non-Christian religions," because, under the name of "Christianity," it is already embracing non-Christian religion and is itself becoming the *new* religion which Berdyaev foresaw, strangely combining "Christianity" and paganism.

The strange "Christian" spirit of the "charismatic revival" is clearly identified in the Holy Scriptures and the Orthodox Patristic tradition. According to these sources, world history will culminate in an almost superhuman "Christian" figure, the false messiah or *antichrist.* He will be "Christian" in the sense that his whole function and his very being will center on Christ, Whom he will imitate in every respect possible, and he will be not merely the greatest enemy of Christ, but in order to deceive Christians will *appear to be Christ,* come to earth for a second time and ruling from the restored Temple in Jerusalem. *Let no one deceive you by any means, for that day shall not come except there come a falling away (apostasy) first, and that man of sin be revealed, the son of perdition, who opposeth and exalteth himself above all that is called God, or that is worshipped; so that he as God sitteth in the temple of God, showing himself that he is God ... even him whose coming is after the working of satan with all power and signs and lying wonders, and with all deceivableness of unrighteousness in them that perish; because they received not the love of the truth, that they might be saved. And for this cause God shall send them strong delusion, that they should believe a lie: that they all might be damned who believed not the truth, but had pleasure in unrighteousness* (II Thess. 2:3–4, 9–12).

The Orthodox teaching concerning antichrist is a large subject in itself and cannot be presented here. But if, as the followers of the "charismatic revival" believe, the last days are indeed at hand, it is of crucial importance for the Orthodox Christian to be informed of this teaching concerning one who, as the Saviour Himself has told us, together with the "false prophets" of that time, *shall show great signs and wonders, insomuch that, if it were possible, they shall deceive the very elect* (Matt. 24:24). And the "elect" are certainly not those multitudes of people who are coming to accept the gross and most unscriptural delusion that "the world is on the threshold of a great spiritual awakening," but rather the "little flock" to which alone our Saviour has promised: *It is your Father's good pleasure to give you the Kingdom* (Luke 12:32). Even the true "elect" will be sorely tempted by the "great signs and wonders" of antichrist; but most "Christians" will accept him without any question, for his "New Christianity" is precisely what they seek.

C. "Jesus is Coming Soon"

Just in the past few years, significantly, the figure of "Jesus" has been thrust into strange prominence in America. On stage and in films long-standing prohibitions against portraying the person of Christ have been abrogated. Sensationally popular musicals present blasphemous parodies of His life. The "Jesus

Movement," which is largely "charismatic" in orientation, spreads spectacularly among teenagers and young people. The crudest form of American popular music is "Christianized" at mass "Jesus-Rock Festivals," and "Christian" tunes for the first time in the century become the most popular in the land. And underlying this whole strange conglomeration of sacrilege and absolutely unenlightened worldliness is the constantly reiterated expression of seemingly everyone's expectation and hope: *"Jesus is coming soon."*

In the midst of this psychic and "religious" devastation of the American land, a symptomatic "mystical" occurrence has been repeating itself in the lives of widely separated Americans. An editor of a "charismatic" magazine relates how he first encountered this occurrence as told by someone at a gathering of like-minded people:

"My friend and his wife were driving up to Boston on Route 3, when they stopped to pick up a hitchhiker. He was young and had a beard, but he wasn't dressed like a hippie. He got in the back seat without saying much, and they drove on. After a while, he quietly said, 'The Lord is coming soon.' My friend and his wife were so startled that they each turned around to look at him. There was no one there. Badly shaken, they pulled into the first gas station they came to. They had to tell someone else, no matter what the reaction. As the attendant listened, he didn't laugh. Instead, all he said was, 'You're the fifth car to come in here with that story.'

"As I listened, in spite of the hazy sunlight, a chill began to creep up my backbone. Yet that was only the beginning. One by one, around the circle, others were led to recount similar incidents, until there were six all told, across the length and breadth of the country, and all had taken place within the past two years"—in Los Angeles, Philadelphia, Duluth (thirteen reports to the police in one night), New Orleans; sometimes the hitchhiker is a man, sometimes a woman. Later an Episcopalian priest told the editor of his own identical experience in upstate New York. To the editor, this all indicates that in fact 'Jesus is coming soon'" (David Manuel, Jr., in *Logos Journal,* Jan.–Feb. 1972, p. 3).

The careful observer of the contemporary religious scene—especially in America, where the most popular religious currents have originated for over a century—cannot fail to notice a very decided air of chiliastic expectation. And this is not only true of "charismatic" circles, but even of the traditionalist or fundamentalist circles that have rejected the "charismatic revival." Thus, many traditionalist Roman Catholics believe in the coming of a chiliastic "Age of Mary" before the end of the world, and this is only one variant on the more widespread Latin error of trying to "sanctify the world," or, as Archbishop Thomas Connolly of Seattle expressed it fifteen years ago, "transforming the modern world into the Kingdom of God in preparation for His return." Protestant evangelists such as Billy Graham, in their mistaken private interpretation of the Apocalypse, await the "millennium" when "Christ" will reign on earth. Other evangelists in Israel find that their millenarian interpretation of the "Messiah" is just what is needed to "prepare" the Jews for his coming.* And the arch-fundamentalist Carl McIntire prepares to build a life-size replica of the Temple of Jerusalem in Florida (near Disneyworld!), believing that the time is at hand when the Jews will build the very "Temple to which the Lord Himself will return as He promised" (*Christian Beacon,* Nov. 11, 1971; Jan. 6, 1972). Thus, even anti-ecumenists

---

* See for example Gordon Lindsay, *Israel's Destiny and the Coming Deliverer,* Christ for the Nations Pub. Co., Dallas, Texas, pp. 28–30.

find it possible to prepare to join the unrepentant Jews in welcoming the false messiah—antichrist—in contrast to the faithful remnant of Jews who will accept Christ as the Orthodox Church preaches Him, when the Prophet Elijah returns to earth.

It is therefore no great consolation for a sober Orthodox Christian who knows the Scriptural prophecies concerning the last days, when he is told by a "charismatic" Protestant minister that, "It's glorious what Jesus can do when we open up to Him. No wonder people of all faiths are now able to pray together" (Harold Bredesen, in *Logos Journal*, Jan.–Feb. 1972, p. 24); or by a Catholic Pentecostal that the members of all the denominations now "begin to peer over those walls of separation only to recognize in each other the image of Jesus Christ" (Kevin Ranaghan in *Logos Journal*, Nov.–Dec. 1971, p. 21). Which "Christ" is this for whom an accelerated program of psychological and even physical preparation is now being made throughout the world?—Is this our true God and Saviour Jesus Christ, Who founded the Church wherein men may find salvation? Or is it the *false Christ* who will *come in his own name* (John 5:43) and unite all who reject or pervert the teaching of the one Church of Christ, the Orthodox Church?

Our Saviour Himself has warned us: *Then if any man shall say unto you, Lo, here is the Christ, or there; believe it not. For there shall arise false Christs, and false prophets, and shall show signs and wonders, so as to lead astray, if possible, even the elect. Behold I have told you beforehand. If therefore they shall say unto you, Behold, he is in the wilderness, go not forth; Behold, he is in the inner chambers, believe it not. For as the lightning cometh forth from the east, and is seen even unto the west, so shall be the coming of the Son of man* (Matt. 24:23–27).

The Second Coming of Christ will be unmistakable: it will be sudden, from heaven (Acts 1:11), and it will mark the end of this world. There can be no "preparation" for it—save only the Orthodox Christian preparation of repentance, spiritual life, and watchfulness. Those who are "preparing" for it in any other way, who say that he is anywhere "here"—especially "here" in the Temple of Jerusalem—or who preach that "Jesus is coming soon" without warning of the great deception that is to precede His Coming: are clearly the prophets of antichrist, the false Christ who must come first and deceive the world, including all "Christians" who are not or do not become truly Orthodox. There is to be no future "millennium." For those who can receive it, the "millennium" of the Apocalypse (Apoc. 20:6) is *now*; the life of grace in the Orthodox Church for the whole "thousand years" between the First Coming of Christ and the time of antichrist.* That Protestants should expect the "millennium" in the future is only their confession that they do not live in it in the present—that is, that they are *outside the Church of Christ* and have not tasted of Divine grace.

D. Must Orthodoxy Join the Apostasy?

Today some Orthodox priests, led by Fr. Eusebius Stephanou, would try to persuade us that the "charismatic revival," even though it began and mostly continues outside the

---

* Such is the Orthodox teaching of Sts. Basil the Great, Gregory the Theologian, Andrew of Caesarea, and many other Fathers. See Archbishop Averky, *Guide to the Study of the New Testament,* Part II (in Russian), Jordanville, New York, 1956, pp. 434–38. [English trans. in *The Apocalypse in the Teachings of Ancient Christianity,* St. Herman of Alaska Brotherhood, Platina, Calif., 1995, pp. 253–54.]

Orthodox Church, is nonetheless "Orthodox," and we are even warned, "Don't be left out." But no one who has studied this movement in the works of its leading representatives, many of whom have been quoted above, can have any doubt that this "revival," in so far as it is "Christian" at all, is *entirely Protestant* in its origin, inspiration, intent, practice, "theology," and end. It is a form of Protestant "revivalism," which is a phenomenon that preserves only a fragment of anything genuinely Christian, substituting for Christianity an emotional "religious" hysteria whose victim falls into the fatal delusion that he is "saved." If the "charismatic revival" differs from Protestant revivalism, it is only in adding a new dimension of crypto-spiritistic phenomena which are more spectacular and more objective than mere subjective revivalism.

This evident fact is only strikingly confirmed by an examination of what Fr. Eusebius Stephanou tries to pass off for an "Orthodox awakening" in his periodical *The Logos.*

This *Orthodox priest* informs his readers that "the Orthodox Church is not sharing in the modern-day Christian awakening" (Feb. 1972, p. 19). He himself now travels about holding Protestant-like revival meetings, together with the Protestant "altar call," which is accompanied by the usual revivalistic "sobs and tears" (April 1972, p. 4). Fr. Eusebius himself with typical revivalistic immodesty, informs us that "I thank and praise God for shedding some of the light of His Spirit into my soul in response to the unceasing prayers I have been sending up night and day" (Feb. 1972, p. 19); and later he openly declares himself to be a "prophet" (April 1972, p. 3). He mentions nothing whatever of the Orthodox interpretation of apocalyptic events, and yet he repeats Billy Graham's fundamentalist Protestant interpretation of the "Rapture" that is to precede the "millennium": "The Great Tribulation day approaches. If we remain true to Christ we will surely be caught up to be with Him at the sound of the glad rapture-shout, and we will be spared the horrible destruction which is to fall upon the world"* (April 1972, p. 22). And yet not even all fundamentalists are agreed on this error,** which has no foundation in Holy Scripture*** and removes from those who follow it all necessity for watchfulness against the deceit of antichrist, from which they imagine they will be spared.

All of this is not even pseudo-Orthodoxy; it is just plain Protestantism, and not even the best kind of Protestantism. One looks in vain in the *Logos* of Fr. Eusebius Stephanou for an indication that his "awakening" is inspired by the sources of the Orthodox ascetic tradition: the Lives of Saints, the Holy Fathers, the Church's cycle of services, the *Orthodox* interpretation of Holy Scripture. Some Orthodox "charismatics," it is true, make use of some of these sources—but alas! they mix them together with "many other books written by devout Christians involved with the Charismatic movement," (*Logos,* March 1972, p. 16) and thus read them "charismatically": like all sectarians, *reading into* Orthodox writings what they have learned from their *new* teaching, which comes from outside the Church.

It is true enough, to be sure, that an Orthodox awakening would be much to be desired in our days, when many Orthodox Christians have lost the salt of true Christianity, and the true and fervent Orthodox Christian life is indeed rarely to be

---

* Compare Billy Graham, *World Aflame,* Doubleday (Pocket Cardinal Ed.), New York, 1966, p. 178; C. H. Mackintosh, *The Lord's Coming,* Moody Press, Chicago, pp. 30–31; and many other fundamentalists.
** See Kurt Koch, *Day X,* Kregel Publications, Grand Rapids, Michigan, pp. 116–17.
*** I Thess. 4:16–17 refers to the Second Coming of Christ, which according to the Holy Fathers comes *after* the "tribulation" and the reign of antichrist.

seen. Modern life has become too comfortable; worldly life has become too attractive; for too many, Orthodoxy has become simply a matter of membership in a church organization or the "correct" fulfillment of external rites and practices. There would be need enough for a *true* Orthodox spiritual awakening, but this is not what we see in the Orthodox "charismatics." Just like the "charismatic" activists among Protestants and Roman Catholics, they are fully in harmony with the spirit of the times; they are not in living contact with the sources of the Orthodox spiritual tradition, preferring the currently fashionable Protestant techniques of revivalism. They are one with the leading current of today's apostate "Christianity": the ecumenical movement. Early in 1978 Archbishop Iakovos of the Greek Archdiocese of North and South America finally gave his official approval to the activities of Fr. Eusebius Stephanou, including permission for him to preach everywhere specifically on the "gifts of the Holy Spirit"; thus the church organization in its most modernist and ecumenist figure joins hands with the "charismatic revival," reflecting the deep kinship that unites them. But true Christianity is not there.

There have been true Orthodox "awakenings" in the past: one thinks immediately of St. Cosmas of Aitolia, who walked from village to village in 18th-century Greece and inspired the people to return to the true Christianity of their ancestors; or St. John of Kronstadt in our own century, who brought the age-old message of Orthodox spiritual life to the urban masses of Petersburg. Then there are the Orthodox monastic instructors who were *truly* "Spirit-filled" and left their teaching to the monastics as well as the laymen of the latter times: one thinks of the Greek St. Symeon the New Theologian in the 10th century, and the Russian St. Seraphim of Sarov in the 19th. St. Symeon is badly misused by the Orthodox "charismatics" (he was speaking of a Spirit different from theirs!); and St. Seraphim is invariably quoted out of context in order to minimize his emphasis on the necessity to belong to the Orthodox Church to have a true spiritual life. In the "Conversation" of St. Seraphim with the layman Motovilov on the "acquisition of the Holy Spirit" (which the Orthodox "charismatics" quote *without* the parts here italicized), this great Saint tells us: "The grace of the Holy Spirit which was given to us all, the faithful of Christ, in the Sacrament of Holy Baptism, is sealed by the Sacrament of Chrismation on the chief parts of the body, as appointed *by the Holy Church, the eternal keeper of this grace."* And again: "The Lord listens equally to the monk and the simple Christian layman, *provided that both are Orthodox."*

As opposed to the true Orthodox spiritual life, the "charismatic revival" is only *the experiential side of the prevailing "ecumenical" fashion*—a counterfeit Christianity that betrays Christ and His Church. No Orthodox "charismatic" could possibly object to the coming "Union" with those very Protestants and Roman Catholics with whom, as the interdenominational "charismatic" song goes, they are already "one in the Spirit, one in the Lord," and who have led them and inspired their "charismatic" experience. The "spirit" that has inspired the "charismatic revival" is *the spirit of antichrist,* or more precisely, those "spirits of devils" of the last times whose "miracles" prepare the world for the false messiah.

E. *"Little Children, It is the Last Hour"*
(I John 2:18)

Unknown to the fevered Orthodox "revivalists," the Lord God has preserved in the world, even as in the days of Elijah the Prophet, *seven thousand men who have not bowed the knee to Baal* (Rom. 11:4)—an unknown number of true Orthodox Christians who are neither spiritually dead, as the Orthodox "charismatics" complain that their flocks have been, nor pompously "spirit-filled," as these same flocks become under "charismatic" suggestion. They are not carried away by the movement of apostasy nor by any false "awakening," but continue rooted in the holy and saving Faith of Holy Orthodoxy in the tradition the Holy Fathers have handed down to them, watching the signs of the times and travelling the narrow path to salvation. Many of them follow the bishops of the few Orthodox churches that have taken strong stands against the apostasy of our times. But there are some left in other Orthodox churches also, grieving over the ever more evident apostasy of their hierarchs and striving somehow to keep their own Orthodoxy intact; and there are still others outside of the Orthodox Church who by God's grace, their hearts being open to His call, will undoubtedly yet be joined to genuine Holy Orthodoxy. These "seven thousand" are the foundation of the future and only Orthodoxy of the latter times.

And outside of genuine Orthodoxy the darkness only grows. Judging from the latest "religious" news, the "charismatic revival" may well be only the faint beginning of a whole "age of miracles." Many Protestants who have discerned the fraud of the "charismatic revival" now accept as "the real thing" the spectacular "revival" in Indonesia where, we are told, there are *really* occurring "the selfsame things that one finds reported in the Acts of the Apostles." In the space of three years 200,000 pagans have been converted to Protestantism under constantly miraculous conditions: No one does anything except in absolute obedience to the "voices" and "angels" who are constantly appearing, usually quoting Scripture by number and verse; water is turned into wine every time the Protestant communion service comes around; detached hands appear from nowhere to distribute miraculous food to the hungry; a whole band of demons is seen to abandon a pagan village because a "more powerful" one ("Jesus") has come to take their place; "Christians" have a "countdown" for an unrepentant sinner, and when they come to "zero" he dies; children are taught new Protestant hymns by voices that come from nowhere (and repeat the song twenty times so the children will remember); "God's tape-recorder" records the song of a children's choir and plays it back in the air for the astonished children; fire comes down from the sky to consume Catholic religious images ("the Lord" in Indonesia is very anti-Catholic); 30,000 have been healed; "Christ" appears in the sky and "falls" on people in order to heal them; people are miraculously transported from place to place and walk on water; lights accompany evangelists and guide them at night, and clouds follow them and give them shelter during the day; the dead are raised.*

Interestingly, in some parts of the Indonesian "revival" the element of "speaking in tongues" is almost totally absent and is even forbidden (although it is present in many places), and the element of mediumism seems sometimes to be replaced by a direct intervention of fallen spirits. It may well be that this new "revival," more powerful than Pentecostalism, is a more developed stage of the same "spiritual" phenomenon (just as Pentecostalism itself is more advanced than spiritism) and heralds the imminence of the dreadful day when, as the "voices" and "angels" in Indonesia also proclaim, "the Lord" is

---

* See Kurt Koch, *The Revival in Indonesia,* Kregel Publications, 1970; and Mel Tari, *Like a Mighty Wind,* Creation House, Carol Stream, Illinois, 1971.

to come—for we know that antichrist will prove to the world that he is "Christ" by just such "miracles."

In an age of almost universal darkness and deception, when for most "Christians" *Christ* has become precisely what Orthodox teaching means by *antichrist,* the Orthodox Church of Christ alone possesses and communicates the grace of God. This is a priceless treasure the very existence of which is not so much as suspected even by the "Christian" world. The "Christian" world, indeed, joins hands with the forces of darkness in order to seduce the faithful of the Church of Christ, blindly trusting that the "name of Jesus" will save them even in their apostasy and blasphemy, mindless of the fearful warning of the Lord: *Many will say to Me in that day, Lord, Lord, have we not prophesied in Thy name? and in Thy name have cast out devils? and in Thy name done many wonderful works? And then will I profess unto them, I never knew you: depart from Me, ye that work iniquity* (Matt. 7:22–23).

St. Paul continues his warning about the coming of antichrist with this command: *Therefore, brethren, stand fast, and hold the traditions which ye have been taught, whether by word, or our epistle* (II Thess. 2:15). *There be some that trouble you, and would pervert the Gospel of Christ. But though we, or an angel from heaven, preach any other gospel unto you than that which we have preached unto you, let him be anathema. As we said before, so say I now again: If any preach any other gospel unto you than that ye have received, let him be anathema* (Gal. 1:8–9).

The Orthodox answer to every new "revival," and even to the final terrible "revival" of antichrist, is this Gospel of Christ, which the Orthodox Church alone has preserved unchanged in an unbroken line from Christ and His Apostles, and the grace of the Holy Spirit which the Orthodox Church alone communicates, and only to her faithful children, who have received in Chrismation, and kept, the true *seal of the gift of the Holy Spirit.* Amen.

2. THE RELIGION OF THE FUTURE

It is deeply indicative of the spiritual state of contemporary mankind that the "charismatic" and "meditation" experiences are taking root among "Christians." An Eastern religious influence is undeniably at work in such "Christians," but it is only as a result of something much more fundamental: the loss of the very feeling and savor of Christianity, due to which something so alien to Christianity as Eastern "meditation" can take hold of "Christian" souls.

The life of self-centeredness and self-satisfaction lived by most of today's "Christians" is so all-pervading that it effectively seals them off from any understanding at all of spiritual life; and when such people do undertake "spiritual life," it is only as another form of self-satisfaction. This can be seen quite clearly in the totally false religious ideal both of the "charismatic" movement and the various forms of "Christian meditation": all of them promise (and give very quickly) an experience of "contentment" and "peace." But this is not the Christian ideal at all, which if anything may be summed up as a fierce battle and struggle. The "contentment" and "peace" described in these contemporary "spiritual" movements are quite manifestly the product of spiritual deception, of spiritual self-satisfaction—which is the absolute death of the God-oriented spiritual life. All these forms of "Christian meditation" operate solely on the psychic level and have nothing whatever in common with Christian spirituality. Christian spirituality is formed in the arduous struggle to acquire the eternal Kingdom of Heaven, which fully begins only with the dissolution of this temporal world, and the true Christian struggler never finds repose even in the foretastes of eternal blessedness which might be vouchsafed to him in this life; but the Eastern religions, to which the Kingdom of Heaven has not been revealed, strive only to acquire psychic states which begin and end in this life.

In our age of apostasy preceding the manifestation of antichrist, the devil has been loosed for a time (Apoc. 20:7) to work the false miracles which he could not work during the "thousand years" of Grace in the Church of Christ (Apoc. 20:3), and to gather in his hellish harvest of those souls who "received not the love of the truth" (II Thess. 2:10). We can tell that the time of antichrist is truly near by the very fact that this satanic harvest is now being reaped not merely among the pagan peoples, who have not heard of Christ, but even more among "Christians" who have lost the savor of Christianity. It is of the very nature of antichrist to present the kingdom of the devil *as if it were of Christ.* The present-day "charismatic" movement and "Christian meditation," and the "new religious consciousness" of which they are part, are forerunners of *the religion of the future, the religion of the last humanity, the religion of antichrist,* and their chief "spiritual" function is *to make available to Christians the demonic initiation hitherto restricted to the pagan world.* Let it be that these "religious experiments" are still often of a tentative and groping nature, that there is in them at least as much psychic self-deception as there is a genuinely demonic initiation rite; doubtless not everyone who has successfully "meditated" or thinks he has received the "Baptism of the Spirit" has actually received initiation into the kingdom of satan. But this is the aim of these "experiments," and doubtless the techniques of initiation will become ever more efficient as mankind becomes prepared for them by the attitudes of passivity and openness to new "religious experiences" which are inculcated by these movements.

What has brought humanity—and indeed "Christendom"—to this desperate state? Certainly it is not any overt worship of the devil, which is limited always to a few people; rather, it is something much more subtle, and something fearful for a conscious Orthodox Christian to reflect on: it is *the loss of the grace of God,* which follows on the loss of the savor of Christianity.

In the West, to be sure, the grace of God was lost many centuries ago. Roman Catholics and Protestants today have not fully tasted of God's grace, and so it is not surprising that they should be unable to discern its demonic counterfeit. But alas! The success of counterfeit spirituality even among Orthodox Christians today reveals how much they also have lost the savor of Christianity and so can no longer distinguish between true Christianity and pseudo-Christianity. For too long have Orthodox Christians taken for granted the precious treasure of their Faith and neglected to put into use the pure gold of its teachings. How many Orthodox Christians even know of the existence of the basic texts of Orthodox spiritual life, which teach precisely how to distinguish between genuine and counterfeit spirituality, texts which give the life and teaching of holy men and women who attained an abundant measure of God's grace in this life? How many have made their own the teaching of the *Lausiac History,* the *Ladder* of St. John, the Homilies of St. Macarius, the Lives of the God-bearing Fathers of the desert, *Unseen Warfare,* St. John of Kronstadt's *My Life in Christ?*

In the Life of the great Father of the Egyptian desert, St. Paisius the Great (June 19), we may see a shocking example of how easy it is to lose the grace of God. Once a disciple of his was walking to a city in Egypt to sell his handiwork. On the way he met a Jew who, seeing his simplicity, began to deceive him, saying: "O beloved, why do you believe in a simple, crucified Man, when He was not at all the awaited Messiah? Another is to come, but not He." The disciple, being weak in mind and simple in heart, began to listen to these words and allowed himself to say: "Perhaps what you say is correct." When he returned to the desert, St. Paisius turned away from him and would not speak a single word to him. Finally, after the disciple's long entreaty, the Saint said to him: "Who are you? I do not know you. This disciple of mine was a Christian and had upon him the grace of Baptism, but you are not such a one; if you are actually my disciple, then the grace of Baptism has left you and the image of a Christian has been removed." The disciple with tears related his conversation with the Jew, to which the Saint replied: "O wretched one! What could be worse and more foul than such words, by which you renounced Christ and His divine Baptism? Now go and weep over yourself as you wish, for you have no place with me; your name is written with those who have renounced Christ, and together with them you will receive judgment and torments." On hearing this judgment the disciple was filled with repentance, and at his entreaty the Saint shut himself up and prayed to the Lord to forgive his disciple this sin. The Lord heard the Saint's prayer and granted him to behold a sign of His forgiveness of the disciple. The Saint then warned the disciple: "O child, give glory and thanksgiving to Christ God together with me, for the unclean, blasphemous spirit has departed from you, and in his place the Holy Spirit has descended upon you, restoring to you the grace of Baptism. And so, guard yourself now, lest out of sloth and carelessness the nets of the enemy should fall upon you again and, having sinned, you should inherit the fire of gehenna."

Significantly, it is among "ecumenical Christians" that the "charismatic" and "meditation" movements have taken root. The characteristic belief of the heresy of ecumenism is this: that the Orthodox Church is not the one true Church of Christ; that the grace of God is present also in other "Christian" denominations, and even in non-Christian religions; that the narrow path of salvation according to the teaching of the Holy Fathers of the Orthodox Church is only "one path among many" to salvation; and that the details of one's belief in Christ are of little importance, as is one's membership in any particular church. Not all the Orthodox participants in the ecumenical movement believe this entirely (although Protestants and Roman Catholics most certainly do); but by their very participation in this movement, including invariably common prayer with those who believe wrongly about Christ and His Church, they tell the heretics who behold them: *"Perhaps what you say is correct,"* even as the wretched disciple of St. Paisius did. *No more than this is required for an Orthodox Christian to lose the grace of God;* and what labor it will cost for him to gain it back!

How much, then, must Orthodox Christians walk in the fear of God, trembling lest they lose His grace, which by no means is given to everyone, but only to those who hold the true Faith, lead a life of Christian struggle, and treasure the grace of God which leads them heavenward. And how much more cautiously must Orthodox Christians walk today above all, when they are surrounded by a counterfeit Christianity that gives its own experiences of "grace" and the "Holy Spirit" and can abundantly quote the Scriptures and the Holy Fathers to "prove" it! Surely the last times are near, when there will come spiritual deception so persuasive as to *deceive, if it were possible, even the very elect* (Matt. 24:24).

The false prophets of the modern age, including many who are officially "Orthodox," ever more loudly announce the approaching advent of the "new age of the Holy Spirit," the "New Pentecost," the "Omega Point." This is precisely what, in genuine Orthodox prophecy, is called the reign of antichrist. It is in our own times, today, that this satanic prophecy is beginning to be fulfilled, *with demonic power.* The whole contemporary spiritual atmosphere is becoming charged with the power of a demonic initiation experience as the "Mystery of Iniquity" enters its next-to-last stage and begins to take possession of the souls of men—indeed, to take possession of the very Church of Christ, if that were possible.

Against this powerful "religious experience" true Orthodox Christians must now arm themselves in earnest, *becoming fully conscious of what Orthodox Christianity is and how its goal is different from that of all other religions, "Christian" or non-Christian.*

Orthodox Christians! Hold fast to the grace which you have; never let it become a matter of habit; never measure it by merely human standards or expect it to be logical or comprehensible to those who understand nothing higher than what is human or who think to obtain the grace of the Holy Spirit in some other way than that which the one Church of Christ has handed down to us. True Orthodoxy by its very nature must seem totally out of place in these demonic times, a dwindling minority of the despised and "foolish," in the midst of a religious "revival" inspired by another kind of spirit. But let us take comfort from the certain words of our Lord Jesus Christ: *Fear not, little flock, for it is your Father's good pleasure to give you the Kingdom* (Luke 12:32).

Let all true Orthodox Christians strengthen themselves for the battle ahead, never forgetting that in Christ the victory is already ours. He has promised that the gates of hell will not prevail against His Church (Matt. 16:18), and that for the sake of the elect He will cut short the days of the last great tribulation (Matt. 24:22). And in truth, *If God be for us, who can be against us?* (Rom. 8:31). Even in the midst of the cruelest temptations, we are commanded to *be of good cheer; I have overcome the world* (John 16:33). Let us live, even as true Christians of all times have lived, in expectation of the end of all things and the coming of our dear Saviour; for *He that giveth testimony of these things saith: Surely I come quickly. Amen. Come, Lord Jesus* (Apoc. 22:20).

Epilogue

JONESTOWN AND THE 1980s

THIS BOOK has been deliberately "understated." Our intention has been to present as calm and objective a view as possible of the non-Christian religious attitudes which are preparing the way for the "religion of the future"; we have hardly touched on some of the "horror stories" that could be cited from some of the cults mentioned in this book: true stories that reveal what happens when one's involvement with the unseen demonic powers becomes complete, and a man becomes the willing tool of their evil purposes.

But then, on the eve of the publication of the new edition of this book, the whole world was suddenly made aware of one of these "horror stories": the mass suicide of Jim Jones and over 900 of his followers in the Marxist-religious commune of "Jonestown" in the jungles of Guyana, South America.

No more striking "sign of the times" could be imagined; Jonestown is a clear warning—and prophecy—of the future of mankind.

The secular press, understandably, did not know quite what to make of this monstrous event. Some of the foreign press took it as merely another example of American violence and extremism; the American press portrayed Jim Jones as a "madman," and the event itself as a result of the evil influence of "cults"; more honest and sensitive journalists admitted that the magnitude and grotesqueness of the whole phenomenon baffled them.

Few observers saw Jonestown as an authentic sign of our times, a revelation of the state of contemporary humanity; but there are many indications that it was indeed such.

Jim Jones himself was unquestionably in touch with the mainstream of today's religious-political world. His religious background as a "prophet" and "healer" capable of fascinating and dominating a certain kind of unsettled, "searching" modern man (chiefly lower-class urban blacks), gave him a respected place in the American religious spectrum, rather more acceptable in our more tolerant times than his hero of an earlier generation, "Father Divine." His innumerable "good deeds" and unexpectedly generous gifts to the needy made him a leading representative of "liberal" Christianity and drew the attention of the liberal political establishment in California, where his influence increased with every year. His personal admirers included the Mayor of San Francisco, the Governor of California, and the wife of the President of the United States. His Marxist political philosophy and commune in Guyana placed him in the respectable political avant-garde; the lieutenant governor of California personally inspected Jonestown and was favorably impressed by it, as were other outside observers. Although there were complaints, especially in the last year or two, against Jones' sometimes violent way of dominating his followers, even this aspect of Jonestown was within the limits allowed by the liberal West for contemporary Communist governments, which are not looked on with too great disfavor even for liquidating some hundreds or thousands or millions of dissenters.

Jonestown was a thoroughly "modern," a thoroughly contemporary experiment; but what was the significance of its spectacular end?

The contemporary phenomenon that is perhaps closest in spirit to the Jonestown tragedy is one that at first sight might not be associated with it: the swift and brutal liquidation by the Cambodian Communist government, in the name of humanity's bright future, of perhaps two million innocent people—one-fourth or more of the total population of Cambodia. This "revolutionary genocide," perhaps the most deliberate and ruthless case of it yet in the bloody 20th century, is an exact parallel to the "revolutionary suicide"* in Jonestown: in both cases the sheer horror of mass death is justified as paving the way for the perfect future promised by Communism for a "purified" humanity. These two events mark a new stage in the history of the "Gulag Archipelago"—the chain of inhuman concentration camps which atheism has established in order to transform mankind and abolish Christianity.

In Jonestown once again the incredible accuracy of Dostoyevsky's 19th-century diagnosis of the revolutionary mind is proved: a key figure in his novel *The Possessed* (more precisely, *The Demons)* is Kirillov, who believes that the ultimate act proving that he has become God is precisely suicide. "Normal" people, of course, cannot understand such a logic; but history is seldom made by "normal" people, and the 20th century has been *par excellence* the century of the triumph of a "revolutionary logic" which is put into execution by men who have become thoroughly "modern" and have consciously renounced the values of the past, and especially the truth of Christianity. To those who believe in this "logic," the

---

* The name given to it by Jones himself and the zealots who helped perform it; see *Time* magazine, Dec. 4, 1978, p. 20.

Jonestown suicides are a great revolutionary act that "proves" there is no God and point to the nearness of the world totalitarian government, whose "prophet" Jones himself wanted to be. The only regret over this act in such minds was expressed by one of the residents of Jonestown, whose last-minute note was found on Jones' body: "Dad: I see no way out—I agree with your decision—I fear only that without you the world may not make it to communism."* All the assets of the Jonestown commune (some seven million dollars) were bequeathed to the Communist Party of the USSR (*The New York Times,* Dec. 18, 1978, p. 1).

Jonestown was not the isolated act of a "madman"; it is something very close to all of us who live in these times. One journalist sensed this when he wrote of Jones (with whom he had some personal contact in San Francisco): "His almost religious and definitely mystical power, its evil well concealed, must somehow be construed as a clue to the mystery that is the 1970s" (Herb Caen, in *The Suicide Cult,* p. 192).

The source of this "mystical power" is not far to seek. The religion of the "People's Temple" was not even remotely Christian (even though Jim Jones, its founder, was an ordained minister of the "Disciples of Christ"); it owed much more to Jones' spiritualist experience of the 1950s, when he was forming his worldview. He claimed not merely to be the "reincarnation" of Jesus, Buddha, and Lenin; he openly stated that he was an "oracle or medium for discarnate entities from another galaxy."** In other words, he gave himself over into the power of

---

* Marshall Kilduff and Ron Javers, *The Suicide Cult,* Bantam Books, 1978, p. xiv.
** Neil Duddy and Mark Albrecht, "Questioning Jonestown," in the periodical *Radix,* Berkeley, Calif., Jan.–Feb. 1979, p. 15.

evil spirits, who doubtless inspired his final act of "logical" madness. Jonestown cannot be understood apart from the inspiration and activity of demons; this, indeed, is why secular journalists cannot understand it.

It is all too likely that Jonestown is but the beginning of far worse things to come in the 1980s—things which only those with the profoundest and clearest Christian faith can even dare think about. It is not merely that politics is becoming "religious" (for the massacres in Cambodia were acts performed with "religious"—that is, demonic—fervor), or that religion is becoming "political" (in the case of Jonestown); such things have happened before. But it may well be that we are now beginning to see, in concrete historical acts, the particular blending of religion and politics that seems to be required for the zealots of antichrist, the religious-political leader of the last humanity. This spirit, to be sure, has already been present to some degree in the earlier totalitarian regimes of the 20th century; but the intensity of fervor and devotion required for *mass suicide* (as opposed to mass murder, which has been committed many times in our century) makes Jonestown a milestone on the path to the approaching culmination of modern times.

Satan, it would seem, is now entering naked into human history. The years just ahead promise to be more terrible than anyone can now easily conceive. This one outburst of satan-inspired energy led nearly 1,000 people to revolutionary suicide; what of the many other enclaves of satanic energy, some much more powerful than this small movement, that have not yet manifested themselves?

A realistic view of the religious state of the contemporary world is enough to inspire any serious Orthodox Christian with fear and trembling over his own salvation. The temptations and trials ahead are immense: *Then shall be great tribulation, such as was not since the beginning of the world to this time, no, nor ever shall be* (Matt. 24:21). Some of these trials will come from the side of pleasing deceptions, from the "signs and lying wonders" which we begin to see even now; others will come from the fierce and naked evil which is already visible in Jonestown, Cambodia, and the Gulag Archipelago. Those who wish to be true Christians in these frightful days had better begin to become serious about their Faith, learning what true Christianity is, learning to pray to God in spirit and in truth, learning to know *Who Christ is,* in Whom alone we have salvation.

Epilogue to the Fifth Edition

FURTHER DEVELOPMENTS IN THE FORMATION OF THE RELIGION OF THE FUTURE

By Hieromonk Damascene

1. The New Age Movement

ONE READER of *Orthodoxy and the Religion of the Future* has aptly observed: "Some years ago, when I read this book, it seemed very 'far-out' to me. I thought: These are just *fringe* movements Fr. Seraphim is describing—this kind of thing can't really be taking over the world. Now, however, I see otherwise. All that Fr. Seraphim was saying is true."

Any thoughtful observer of the world today can see that the formation of a "new spirituality" has progressed precisely along the lines which Fr. Seraphim described. When *Orthodoxy and the Religion of the Future* was first published in 1975, the form of neo-paganism in Western society was only beginning to be delineated. Today it has taken on a more definite shape, being seen most clearly in what has come to be known as "New Age" spirituality. In 1975 the term "New Age," though indeed familiar in Masonic, esoteric, and countercultural groups, was not common parlance. Now it is a banner term for a whole worldwide movement—and a multi-billion dollar business.

Unlike most formal religions, the New Age movement has no central organization, membership, geographic center, dogma or creed. Rather, it is a loose network of people who share similar ideas and practices, and who align themselves with the worldview of the "new religious consciousness."*

Because the New Age movement has no single set of beliefs, it is difficult to offer a blanket definition of it. New Agers can hold to any number of neo-pagan beliefs, from pantheism, panentheism, monism, reincarnation and karma, to a belief in a World-Soul and in Mother Earth (Gaia) as a goddess or living entity. Various psychotechnologies (e.g., guided imagery, possibility thinking, hypnosis, "dream work," "past-life regression," Yoga, Tantra, and hallucinogenic drugs), divination (tarot, astrology), and spiritistic practices (now usually referred to as "channeling") are undertaken in order to raise practitioners to new levels of consciousness, to develop new "mind-body-spirit" potentials, to effect "inner healing," or to attain psychic powers.

Chiliastic at its core, the New Age movement is commonly associated with what popular author Joseph Campbell has called a "new planetary mythology": a mythology which maintains that man is not fallen, that he is ultimately perfectible through the process of "evolution," and that through leaps of consciousness he can realize that he is God and thus actualize the Kingdom of God on earth.

According to New Age thinking, since man and everything else is God, only one reality exists; and therefore all religions are only different paths to that reality. There is no one correct path, for all paths reach the Divine. New Agers anticipate that a new

---

* B. A. Robinson, "New Age Spirituality," Ontario Consultants on Religious Tolerance, Ontario, Canada, 1995.

universal religion which contains elements of all current faiths will evolve and become generally accepted worldwide.

2. The Revival of Paganism

As the New Age "religion of the future" takes shape, we see in our Western, post-Christian society the continued rise of neo-paganism in every possible form. The Eastern religions that Fr. Seraphim wrote about—especially Hinduism and Buddhism—continue to gain followers, receiving endorsements from high-profile celebrities and being publicized through television talk shows, news magazines, and other media outlets.

Yoga, Ayurvedic medicine, and other such Hindu practices have now been accepted into mainstream society. New Age self-help gurus such as Deepak Chopra (formerly a spokesman for the TM movement) promote them exclusively as a means toward "mind-body" health. However, as Fr. Seraphim observed* and as every true Hindu knows, these practices cannot be divorced from their religious context, for they were devised precisely in order to dispose the practitioner toward Hindu religious attitudes and experiences. This fact is now playing itself out in the Western Yoga community, which, having arisen largely out of a quest for "mind-body" health, is steadily introducing the ritual worship of Hindu deities, together with a study of the Hindu Vedas and Jyotish astrology.

Tibetan Buddhism has also seen a considerable gain in popularity among Westerners; it is now much more visible than Zen, which was the leading form of Buddhism among Westerners during Fr. Seraphim's time. Combining Buddhism with the form of shamanism indigenous to Tibet (the Bon

---

* See p. 39 above.

religion), Tibetan Buddhism contains more overtly occult elements than does Zen, including temporary spirit-possession by Tibetan deities.

As Eastern religions continue to grow in the West, we see today an equal if not greater interest in *Western* forms of paganism. Witchcraft, Druidical magic, gnosticism and Native American shamanism have gained enormous popularity among Westerners who find them closer to their own roots than Eastern religions. Kabbalah, the Jewish system of occultism developed after the time of Christ, has also attracted widespread interest; its adherents now include many celebrities from the movie and rock music industries.*

While many people merely dabble in the various forms of paganism that are readily available in today's spiritual supermarket, a growing number have entered deeply into their practice, thus taking part in the pagan "initiation experience" that Fr. Seraphim said would characterize the religion of the future.

3. The Rise of Witchcraft

In the youth culture of America and England, witchcraft has become an extremely popular theme. The phenomenal success of the Harry Potter books—with over 250 million copies sold around the world since 1997, and over half the children in the U.S. having read at least one of the books—has been a catalyst in this trend. Under the cloak of innocent fantasy, these books introduce the young to real occult practices and real figures in the history of witchcraft. The seven projected books in the series trace Harry Potter's seven-year

---

* Alison Lentini, "Lost in the Supermarket: Pop Music and Spiritual Commerce," *Spiritual Counterfeits Project Newsletter,* 22:4–23:1, 1999, p. 25.

training in witchcraft, the curriculum of which closely resembles the seven-year program of the Ordo Anno Mundi, an occult group based in London. While author J. K. Rowling disavows any personal involvement in the occult, she admits to having done much research into witchcraft in order to make her books more realistic, and acknowledges that more than one third of her books are based on actual occult practices.* Intentionally or not, her books—together with the movies and franchise based on them—are a portal into the occult for those wishing to take the next step.**

The Harry Potter phenomenon represents only one of many vehicles by which witchcraft is being popularized in the youth culture. Movies (e.g., *The Craft, Practical Magick*) and television shows (e.g., *Buffy the Vampire Slayer, Sabrina the Teenage Witch, Charmed*) target young audiences with the allure of how powerful and "hip" one can be through occult practices, and a plethora of books (e.g., *The Real Witch's Handbook, Teen Witch*) and websites offer detailed instruction and guidance in how one can become a witch.***

The youth are taking the bait. Since the release of *The Craft* in 1996, there has been a dramatic rise in the number of young people contacting Neopagan groups and Web sites, such as Covenant of the Goddess (cog.com) and Witch's Voice (witchvox.com). The Witch's Voice Web site, which claims to be "the busiest religious Web site in the world," has had over

---

* Radio interview with J.K. Rowling on *The Diane Rheim Show,* WAMU, National Public Radio, October 20, 1999. Quoted in Richard Abanes, *Harry Potter and the Bible,* Horizon Books, Camp Hill, Penn., 2001, p. 205.
** Monk Innocent, "Potter's Field: Harry Potter and the Popularization of Witchcraft," *The Orthodox Word,* no. 220, 2001, pp. 241–55.
*** Linda Harvey, "How Sorcery Chic Permeates Girl-Culture," *Spiritual Counterfeits Project Newsletter,* 27:2, 2002–2003, pp. 1–15.

100 million hits since its inception in 1996; according to a survey conducted in 1999, 60 percent of the respondents have been under 30, and 62 percent have been female. In acknowledgment of this trend, the youth magazine *Spin* has ranked witchcraft as the top interest among teenage girls in America.*

The same phenomenon is occurring in England as it is in America. In 2001, the Pagan Federation of England appointed its first youth officer to deal with the increased number of queries from young people. The Federation's media officer, Andy Norfolk, attributed the youth's increasing interest in witchcraft to the Harry Potter books and to the other books, articles and television shows that make witchcraft look attractive. He further stated that, after every article on witchcraft or paganism appears, "we have a huge surge of calls, mostly from young girls."** A survey in the year 2000 of secondary-school children in England found that over half were "interested" in the occult, and over a quarter were "very interested."***

Today in America, the most popular form of witchcraft is Wicca. Its founder, British occultist Gerald Gardner (1884–1964), was a personal friend of the notorious satanist Aleister Crowley, a member of Crowley's Ordo Templi Orientalis, and a member of the Fellowship of Crotona, a co-Masonic organization. In the Fellowship of Crotona, Gardner was supposedly initiated into a coven of witches who claimed to belong to a lineage going back hundreds of years, and who worshipped the "goddess" and the "horned god." In 1951 the law against witchcraft was repealed in England, and

---

* Brooks Alexander, *Witchcraft Goes Mainstream* (Eugene, Oregon: Harvest House, 2004), pp. 48–49, 68.
** "Potter Fans Turning to Witchcraft," *This is London,* Associated Newspapers, Ltd., August 4, 2000.
*** "Occult Sites 'Lure' Teenagers," *BBC News,* April 22, 2000.

shortly thereafter Gardner began to publicly promote witch-craft under the old British name "Wicca." Gardnerian Wicca combined the practices and ideas of his coven together with those of the Ordo Templi Orientalis, Eastern philosophy and Freemasonry. Today, having been impacted by various spiritual and cultural trends, Wicca has become an amalgam of medi-eval witchcraft, feminism, goddess worship, pantheism, "deep ecology," and worship of the earth.

In terms of percentage, Wicca is the fastest growing reli-gion in the United States and Canada. Numbers of adherents went from 8,000 in 1990 to 134,000 in 2001. With adherents being inducted from among the old and young alike, it is esti-mated that the number of Wiccans in the U.S. and Canada is doubling every thirty months.* According to polls taken by the Covenant of the Goddess, the total number of self-styled pa-gans in the United States, including witches, is now nearing a million and a half.**

Tragically, the phenomenal increase in the number of witches coincides with a *decrease* in the number of Christians in America. A poll conducted in 2001 found that, during the previous eleven years, the number of Christians in the U.S. had been decreasing by two million every year.***

Wicca is but one of the varied expressions of New Age spirituality. As Wiccan author Carol LeMasters explains: "The impact of New Age spirituality on the goddess community has also been incalculable. Emerging approximately at the same time, the two movements have now become so intertwined as to appear indistinguishable."

---

* American Religious Identification Survey, Feb.–April 2001.
** Brooks Alexander, *Witchcraft Goes Mainstream,* p. 47.
*** American Religious Identification Survey, Feb.–April 2001.

4. The Leaven of New Age Spirituality

New Age/neo-pagan gatherings take place on a regular basis throughout the world. In America the most prominent of these are the Rainbow Gatherings held in various parts of the country, and the Burning Man Festivals held in the Black Rock Desert of Nevada. Drawing New Agers, Wiccans, goddess-worshippers, earth-worshippers and outright satanists together with curiosity-seekers and party-goers, the Burning Man Festivals increase in size every year; in 2004 there were 35,000 participants. The Festivals conclude each year with the torching of a forty-foot-high sacrificial wooden man, reminiscent of the ancient "wicker man" sacrifice practiced by the Druids on the feast of Samhain.

While such gatherings are a significant indicator of the growing normalization of paganism in our society, more significant is the fact that New Age *ideas and practices* are entering more and more into all spheres of human thought and activity, shaping the lives of millions who may not consciously identify themselves as neo-pagans or New Agers.

Thus, the "New Age" has become less a movement than a cultural trend, a leaven insinuating itself everywhere: into psychology, sociology, history, the arts, religion, health care, education, and government. Mental hospitals throughout the country have instituted New Age programs: Eastern meditation, transpersonal psychology, biofeedback, and music meditation. Many senior citizen centers have adopted Yoga as a way to promote "mind-body" health. A large number of major corporations have sponsored New Age seminars for their employees, where visualization, hypnosis, "psychic healing," "dream work," contacting "spirit guides," and other "consciousness-raising" practices have been taught. Even in public, government-funded schools, mediumism under the name of "channeling" has been taught as a means of "inner healing." A consortium of concerned parents in Connecticut has described what has been happening in the classroom: "In the name of discovering their 'life purpose,' children are encouraged into trance-like states of mind where they communicate with 'guardian spirits.' The use of Yoga exercises and mind control techniques are other examples of the format of this program."*

Christian churches, sadly, follow the same dangerous trends, trailing in the dust of the world's march of apostasy. In the mid-1970s Fr. Seraphim had written: "The profound ignorance of true Christian spiritual experience in our times is producing a false Christian 'spirituality' whose nature is closely kin to the 'new religious consciousness.'" Years before "channeling" of disembodied entities had become a New Age fad, Fr. Seraphim had quoted "charismatics" speaking about how they "channeled" the "Holy Spirit." But even if we omit the issue of the "charismatic revival," the prognosis he made has been borne out in other areas. As New Ager Marilyn Ferguson writes in her book *The Aquarian Conspiracy:* "An increasing number of churches and synagogues have begun to enlarge their context to include support committees for personal growth, holistic health centers, healing services, meditation workshops, consciousness-altering through music, even biofeedback training."**

In the city of Detroit, for example, "Silva Mind-Control" courses have been taught by a Roman Catholic priest and nun. In New York City, the Episcopal Cathedral of St. John the Divine has featured sermons by David Spangler—a leading mem-

---

* Connecticut Citizens for Constitutional Education, January 22, 1980.
** Marilyn Ferguson, *The Aquarian Conspiracy,* J. P. Tarcher, Inc., Los Angeles, 1980, p. 369.

ber of the Findhorn Foundation who has said that a "Luciferian Initiation" would be required to enter the New Age. In Oakland, California, the "University of Creation Spirituality," under the leadership of Episcopal priest Matthew Fox, advocates a redefined "Christianity" that rejects the traditional Christian theology and the ascetical Christian worldview while embracing Wiccan spirituality. Here, "rave masses" (also known as "techno-cosmic masses") are held every month, having been originally launched at Grace Episcopal Cathedral in San Francisco. Described by one observer as "a syncretistic brew of paganism, witchcraft, nature-worship, drama, art and dance," these multi-media "masses" are attended by well over a thousand people.*

Concurrently, there is now a movement in contemporary Roman Catholicism to assimilate the teachings of Carl Jung, one of the founding fathers of the New Age movement. Jung, who participated in séances and admitted to having "spirit guides," taught that the exclusion of the "dark side" is a fatal flaw in Christianity, and that therefore there needs to be a fourth *hypostasis* added to the Holy Trinity—Lucifer! His theories are being extolled in Roman Catholic seminars and workshops, and his psychotherapy is being practiced in some Roman Catholic churches, and by monks and nuns in some monasteries.** Episcopal and Protestant (especially Methodist)

---

* Catherine Sanders, "Matthew Fox's Techno-cosmic Masses," *Spiritual Counterfeits Project Newsletter,* vol. 26:3, Spring 2002, p. 4.
** Deborah Corbett, "The Trouble with Truth: A Review of *The Illness That We Are: A Jungian Critique of Christianity* by John P. Dourley," *Epiphany Journal,* Spring 1986, pp. 82–90; "Jungian Psychology as Catholic Theology," *St. Catherine Review,* May–June 1997; and Mitch Pacwa, S.J., *Catholics and the New Age,* Servant Publications, Ann Arbor, Mich., 1992.

churches have also entered this movement; a number of Protestant ministers also work as Jungian analysts.*

Within many mainline Christian churches, there is a strong and determined movement to "re-imagine" the Christian faith along the lines of radical feminist theology, neo-pagan goddess worship, and a New Age worldview. In 1993 the first "Re-imagining" conference was held in Minneapolis, Minnesota, in conjunction with the World Council of Churches' Ecumenical Decade of Churches in Solidarity with Women. The conference was attended by over two thousand participants from twenty-seven countries and fifteen mainline denominations, most prominently the Presbyterian, Methodist, Lutheran, Roman Catholic, United Church of Christ and American Baptist. One third of the participants were clergy. Speaking of the need to "destroy the patriarchal idolatry of Christianity," the conference speakers rejected and at times ridiculed the Christian dogmas of the Holy Trinity, the Fall of man, the unique incarnation of God in Jesus Christ, and the redemption of man by Christ's death on the Cross. In place of these articles of faith, the conference promoted pantheism, shamanism, and homosexual rights. The participants took part in a "liturgy" wherein milk and honey were used rather than bread and wine, and the goddess "Sophia" was worshipped rather than Jesus Christ. The chant was repeated: "Our Maker Sophia, we are women in your image ... with our warm body fluids we remind the world of its pleasure and sensations."** At a later Re-imagining conference held in 1998, Sophia-worship-

---

* Deborah Corbett, "The Jungian Challenge to Modern Christianity," *Epiphany Journal,* Summer 1988, pp. 33–40.
** Craig Branch, "Re-imagining God," *Watchman Expositor,* 11:5, 1994, pp. 4–6, 19.

ping participants also shared biting into large red apples to express their solidarity with Eve, whom they regard as a heroine for having partaken of the forbidden fruit.

Although conservative Christians have spoken out against the conferences, the Re-imagining community remains influential within mainline churches, holding inter-denominational caucuses to discuss strategies for expansion. Worship of the goddess Sophia continues within these churches. As recently as June 2004, during the Presbyterian General Assembly in Richmond, Virginia, a "Voices of Sophia" meeting was held in which Sophia was invoked as a goddess.*

More significantly, feminist theology has become the most prominent trend on mainline seminary campuses today, and is a driving force within the ecumenical movement.** The main coordinator of the 1993 Re-imagining conference, Mary Ann Lundy, is now the Deputy Director of the World Council of Churches. At the 1998 Re-imagining conference, she made clear the agenda of both feminist theology and modern-day ecumenism: "We are learning that to be ecumenical is to move beyond the boundaries of Christianity. You see, yesterday's heresies are becoming tomorrow's *Book of Order.*"*** As we have seen, this is also the agenda of the New Age movement.

5. *The Toronto Blessing*

Since Fr. Seraphim first wrote about the "charismatic movement" that was sweeping Christian churches, the move-

---

* Parker T. Williamson, "Staying Alive: Re-imaginers Gather," *The Presbyterian Layman,* July 2004, p. 9.

** Diane L. Knippers, "Ye Goddesses!", *Foundations,* May 28, 1998.

*** Parker T. Williamson, "Sophia Upstages Jesus at Re-imagining Revival," *The Presbyterian Layman,* 31:3, May–June 1998.

ment has grown at a phenomenal rate. Worldwide, Pentecostalism is the fastest growing segment of Christianity: it is increasing at a rate of thirteen million people per year—primarily in Asia, Africa and South America—and now claims nearly a half billion adherents.*

Fr. Seraphim's observations about charismatic experiences have been borne out most strikingly in the "holy laughter movement" that mushroomed in the 1990s. About "laughter in the Holy Spirit," Fr. Seraphim had written: "Here perhaps more clearly than anywhere else the 'charismatic revival' reveals itself as not at all Christian in religious orientation." This is precisely the charismatic phenomenon that has seen the greatest increase in the last decade.

The rise of the current laughter movement can be traced to another movement that arose within Pentecostalism: the so-called Faith (or Word-Faith) Movement in the 1980s. Also known as the "health, wealth and prosperity gospel" because of its teaching that Christ has delivered believers from the curse of poverty and sickness, the Faith Movement contains strange tenets which resemble those of the New Age movement, such as belief in the power of creative visualization (visualizing what you want, and then "claiming" it), the belief that a person can become as much an incarnation of God as Jesus Christ was, and the denial that Christ redeemed man through His death on the Cross.**

Through the ministries of leaders such as Kenneth Copeland, Benny Hinn, Rodney Howard-Browne, Kenneth Hagin, Morris Cerullo, Paul Yonggi Cho, and Marilyn Hickey, the

---

* "The Rise of Pentecostalism," *Christian History,* no. 58, 1998, p. 3.
** Dr. Nick Needham, "The Toronto Blessing," *The Shepherd,* 16:3, December 1995.

Faith Movement has spread its heresies and attendant charismatic phenomena throughout the world. Since the spring of 1993, the movement has had a profound impact, not only on Pentecostal churches, but on mainline Christian churches as well. It was then that Faith Movement leader Rodney Howard-Browne drew widespread attention to his televised "laughing revival" at an Assemblies of God church in Lakeland, Florida. Thousands came from around the world to take part. Howard-Browne would walk through the crowds, placing his hands on people, and saying such things as "Fill! Fill! Fill!", whereupon many would collapse on the floor, laughing uncontrollably, cackling and hooting. Others would writhe on floor screaming hysterically, act as if drunk, be stuck to the floor with what Howard-Browne called "Holy Ghost glue," or be "slain in the Spirit," that is, fall to the ground on their backs, often into unconsciousness.* Each of these manifestations would often last for up to several hours, and sometimes (as in the case of uncontrollable laughter) for several days.

Calling himself a "Holy Ghost bartender" who is "drunk all the time," Howard-Browne showed disdain for any attempts to *test the spirits to see whether they are of God* (I John 4:1). "I'd rather be in a church where the devil and the flesh are manifesting," he stated, "than in a church where nothing is happening because people are too afraid to manifest anything.... And if a devil manifests, don't worry

---

* *The Dictionary of Pentecostal and Charismatic Movements* notes that Kathryn Kuhlman (1906–1976) was the person responsible for introducing the modern phenomenon of being "slain in the Spirit." Whereas earlier manifestations of being "slain in the Spirit" usually lasted for a few minutes, at the touch of Rodney Howard-Browne people have been "out" for several hours.

about that, either. Rejoice, because at least something is happening!"*

In August 1993, Randy Clarke, pastor of the "Vineyard" charismatic church in St. Louis, Missouri, attended a Faith Movement meeting led by Howard-Browne in Tulsa, Oklahoma. Four months later, Clarke brought the "laughing revival" to the Airport Vineyard Church of Toronto, Ontario. What began as a four-day series of meetings expanded into months of nightly services that sometimes lasted until 3 a.m. At this point the laughter movement skyrocketed, eliciting massive coverage by the worldwide media. Dubbed the "Toronto Blessing," the "holy laughter" meetings were billed as the top tourist attraction of 1994. Hundreds of thousands of Christians came to the Toronto church from all over the world—not only Pentecostals, but also Mennonites, Nazarenes, Methodists, Anglicans, Baptists, Roman Catholics, etc.**

In Toronto, the manifestations of the Faith Movement-inspired "laughing revival" grew even more bizarre than those reported earlier. In addition to the phenomena already described, people were seen to crawl on the ground and roar like lions, bark like dogs, paw the ground and snort like bulls, oink, howl, moo, crow, growl and emit other animal noises.*** Other manifestations of the "revival" included jerking and shaking of the head and body, karate chopping motions, imitating warriors, dancing uncontrollably, abdominal spasms, in-

---

* Rodney Howard-Browne, *The Coming Revival*, R.H.B.E.A. Publications, Louisville, Kentucky, 1991, p. 6.
** Paul Carden, "'Toronto Blessing' Stirs Worldwide Controversy, Rocks Vineyard Movement," *Christian Research Journal*, Winter 1995, p. 5.
*** Deacon R. Thomas Zell, "Signs, Wonders, & Angelic Visitations," *Again*, September 1995, p. 6.

tense chest pain, "vomiting in the spirit," and "birthing" (going through a mock labor and delivery).*

Of the hundreds of thousands of people who have taken part in the "Toronto Blessing," 15,000 have been Christian ministers and pastors. They have subsequently brought the movement to their congregations throughout the world, causing such phenomena as "holy laughter" and being "slain in the Spirit" to multiply at a rapid rate on five continents. In England alone, 7,000 churches, including those of the Church of England, have embraced the Toronto Blessing. The manifestations of the laughter movement have now swept what has long been regarded as mainstream Christianity. In July of 1995, Pat Robertson's *700 Club* featured a Pentecostal and several Protestant and Roman Catholic charismatic scholars who defended the animal noises as either manifestations of the Holy Spirit or human responses to the Holy Spirit's working.**

The widespread acceptance of these manifestations reveals an utter ignorance of the traditional Christian standards of spiritual life. In the Orthodox Church, most of these manifestations have been historically regarded as clear signs of demonic possession. In Orthodox Christian countries even today, such behaviors are exhibited by possessed individuals during services of exorcism performed by Orthodox priests. An American Orthodox nun, who attended such exorcisms in Russia in 1995, records that "Once the services are underway, the demons begin to show themselves. One woman rages in a male voice, another person shakes violently, another shrieks, another is

---

* Curt Karg, "Rodney Howard-Browne/Toronto Airport Vineyard Phenomena," Position Paper: October 1996, available from Spiritual Counterfeits Project.
** Timothy Brett Copeland, "Discerning the Spirit: Reflections of a Charismatic Christian," *Again,* September 1995, p. 9.

thrown to the floor, losing consciousness ... yet another looks as though he is in distress and pain, just before vomiting on the floor.... They scream their hatred for the priest, vowing to have their revenge, as he douses them with holy water. Some demons make jokes, others are just raw anger and hatred. But the loudest noise always seems to be that of animals: mooing, crowing, and especially barking and growling."*

Although, as Fr. Seraphim Rose has noted in this book, charismatics would disclaim any association with occultism and paganism,** it is noteworthy that the same manifestations of the "holy laughter" movement are found in the New Age movement. The Indian guru Bhagwan Shree Rajneesh, called by his disciples the "divine drunkard," encouraged his devotees to come and "drink" from him. His spiritual "wine" was often passed on with a single touch to the head (known as the *shakti-pat*), at which his followers would collapse in ecstatic laughter. Another famous guru, Swami Muktananda, would hold meetings at which thousands of his followers from around the world came to receive his touch. They experienced uncontrollable laughing, roaring, barking, hissing, crying, shaking, as well as falling unconscious.*** Muktananda was only imparting to his disciples experiences that he himself had undergone: roaring like a lion and other involuntary animal behaviors, which he attributed to spirit-possession by the goddess Chiti.****

It is also noteworthy that prominent New Agers have spo-

---

* Nun Cornelia, "Exorcisms in Russia Today," *Death to the World,* no. 10, 1995, p. 10.
** See p. 149 above.
*** Testimony of former Muktananda disciple Joy Smith, in *Focus* magazine, no. 12, Winter 1995/1996.
**** Quoted in Tal Brooke, *Riders on the Cosmic Circuit,* Lion Publishing, Batavia, Illinois, 1986, p. 45.

ken out in favor of the "holy laughter" movement that has entered Christian churches. One such spokesman, Benjamin Creme, well known for his predictions of the imminent coming of a New Age Messiah, has said the following about the "Toronto Blessing": "People are reacting to new energies invading our planet. Energies emanating from the 'christ' give them a sense of peace."*

Popular evangelist Oral Roberts, who hosted a revival led by Rodney Howard-Browne, has called the "holy laughter" movement the beginning of "another level of the Holy Spirit."** Howard-Browne himself has said the movement marks a "powerful new wind of the Spirit," bringing with it "the exciting sound of joy, joy, joy, joy!" that is "energetically stirring us to higher levels with God."*** This is remarkably similar to claims made by today's New Age "prophets." At the same time "holy laughter" began to ripple through the churches, New Age leader Barbara Marx Hubbard wrote that the human race was soon to experience a leap in evolution which she called "The Planetary Pentecost" or "The Planetary Smile."**** "From within," she wrote, "all sensitive persons will feel the joy of the force flooding their systems with love and attraction. As this joy floods though the nervous systems of the most sensitive persons on earth, it will create a psychomagnetic field of empathy.…

---

* Quoted in Tony Pearce, *"Holy Laughter" and the New Age Movement,* Light for the Last Days, London, p. 3.
** Julia Duin, "An Evening with Rodney Howard-Browne," *Christian Research Journal,* Winter 1995, p. 44.
*** Quoted in Charles and Francis Hunter, *Holy Laughter,* Hunter Books, Kingwood, Texas, 1994, p. 5.
**** Barbara Marx Hubbard, *Teachings from the Inner Christ for Founders of a New World Order of the Future,* Foundation for Conscious Evolution, Greenbrae, Calif., 1994.

This massive sudden emphatic alignment will cause a shift of consciousness of Earth." As a result of this, she says, "The 'christ' will appear to you all at once."*

With mainline Christians having the same experiences and harboring the same expectations as neo-pagans, we see the fulfillment of Fr. Seraphim's words about how many Christians will be deceived into accepting a pagan initiation experience.

6. UFOs in the Contemporary Mind

In the area of UFOs, Fr. Seraphim's conclusions have also been borne out by new developments. Now there is a growing consciousness, not only on a scientific but on a *popular* level as well, that the UFO phenomenon is not just a matter of beings from other planets in spaceships, that it is somehow involved in the psychic and occult realm, and that the "aliens" are somehow inhabiting the earth with us. Also, the image—promoted by director Steven Spielberg in his films *Close Encounters* and *E.T.*—of benevolent and even "cuddly" aliens, is now being replaced by an image closer to the truth. With the experiences described by Whitley Strieber in his book *Communion: A True Story* (1987), the public has been shown that these so-called "visitors" are in fact cruel, malicious beings who wreak psychic havoc on those who contact them. (This aspect of the phenomenon also corresponds very closely with the evidence amassed by the scientists Vallee and Hynek.) "I felt an indescribable sense of menace," Strieber writes. "It was hell on earth to be there, and yet I couldn't move, couldn't cry out, and

---

* Barbara Marx Hubbard, *The Revelation: A Message of Hope for the New Millennium,* 2nd edition, Nataraj Publishing, 1995.

couldn't get away. I lay as still as death, suffering inner agonies. Whatever was there seemed so monstrous and ugly, so filthy and dark and sinister...." Strieber also describes peculiar smells associated with his "visitors"—among them, a "sulfur-like" odor such as is mentioned when the ancient Lives of Saints speak of demonic encounters.*

Since the publication of *Communion*, hundreds of thousands of UFO "abductees" have come forward with accounts of their contact with aliens.** Today they have formed a substantial network, sharing their views and experiences through the internet and call-in radio shows.

Perhaps not surprisingly, this UFO network has found itself segueing into the New Age movement. Whitley Strieber is himself an indication of this. Now one of the leading spokesman of the UFO network, he has in more recent books offered reflections on how contact with aliens can help usher in a New Age. As one UFO "abductee," Col. Philip J. Corso, writes in his endorsement of Strieber's latest book, *Confirmation* (1999): "During an 'alien encounter,' the message that they were offering mankind, 'A new world—if you can take it," was conveyed to me.... It took an intellect like Whitley Strieber to give this message's meaning to me and the world."***

Setting forth the evolutionist view that "we are passing into a great change of species," Strieber writes: "As we express ourselves into the next age, we will come to a prime moment of this species, when mankind gains complete mastery over time and space and lifts his physical aspect into eternity, inducing

---

* Whitley Strieber, *Communion: A True Story,* HarperCollins, New York, 1987; revised edition, Avon, 1995.
** Whitley Strieber, *The Secret School,* HarperCollins, New York, 1997, p. xv.
*** Whitley Strieber, *Confirmation: The Hard Evidence of Aliens among Us,* St. Martin's Press, New York, 1999.

the ascension of the whole species into a higher, freer, and richer level of being.... As mind frees itself from time and thus approaches singularity of consciousness, nations as we know them—directed by power politics, greed and lies—will end."*

Strieber sees this utopian dream being realized as mankind leaves behind the "the old hierarchies" of the past: "The absolute blackness of the past symbolizes the rigidly authoritarian nature of the past civilization. Indeed, its customs have echoed forward all the way to the present, where they persist still in our governments, our ritual-encrusted religions, and our moral lives with their emphasis on sin."** As humanity abandons the "religious mythology" of those who "identify [aliens] with their version of demons,"*** it will become open to the "new world" offered by the visitors: "As we move into [the Age of] Aquarius, we do indeed see authority weakening in almost every human culture and institution. The new willingness to entertain notions like the presence of visitors and to largely reject the refusal of the old authorities to deal rationally with such matters signals a new eagerness to form opinions outside the traditional control mechanisms. As those mechanisms fade, the unknown uses their weakness to attempt to break through into the conscious world, and we find ourselves inundated with reports of UFOs, aliens, and all sorts of weird and wonderful things."****

In order to reconcile the obvious contradiction between the apparently sinister nature of the "visitors" and his own utopian ideas about aliens helping to usher in a New Age, Strieber attempts to blur the distinction between good and evil: "We

---

* Strieber, *The Secret School*, pp. 229, 225–26, 233.
** Ibid., pp. 226, 228–29.
*** Strieber, *Confirmation*, p. 286.
**** Strieber, *The Secret School*, p. 226.

live in an ethical and moral world that is like the ethical context of the [UFO] phenomenon, full of ambiguities, a place in which plain good and plain evil are rare."*

Strieber's view, which is shared by many in today's UFO network, is that the "visitors" are highly evolved beings which want us also to evolve—for their sake as well as ours. He speculates that, in their often terrifying encounters with humans, the visitors are exploiting us and at the same time "tempting" us to advance further in our evolution, to "close the gap" between us and them, so that we may "join [them] as a cosmic species": in other words, that we may become like them. This, he says, "explains why many people are taken to an evolutionary edge in their experiences" of aliens.**

Strieber notes that "In all the past fifty years, there has been no instance of the visitors directly adding resources. Nobody gets the plans to a starship. Nobody gets a map back to the home world. What we get instead are fear, confusion, cryptic messages, and a feeling of being pushed around—and the sense of something beyond price, lying just out of reach.... Rather than satisfying us, they are likely to tempt us further and further—with outrages, with dazzling displays, with promises—with whatever it takes."***

Perhaps the saddest "sign of the times" in our post-Christian age is the fact that great numbers of spiritually impoverished people now find it preferable to be in contact with these monstrous "visitors" than to feel all alone in what seems to them an impersonal universe. As a journal called *The Communion Letter* states, "People all across the world are encountering

---

* Strieber, *Confirmation*, p. 279.
** Ibid., pp. 287–88.
*** Ibid., pp. 288–89.

strange beings in their homes and even in the streets ... along the roads of dream and night." The journal asks people to "learn to respond usefully and effectively to the visitors if they appear in your life.—Discover the mystery, the wonder, and the beauty of the experience ... the things the ordinary media will not reveal ... the strange and wonderful truths that are rushing up out of the darkness."

In the face of all this, the Christian believer can hardly doubt Fr. Seraphim's words that "satan now walks naked into human history." Whitley Strieber is likewise correct when he observes that, with the decline of the "control mechanisms" of traditional Christian civilization, the "visitors" are attempting more and more to "break into the conscious world." But instead of leading us to the New Age that Strieber envisions, these attempts will help to usher in precisely what he described of his first encounter with aliens: "hell on earth."

7. The Plan for the New Age

It is interesting to note that 1975, the year that *Orthodoxy and the Religion of the Future* came out, was a banner year for the "new religious consciousness." This was the year which the deceased occultist Alice Bailey (1880–1949)—one of the major builders of the present-day New Age movement and an avowed enemy of orthodox Christianity—had designated for her disciples to publicly disseminate hitherto secret teachings to all available media. During that year David Spangler and a host of other New Age spokesmen and organizations began their public work.

The goals of today's New Age movement were mapped out well in advance in the writings of occultist and medium Helen Blavatsky, who founded the Theosophical Society in

1875,* and later by Alice Bailey, Nicholas Roerich (author of the Agni Yoga writings), Teilhard de Chardin (the evolutionary thinker and paleontologist mentioned in chapter 2 above), and H. G. Wells. In the words of Teilhard, these goals include a "convergence of religions" in tandem with a "confluence" of political and economic forces toward World Government.** Today, some New Age circles speak of "The Plan" for a "New World Order," which would include a universal credit system, a universal tax, a global police force, and an international authority that would control the world's food supply and transportation systems. In this utopian scheme, wars, disease, hunger, pollution, and poverty will end. All forms of discrimination will cease, and people's allegiance to tribe or nation will be replaced by a planetary consciousness.

According to some of the major architects of the New Age movement, this "Plan" can be traced back to the fall of Lucifer and his angels from heaven. Alice Bailey wrote that the revolt of the angels against God was part of "the divine plan of evolution," for by it the fallen angels "descended from their sinless and free state of existence in order to develop full divine awareness on earth."*** In this total reversal of Christian theology, the Fall of man was really an ascent to knowledge, for by it

---

* According to Blavatsky, the purpose of the Theosophical Society was "to oppose the materialism of science and every form of dogmatic theology, especially the Christian, which the Chiefs of the Society regard as particularly pernicious." (Blavatsky, *The Secret Doctrine,* vol. 3, 1888, p. 386). Incidentally, Blavatsky appears as a character in the above-mentioned Harry Potter books, under the anagram "Vlabatsky."

** Teilhard de Chardin, *How I Believe,* Harper & Row, New York, 1969, p. 41.

*** Alice Bailey, *The Externalization of the Hierarchy,* Lucis Publishing Company, New York, 1957, p. 118.

man's "eyes were opened" to good and evil.* Thus, wrote Helen Blavatsky: "It is but natural ... to view Satan, the Serpent of Genesis, as the real creator and benefactor, the Father of Spiritual mankind. For it is he who was the 'Harbinger of Light,' bright radiant Lucifer, who opened the eyes of the automaton created by Jehovah.... Indeed, [mankind] was taught wisdom and the hidden knowledge by the 'Fallen Angel.'"** As man's "benefactor," Lucifer continues to assist man's evolution. In the words of David Spangler, a disciple of the writings of Blavatsky and Bailey, Lucifer is "the angel of man's evolution."***

Within New Age esoteric societies it is taught that, for the furtherance of "The Plan," mass "planetary initiations" will occur. According to Benjamin Creme—another follower of Blavatsky and Bailey—"revitalized" Christian churches and Masonic lodges will be used for the purpose of giving these initiations. And as we have seen, David Spangler has stated that these initiations will be "Luciferic" at their esoteric core. Reiterating the teachings of Alice Bailey, who "channeled" them from a discarnate entity called "Djwhal Khul," Spangler writes: "Lucifer works within each of us to bring us to wholeness as we move into the New Age ... each of us is brought to that point which I term the Luciferic initiation.... Lucifer comes to give us the final ... Luciferic initiations ... that many people in the days ahead will be facing, for it is an initiation into the New Age."****

As "The Plan" approaches fulfillment, the one-world reli-

---

* This is also the view of the feminist theologians of the Re-imagining movement, who honor Eve for having partaken of the forbidden fruit.
** Blavatsky, *The Secret Doctrine,* vol. 2, The Theosophical Publishing House, Wheaton, Illinois, 1888; revised ed. 1970, pp. 243, 513.
*** David Spangler, *Reflections on the Christ,* Findhorn Community Press, Scotland, 1978, p. 37.
**** Ibid., pp. 40, 44.

gion acquires its final shape. "The day is dawning," wrote Alice Bailey, "when all religions will be regarded as emanating from one great spiritual source; all will be seen as unitedly providing the one root out of which the universal world religion will inevitably emerge."* Helen Blavatsky said that this universal religion was "the religion of the ancients," the memory of which was "the origin of the Satanic myth" of Christians. "The religion of the ancients," Blavatsky wrote, "is the religion of the future."**

"The Plan" reaches its apotheosis with the coming of the New Age Messiah: the so-called "Maitreya—the Christ." David Spangler speaks in anticipation of this event: "From the depths of the race a call is rising for the emergence of a saviour, an avatar, a father-figure ... who can be for the race what the ancient priest-kings were in the dawn of human history."*** According to Alice Bailey, "angels" will appear with this false Christ in order to convince people that they should follow him. Thus, the final stage of the "New Age" reversal of Christianity will be the worship of the antichrist, *whose coming is after the power of satan with all power and signs and lying wonders* (II Thes. 2:9).

It should be pointed out that many New Agers today would not be aware of, much less subscribe to, all the points of "The Plan." As we have seen, the movement incorporates a diverse array of groups, ideas and practices. If it can be called a "conspiracy," this is certainly not because all New Agers are

---

* Alice Bailey, *Problems of Humanity,* Lucis Publishing Company, New York, 1947; revised ed. 1964, p. 140.
** Blavatsky, *The Secret Doctrine,* vol. 2, p. 378; *Isis Unveiled,* vol. 1, The Theosophical Publishing House, Wheaton, Illinois, 1877; revised ed. 1972, p. 613.
*** David Spangler, *Explorations: Emerging Aspects of the New Culture,* Findhorn Publications Lecture Series, 1980, p. 68.

working together secretly, on an organizational level, toward fulfillment of "The Plan." Ultimately, "The Plan" is being orchestrated not on a human but on a demonic level, and the architects of the New Age movement are, to a large degree, only mouthpieces of ideas that are not their own.

8. Globalism

The New Age movement is only the "spiritual" side of a much broader movement which has mushroomed in the decades since Fr. Seraphim's death. This is the multi-faceted movement toward "globalism," which is very much in the interest of those whose goals may not be religious at all.

In recent years international investment bankers and corporations have made enormous strides toward their goal of a hegemony of world finance and a global economic system. In 1980 the following warning was issued by Admiral Charles Ward, a former member of the elite Council on Foreign Relations, which includes major government figures, heads of multinational corporations, and representatives of the largest banking firms in the world: "The most powerful cliques in these elitist groups have an objective in common—they want to bring about the surrender of the sovereignty and the national independence of the United States. A second clique of international members in the CFR ... comprises the Wall Street International bankers and their key agents. Primarily, they want the world banking monopoly from whatever power ends up in the control of global government."* More recently, in 1993, the President of the Council on Foreign Relations, Les Gelb, announced on television: "You had me on [before] to

---

* Rear Admiral Chester Ward, *Review of the News,* April 9, 1980, pp. 37–38.

talk about the New World Order.... I talk about it all the time.... It's one world now.... Willing or not, ready or not, we are all involved.... The competition is about who will establish the first one-world system of government that has ever existed in the society of nations. It is control over each of us as individuals and over all of us together as a community."*

This vision of the future has been shaping the foreign policy of many governments, not least that of the United States. A clear declaration of the globalist agenda was made in 1992 by Strobe Talbott, longtime personal friend of President Bill Clinton, Deputy Secretary of State during the Clinton administration, and one of the chief architects of the U.S.-led military intervention in the Balkans: "Nationhood as we know it will be obsolete; all states will recognize a single, global authority." In Talbott's view, nations are nothing more than social arrangements: "No matter how permanent and sacred they may seem at any one time, in fact they are all artificial and temporary.... It has taken the events in our own wondrous and terrible [20th] century to clinch the case for world government."**

With the establishment and expansion of the European Union, the creation of the Euro currency, the advances toward a cashless society, the control of former Eastern-bloc countries by Western financial interests, the formation of an international criminal tribunal by the United Nations, and the consolidation of state armies as "peacekeeping" forces under the United Nations and NATO, we see what appear to be the forerunners of such a one-world system. Some of these developments are not

---

* *The Charlie Rose Show,* May 4, 1993. Quoted in Tal Brooke, *One World,* End Run Publishing, Berkeley, Calif., 2000, pp. 7–8.
** Strobe Talbott, "The Birth of a Global Nation," *Time* magazine, July 20, 1992.

necessarily evil in themselves. Taken together, however, they help to set up a global apparatus which can make way for the rising "religion of the future." Such was the expectation of Alice Bailey, who in the 1940s wrote: "The expressed aims and efforts of the United Nations will be eventually brought to fruition, and a new church of God, gathered out of all religions and spiritual groups, will unitedly bring to an end the great heresy of separateness."* Robert Muller, former Assistant Secretary General of the United Nations, expressed the same belief on the fiftieth anniversary of the United Nations in 1995: "At the beginning the United Nations was only a hope. Today it is a political reality. Tomorrow it will be the world's religion."** A proponent of the teaching of both Alice Bailey and Teilhard de Chardin, Muller says that mankind's goal should be "to see the religions globalize themselves urgently in order to give us a universal, cosmic meaning of life on Earth and give birth to the first global, cosmic, universal civilization."***

Today, those with a globalist agenda in the political and financial sectors work alongside globalists in the religious sector, particularly with "interfaith" organizations such as the United Religions Initiative (founded as a religious counterpart to the United Nations), the Temple of Understanding (an official consultant of the United Nations Economic and Social Council), and the Council for a Parliament of the World's Religions (a revival of the World's Parliament of Religions,

---

* Alice A. Bailey, *The Destiny of the Nations,* Lucis Publishing Company, New York, 1949, p. 52.
** Robert Muller, *My Testament to the UN: A Contribution to the 50th Anniversary of the United Nations,* World Happiness and Cooperation, Anacortes, Washington, 1995, p. 4.
*** Robert Muller, *2000 Ideas and Dreams for a Better World,* Idea 1101, July 16, 1997.

mentioned in chapter 2 above, which first convened in Chicago in 1893).*

Although "interfaith" organizations usually affirm that their only aim is to promote "understanding" and "dialogue" among religions, it is apparent that in some cases this aim is only a first step in a larger program: the "convergence of religions" in the New Age. As William Swing, Episcopal Bishop of California and founder/director of the United Religions Initiative, expressed it in his book *The Coming United Religions:* "The time comes ... when common language and a common purpose for all religions and spiritual movements must be discerned and agreed upon. Merely respecting and understanding other religions is not enough."** Bishop Swing imagines all the world's religions as paths up a mountain, converging from below on a single point, a "unity that transcends the world." At the top of the mountain, the esoteric believers from each faith would "intuit that they were ultimately in unity with people from other religions because all come together at the apex, in the Divine. Everyone below the line would be identified as ex-

---

* In the last decade, witchcraft has played an prominent role in the interfaith movement. At the centennial conference of the Parliament of the World's Religions, held in Chicago in 1993, Wicca took center stage. As "Covenant of the Goddess" officer Don Frew notes, "We Witches found ourselves the media darlings of the conference!... By the end of the nine days, the academics attending the Parliament were saying, 'In 1893, America was introduced to the Buddhists and Hindus; in 1993, we met the Neopagans.'... From that point on, Neopagans would be included in almost every national or global interfaith event." (Don Frew, "The Covenant of the Goddess & the Interfaith Movement," quoted in Brooks Alexander, *Witchcraft Goes Mainstream,* p. 211.)

** Bishop William Swing, *The Coming United Religions,* United Religions Initiative and CoNexus Press, 1998, p. 63.

oteric."* Like Blavatsky, Bailey and Teilhard before him, Bishop Swing looks to this convergence of religions with messianic expectancy. In his opening address to the 1997 summit conference of the United Religions Initiative, he proclaimed: "If you have come here because a spirit of colossal energy is being born in the loins of the earth, then come here and be a midwife. Assist, in awe, at the birth of new hope."

9. Denatured Christianity

Although not all globalists and globalist organizations share specifically religious goals, they are certainly united in their view of what kind of religion will *not* fit into the one-world system they are working to create. Conservative, traditional adherents of a religion, who believe that their religion is a unique revelation of the fullness of truth, will not be welcome in the "global village." As Paul Chaffee, board member of the United Religions Initiative, said in 1997: "We can't afford fundamentalists in a world this small." The same view was expressed at the 1998 State of the World Forum (sponsored by a host of international investors and corporations), where Forum president Jim Garrison announced: "If my theology is an impediment, then I have to get rid of my theology.... I think history is moving beyond dogma.... During times of transition, orthodoxies fall and the heretics and mavericks are the people creating the new orthodoxy."**

Also in 1998, this subject was discussed in some detail by one of the more recent ideologues of the "new religious consciousness," Ken Wilber. A popular author whose works have

---

* Ibid., pp. 58–59.
** State of the World Forum, "A New Spirituality"; quoted in Lee Penn, "The United Religions: Foundation for a World Religion," *Spiritual Counterfeits Project Journal,* 22:4–23:1, 1999, pp. 64–65.

been praised and avidly studied by both former President Clinton and former Vice President Al Gore, Wilber outlined the agenda that the world must follow in order to combine science with religion, as well as to establish a "universal theology" which all religions can embrace without losing their outward differences. "Religions the world over," he writes, "will have to *bracket their mythic beliefs,*" and he cites as examples Moses parting the Red Sea, Christ being born of a Virgin, and the creation occurring in six days. Further, he says that "religion will also have to adjust its attitude toward evolution in general," and "any religion that attempts to reject evolution seals its own fate in the modern world."*

As we have seen, evolution is a key element in the New Age utopian dream. A panentheist, Wilber believes that the entire universe is God, evolving throughout billions of years toward Teilhard de Chardin's "Omega Point." Man, having evolved from a primordial soup, now evolves toward total God-consciousness, and in this way even God is in the process of becoming. According to New Age thought, with Darwin's "discovery" of physical evolution, and even more so with the "discovery" of spiritual evolution, evolution has *become conscious of itself,* and this new paradigm shift will accelerate the process of cosmic evolution.** Thus it is that, in Wilber's view, those religious believers who reject evolution and "pledge allegiance to a mythic

---

* Ken Wilber, *The Marriage of Sense and Soul: Integrating Science and Religion,* Random House, Broadway Books, New York, 1998, pp. 204–5, 211.
** This idea of conscious evolution is extremely popular today among New Age circles. Earlier expositions of it can be found in the writings of Teilhard de Chardin ("Man discovers that he is nothing else than evolution become conscious of itself" [*The Phenomenon of Man,* 1961, p. 221]), and in those of Alice Bailey ("For the first time" mankind is "intelligently participating in the evolutionary process" [*The Externalization of the Hierarchy,* 1957, p. 685]).

Eden in any actual sense" are destined for extinction.* Only those who embrace the new religious consciousness, or who at least "bracket" their religious beliefs, will survive in the coming global society, which Wilber says will be marked by a "worldcentric" awareness based in "universal pluralism."**

Since traditional Christianity is an obstacle to the dreams of globalists on both the secular and "spiritual" fronts, there is now a concerted effort to *reinterpret* and *denature* the Christian faith—to transform Christ from the Divine-human, unique Saviour of Christian orthodoxy to a mere "spiritual guide" of the New Age variety.

We have already discussed how the feminist theologians of the Re-imagining movement have sought to reinvent Christianity: for them, Christ is not particularly unique, but is only one of the many "expressions" or "servants" of the goddess Sophia.*** These theologians, however, represent only one facet of the cultural trend to denature Christianity.

If, according to the neo-pagan view, we and everything else are but emanations of God, then there is nothing for Christ to do but guide us back to *gnosis* of what we already are. This idea is precisely what is being promoted today under the guise of being the authentic, esoteric teaching of Christ. In actual fact, it is but a revival of the ancient gnostic heresy, based on pagan philosophy, that was rightly condemned by the early Fathers of the Orthodox Church. This message of gnostic "Christianity" is being publicized today through the writings and media appearances of scholars with an obvious

---

* Ken Wilber, *The Marriage of Sense and Soul,* p. 206.
** Ken Wilber, *One Taste,* Shambhala Publications, Boston, 1999, pp. 311, 345.
*** Parker T. Williamson, "Sophia Upstages Jesus at Re-imagining Revival," *The Presbyterian Layman,* 31:3, May–June 1998.

bias against traditional Christianity, chief among whom is Elaine Pagels, author of *The Gnostic Gospels* and *Beyond Belief.* The same message has recently received much attention through the quasi-historical novel *The Da Vinci Code* by Dan Brown: a blasphemous assault on traditional Christianity that has sold over twelve million copies since its publication in 2003.

Ken Wilber speaks of the teachings that are being "rediscovered" in the ancient gnostic texts: "It is obvious from these texts that Jesus' primary religious activity was to incarnate in and as his followers, in the manner, *not* of the *only* historical Son of God (a monstrous notion), but of a true Spiritual Guide helping all to become sons and daughters of God.... Elaine Pagels points out that there are three essential strands to the esoteric message of Christ, as revealed in the Gnostic Gospels: (1) 'Self-knowledge is knowledge of God; the [highest] self and the divine are identical.' (2) 'The "living Jesus" of these texts speaks of illusion and enlightenment, not of sin and repentance.' (3) 'Jesus is presented not as Lord but as spiritual guide.' Let us simply note that those are precisely tenets of Dharmakaya religion."*

Here is a clear outline of the "new Christianity" that can easily be accommodated by the "religion of the future"—an imitation Christianity that leads not to Christ but to antichrist. Here, Christ is seen as a vague concept of ultimate Good, the belief in Him as the only begotten Son of God is rejected as a "monstrous notion," and the idea is put forth that

---

* Ken Wilber, *Up from Eden: A Transpersonal View of Human Evolution,* The Theosophical Publishing House, Wheaton, Illinois, 1981, p. 256; quoting from Elaine Pagels, "The Gnostic Gospels' Revelations," *New York Review of Books,* 26:16–19, 1979.

we ourselves can be just like Him.* This is a crucial element in the "religion of the future," for by it the antichrist will actually be convinced that he is another incarnate Son of God.

In one sense, the imitator of Christ will appear as a kind of saviour, solving man's economic and political problems and offering to satisfy his spiritual aspirations through what Fr. Seraphim called a "melting pot" of science and world religions. According to the worldview of the "new religious consciousness," however, the ultimate saviour will be evolution itself, moving forward in a natural development of this world into the Kingdom of God. The last great deceiver, who in the end will pretend to be Christ, will be seen as but another magnificent product of evolution.

10. The Vague Expectancy of the "New Man"

If, as we have said, the worldview of the "new religious consciousness" is entering into all aspects of human thought, what are some of the signs by which one can identify it? It can be seen, first of all, in the common sentiment that all religions are one, all are equal, and all are saying the same thing, only in different ways. On the surface this idea appears attractive because it seems to give everyone a fair shake. On a deeper level, however, it can be seen how this concept, under the pretense of fostering "unity in diversity," actually destroys diversity. If an adherent to a religion believes that all other religions are equal to his own, he can no longer truly hold to that religion; he can no longer be who he is. Instead, while perhaps holding to some

---

* It will be remembered that these same ideas are found, in an only slightly different form, in the Faith Movement that spawned the "holy laughter" revival.

outward cultural artifacts, he becomes essentially a blank—a blank waiting to be filled by some new revelation. He has become as blank as everyone else who has been infected with the same modern mentality. Thus there is no true unity *or* diversity, only sameness based on blankness. This false "unity in blankness" is precisely what satan will use in order to hypnotize the mass mind in the last days. As Fr. Seraphim once pointed out in a lecture: "Such a vague thing is exactly what the devil likes to grab hold of. In any particular religious belief you may be mistaken, but at least you put your heart into it, and God can forgive all kinds of mistakes. But if you do not have any particular religious belief and you give yourself over to some kind of vague idea, then the demons come in and begin to act."*

The religious mentality of modern man is becoming more amorphous and hazy all the time. A poll taken in 2002 indicates that 33% percent of Americans consider themselves "spiritual but not religious," which is to say that they do not identify with an organized religion but are creating their own personal spirituality. According to the same poll, the number of such people is increasing by over two million every year, even as the number of those who consider themselves religious is declining at the same rate.**

The new, "spiritual" man of today can browse through bookstores or surf the internet to find any religious idea or practice that strikes his fancy, from Western to Eastern, from Sufism to satanism. The more data he stores in his head, however, the more vague his worldview becomes. He has religious

---

* Fr. Seraphim Rose, "Contemporary Signs of the End of the World" (a talk given at the University of California, Santa Cruz, May 14, 1981), in *The Orthodox Word,* no. 228, 2003, p. 32.
** *USA Today*/Gallup poll, 2002.

interests in several areas, but he basically believes that all is relative: i.e., "My ideas work for me, your ideas work for you." He believes in everything at once, but in nothing very deeply, and in nothing that will demand a sacrifice from him. He has nothing worth dying for. But his antennae are out, feeling for something else that will strike his fancy, that will satisfy his vague unrest without asking that he honestly look at himself and change, without disturbing his constant endeavor to satisfy his ego. His spiritual interest is intimately connected to his quest for ego gratification, and thus he stands poised to receive anything from anywhere that will provide this gratification. He is as clay in the hands of the spirit of antichrist, which, as the Apostle teaches, *is already in the world* (I John 4:3). He is a candidate—or rather a target—for the "religion of the future" about which Fr. Seraphim wrote.

A sad indicator of the spiritual condition of contemporary man is seen in the enormous popularity of the *Conversations with God* books by Neale Donald Walsch, which have sold over seven million copies since the first book appeared in 1995. At the 1997 summit conference of the United Religions Initiative, Walsch said of himself, "I represent the new paradigm of a religionless religion—a religion without structure—a spirituality that transcends all boundaries." Walsch claims to channel a being whom he calls "God." Flattering readers with the idea that they too are God, Walsch's "God" tells them there is no such thing as sin and no need for repentance, for the "Original Sin" was really the "Original Blessing"—an ascent to knowledge.* Walsch's "God" speaks to the blank mind of the new, "spiritual"

---

* Neale Donald Walsch, *Conversations with God: An Uncommon Dialogue,* book 2, Hampton Roads Publishing Co., Inc., Charlottesville, Virginia, 1997, p. 57.

man: "You may want to consider the possibility that what would work for the world right now—given what the world says it wants to experience, which is peace and harmony—is a New Spirituality based on New Revelations.... A spirituality that enlarges upon organized religion in its present form. For it is many of your old religions, with their inherent limitations, that stop you from experiencing God as God really is. They also stop you from experiencing peace, joy, and freedom—which are *other* words for God as God really is.... The world is hungry, the world is starving, for a new spiritual truth."*

In these revelations from Walsch's "God," one can recognize the same basic message that was channeled by earlier occultists such as Alice Bailey. But while this message resonated with a relatively small number of occultists during Bailey's time, today it resonates with mainstream society, with the emerging "global consciousness."

If one perceives a common thread among occult and New Age teachings spanning generations, this is because there is a single mind directing the formation of the new religious consciousness. It is the mind of the same fallen angel who tempted Adam and Eve in the Garden with the words: *Ye shall be as Gods* (Genesis 3:5). But while the evil one's servant, the antichrist, will appear to triumph for a time, in the end it is he *whom the Lord shall consume with the spirit of His mouth, and shall destroy with the brightness of His coming* (II Thes. 2:8).

11. Conclusion

From all that has been said above, it can be seen how, in the years following the publication of Fr. Seraphim's book, the

---

* Neale Donald Walsch, *The New Revelations: A Conversation with God*, Simon & Schuster, Atria Books, New York, 2002, pp. 142–43, 258.

formation of an actual "religion of the future" has become increasingly real and believable. Now we can see even more clearly how humanity is being made open to the "demonic pentecost" that Fr. Seraphim predicted, in which the multitudes of the world—including those who call themselves Christians—can actually be initiated into the realm of demons.

Only Orthodox Christianity—with its Patristic standard of spiritual life and its thoroughly refined teachings on spiritual discernment—can cut through all the deceptions of our times at once. For this reason, satan sees it as his greatest enemy, and is doing all in his power to undermine it. But for the same reason we must do all that we can to cling to it, as Fr. Seraphim exhorts us.

"He who does not experience the Kingdom of God within him," writes St. Ignatius Brianchaninov, "will not be able to recognize the antichrist when he comes." In Orthodoxy we behold Christ undistorted. We can know Who He is, and we can know His Kingdom within us, without fantasies, hysteria, heated emotional states, and without any mental images. Knowing this, we will not be starving for a new spiritual truth, for we have found the Truth, not as an idea but as a Person—and we partake of Him in Holy Communion. We will not be a blank waiting to be filled, for we will already be filled with *Christ, Who is all, and in all* (Col. 3:11). Having Christ's Kingdom within us, we will inherit it for eternity.

General Index

Abraham (Righteous Forefather), 3–6
absolutism, 23
Advaitins, 10, 14, 23
aerial realm, 111
Africa, 80, 137, 212
"Age of Mary," chiliastic, 177
Al Montada, xxviii
Albrecht, Mark
—"Questioning Jonestown," 198n
Ambartsumyam, Victor, 83
Ambrose, St., Starets of Optina, 129
Anatolius, monk, 104
Ancient of Days, 4
Andrew of Caesarea, St., 179n
"angel of light," 12, 18, 42, 144
   devil appearing as, 165
"angels," 104, 106–8, 114, 144–45, 148,
   184, 226
   evil spirits appear as, 149
   in Indonesia, 185
Anthony the Great, St., 104
Anti-Trinitarians, 3
antichrist, 6, 109–10, 179, 181, 186,
   188, 226, 235, 239
   as false messiah, 174, 178
   "great signs and wonders" of, 175
   Orthodox teaching on, 175, 186
   reign of, 181n, 192
   religion of, xxii, 114
      forerunners of the, 188
   spirit of, 183, 237
Apocalypse (Revelation) of St. John the
   Theologian, 177, 179
apostasy, 6, 170, 184, 186, 188, 209
"Aquarian Age," 59, 62, 221
"Aquarian nation," 59
Arminianism, 121
Arnold, Kenneth, 79

Arrupe, Fr., S. J. (General of the Society
   of Jesus), 27
Ashtavakra Samhita, 8
Assemblies of God, 119
Association of United Religions, xxvi, 1
Asia, 80, 212
astral travelling, 64
astrology, 64, 202–3
atheism, 197
Athenagoras, Patriarch of Constantino-
   ple, xxiv, 171
Augustine, Blessed
   —*Homilies on John,* 125
Aurobindo, Sri, 28n
Averky (Taushev), Archbishop of
   Syracuse
   —*The Apocalypse in the Teachings of
   Ancient Christianity,* 179n
   —*Guide to the Study of the New Testa-
   ment, Part II,* 179n
Ayurvedic medicine, 203

Babel, Pastor, xxvi
Bailey, Alice, 223–26, 228–29, 232n,
   238
Baki (ritualistic magic) ceremony, 16–17
"Baptism of the Holy Spirit," 117–18,
   120, 134–36, 143, 146, 159, 162,
   188, 190
   can be had without Christ, 172
   commonest responses to, 139, 151,
   156, 163, 171–72
   "ecstatic" experiences of, 156, 158
   other physical reactions to, 154
Baptist church, 211, 215
Barsanuphius and John, Sts., 153
   writings of, 169
Basil the Great, St., 6

Berdyaev, Nicholas, xxxii–xxxiv, 130, 143, 173–74
Bhagavad Gita, 8, 21–22, 55
Bhajan, Yogi, "3HO" founder, 60–61
Bhaktivedanta, A. C., "Krishna Consciousness" movement founder, 55
Bigfoot, 109n
biofeedback, 67, 208–9
black magic, 16, 18
Blackmore, Simon A., S. J.
　—*Spiritism Facts and Frauds,* 131n, 157, 163n
Blake, Eugene Carson, Dr., xxvi
blasphemy, 149, 167, 176, 186, 234
Blavatsky, Helen, 132, 223–26, 230
Bon religion, 203–4
breath control, 19, 39, 43
Bredesen, Harold, 178
Brown, Dan, 234
Buddha, 65
　"-nature" within one, 63
Buddhism. *See* Zen Buddhism; Tibetan Buddhism
Burdick, Donald W.
　—*Tongues: To Speak or Not to Speak,* 128n, 167
Burning Man Festivals, 207
Byashyananda, Swami, 24
Bykov, V. P.
　—*Tikhie Priyuty,* 129n

Caen, Herb, 198
Calvinism, 121
Cambodia, 197, 199
Campbell, Fr. Robert, 24–25
Campbell, Joseph, 202
Canadian UFO Report, 101
Catholicism. *See* Roman Catholicism
Catoe, Lynn G.
　—*UFOs and Related Subjects: An Annotated Bibliography,* 102n
Cerullo, Morris, 213
Chadwick, Owen
　—*Western Asceticism,* 147n
Chaffee, Paul, 231

"channels," "channeling," 135, 202, 209, 225, 237–38
"charismatic" movement, xx, 135, 141, 143, 146, 150, 160, 181, 188, 191, 212–17
"charismatic revival," xiv, xvii, xx–xxii, xxxv, 35, 44, 116–24, 128, 133–44, 146, 149, 152, 154, 158–59, 162–66, 170–71, 173–74, 176–77, 179–84, 187, 209, 212–16. *See also* Pentecostal; Pentecostalism
　apologists of, 152, 155–56, 170, 172
　attitude of Orthodox followers of, 149
　conference of, in Ireland, 118
　distinctive characteristics of, 119
　interdenominational, 115, 151, 163
　"new spirituality" of, 143
　"Orthodox," 181–82
　"prophecies and interpretations" of, 137
Chiti, goddess, 217
Chopra, Deepak, 203
Chrismation, Sacrament of, 122–23, 143, 183, 187
Christenson, Larry, 127, 149
　—*Speaking in Tongues,* 169
Christian Beacon, 177
Christian Century, xxvii
"Christian" America, 56, 58, 67
"Christian Science," 67
Christianity, xxv, xxix, xxxiv, 2–3, 8–9, 13–15, 22–23, 26, 38, 43–44, 50–52, 67–68, 75, 101, 117, 133, 140, 154, 165, 169–71, 174, 181–82, 187–89, 196–98, 207, 216, 223
　counterfeit, 183, 191
　deformation of, 29
　denatured, redefined, 209–12, 225, 230–35
　dogmas of, 9, 14–15, 211
　Eastern religion combined with, 69
　genuine, 130
　gnostic heresy of, 233

GENERAL INDEX

liberal, 24–25
"New," xxxiii, 130, 173, 175, 234
Orthodox, xii, xxviii, xxxiii, xxxv,
 36–37, 137, 143, 156, 165, 173,
 192, 239 (*see also* Orthodoxy)
"universal," 14
Western, 43
"Churches of God," 119
clairvoyance, 129
Clarke, Arthur C.
 —*Childhood's End,* 74
Clarke, Randy, 215
Clinton, Bill, 227, 231
"close encounters," 84, 87–90, 92–94, 97
Close Encounters of the Third Kind, 72,
 91, 110, 219
Communion Letter, The, 222
Communism, 77, 197–98
"Condon Report," 81–82
Conference on "Divine Gifts," 146
Connolly, Archbishop Thomas, of Seat-
 tle, 177
consciousness, 60, 67, 69–70
 altered, 209
 "global," 238
 human, 109
 "leaps" of, 202
 "new levels" of, 49, 202
 "transcendental," 61
 of the West, 67
Convocation of Religion for World
 Peace, xxv
Copeland, Kenneth, 213
Corbett, Deborah
 —"The Trouble with Truth," 210n
 —"The Jungian Challenge to Modern
 Chrristianity," 211n
Cornelius the Centurion, 37, 123n
Corso, Col., Philip J., 220
Cosmas of Aitolia, St., 182
Council on Foreign Relations, 227
Covenant of the Goddess, 205, 230n
Creme, Benjamin, xv, 218, 225
Crowley, Aleister, 206
cults, 61–62, 70, 195–96

"consciousness," 68–69
Eastern religious, xxi, 61, 67, 70
Hindu, 62
new, 69
secular, 68
UFO, 94, 98
Cumbey, Constance E.
 —*The Hidden Dangers of the Rainbow,*
 xiv
Cyprian of Carthage, St., 6, 104

Damascene (Christensen), Hieromonk
 xviii, 201
Daniel, Prophet, 4
Darwin, Charles, 232
David, Prophet-King, 4
Da Vinci Code, 234
Davis, Rennie, 57
de Chardin, Teilhard, 21, 224, 229, 232
 "the new religion" of, 27
 New Christianity of, 26, 28–29
 "Omega Point" of, 29, 192, 232
deception, xxii, 150, 179, 186
 "charismatic," 159, 166
 demonic, xi, 104–5, 114, 159
 self-, 111, 159, 163, 174, 188
 spiritual, xiii, 41, 149, 157, 162, 165,
 170, 187, 191
Dechanet, J. M.
 —*Christian Yoga,* 38n, 41–42, 45
Deir, Costa, 115
delusion, 18, 69, 175
demonic, 69, 75, 102, 109–13, 141,
 169, 189, 192, 195, 226
 activity, true stories of, 107
 deception, xi, 104–5, 114, 159
 encounters, 219–22
 initation, 188, 192, 238 (*see also*
 initiation)
 "kidnapping," 106
 manifestations, 104, 112
 "pentecost," xi, 213, 238
 power, 104, 130, 140, 192
 possession, 51, 102, 128–29, 157,
 192, 216–17

GENERAL INDEX

demons, 11–12, 36, 42, 68–69, 75, 102, 104–9, 113–14, 144, 146, 149, 152, 162, 166, 174, 185, 220, 236
  activity of, 108
  and angels, Orthodox doctrine of, 104n. *See also* angels
  contact with, 110
  escaping the nets of, 108
  in human form, 113
  inspiration and activity of, 199
devil, 105, 131n, 162, 173, 183, 235, 238. *See also* Lucifer; Satan
  appearing as an "angel of light," 165
  gains initiates, 110
  grants great "visions," 144
  loosed for a time, 188
  wiles of the, 113, 141
Diakonia, xxiv
discernment, 12, 149, 238
"Disciples of Christ," 198
divination, 130, 202
"Divine Light Mission," 56–57, 68
"Djwhal Khul," 225
dogma, 14–15, 161, 202, 211, 231
  as a derisive term, 13
"doors of perception," 68
Dostoyevsky, Fyodor M.
  —*The Possessed (The Demons),* 197
"dream work," 202, 208
Druidism, 204, 208
Du Plessis, David J., 120, 124–25, 162
  —*The Spirit Bade Me Go,* 169
Duddy, Neil
  —"Questioning Jonestown," 198n

earth/nature worship. *See* Gaia (earth) worship
Eastern religions. *See* religions, Eastern
ecology, "deep," 207
ecumenical
  activists, xxiv
  "Christians," 191
  fashion, xx, 183

movement, xxiii–xxvi, 120–21, 170, 182, 191, 212
  spirituality, xx–xxi
ecumenism, xxviii, 23, 120, 123, 211
  "charismatic revival" comes to, 171
  "Christian," xxv, xxviii–xxix
  heresy of, xix, 191
  ideology behind, xxv
Efremov, Ivan, 76–77
Elijah the Prophet, 178, 184
Emilianos, Metropolitan of the Patriarchate of Constantinople, xxvi
"Enlightenment," 76, 107
  the modern age of, 113
Ephraim the Syrian, St., 153
Episcopalianism, 115, 117, 121, 209–10, 215, 230
equinox rites, 63
"Erhard Seminars Training," 67
E. T.: The Extra Terrestrial, 219
evolution, evolutionism, 10, 27–28, 73–75, 77, 91, 202, 218, 220–21, 224, 232, 235
"exotheology" (theology of outer space), 74
exorcism, 216–17
extraterrestrial beings, 73, 103
  hypothesis of origin of, 79, 99
  and the idea of intelligent life, 98
  myth of, 108
  "races" of, 74

fakir, xvi, 32, 34–35, 87, 132
"Faith Movement," 213–15, 235n
fall of man, 202, 211, 224
"fancy," 166–67
  deception known as, 165
  a second form of *prelest,* 162
"Father Divine," 196
Father Seraphim Rose: His Life and Works (Hieromonk Damascene), xiii(n), xvii
Fellowship of Crotona, 206
feminism/feminist theology, 207, 211–12, 225n, 233

General Index

Ferguson, Marilyn
—*The Aquarian Conspiracy,* 209
fetishism, 23
Findhorn Foundation, 210
Finsaas, Clarence, 121
Fisher, David
—*Tranquility without Pills* (All about Transcendental Meditation), 46n
"flying saucers." *See* unidentified flying objects
Ford, J. Massingberd, 160
—*The Pentecostal Experience,* 167
fortune tellers, 98. *See also* divination
Francis of Assisi, 158
Freemasonry, xxvi, 201, 206–7
  ideology, undisguised aim of, xxv
  lodges of, xxxii, 225
"Full Gospel Business Men's Fellowship International," 119, 161
Fuller, John
—*The Interrupted Journey,* 95

Gaia (earth) worship, 202, 206–8
Gardner, Gerald, 206
Garrison, Jim, 231
Gelb, Les, 227
Gelpi, Donald L., S. J.
—*Pentecostalism, A Theological Viewpoint,* 169
genocide, "revolutionary, " 197
Georges (Khodre), Metropolitan of Lebanon, xxvii, xxix–xxx, 20
Ghandi, philosophy of, xxvii
globalism, 226–30, 232, 237
gnosticism, 204, 233–34
goddess worship, 202, 206, 208, 210–11, 217, 232
Gore, Al, 231
Grace Episcopal Cathedral, San Francisco, 209
Graham, Billy, 177
  interpretation of the "Rapture," 180
—*World Aflame,* 181n
Grebens, G. V.
—*Ivan Efremov's Theory of Soviet Science Fiction,* 76n
Greek Orthodox Archdiocese of North and South America, xxv, xxviii, 182
Greek Orthodox Church, 115–16
Greenfield, Robert
—*The Spiritual Supermarket,* 57–58
Gregerson, J.
—"Nicholas Berdyaev, Prophet of a New Age," xxxii(n)
Gregory of Sinai, St., 11, 150, 179
Gregory the Theologian, St., 179n
"guitar masses," 120
Gulag Archipelago, 197, 200
gurus, 19, 48
  "Eastern," of the newer school, 56
  Indian, 53, 216–17
  Western, 53

Hagar the Egyptian, 3–4
Hagin, Kenneth, 213
Haight-Ashbury, San Francisco, 54
Hare Krishna sect. *See* "Krishna consciousness" movement
Harper, Michael
—*Life in the Holy Spirit,* 168
Harry Potter books, 204–5, 224n
"health, wealth and prosperity gospel," 213
Hellenic Chronicle, xxiv
Herman of Alaska, St., 140
Hickey, Marilyn, 213
Himalayas, 16, 53
Hinduism, xxxiv, 7–10, 12–13, 15, 19–20, 26–27, 29, 66, 76, 137, 203
  conversion from, to Orthodox Christianity, xxxiv
  philosophical construct of, 10
  power it holds over devotees, 143
  success of, 25
  system of practices of, 18
  Vedantic, 21
Hinn, Benny, 213
hippies, 53, 61
Hoare, F. R., 105
—*The Western Fathers,* 105n

"Holiness" sect, 119, 132
Holy Baptism, Sacrament of, 183
Holy Communion, Sacrament of, xxiv, 239
"holy laughter" movement, 212–18, 235n. *See also* Holy Spirit, "laughter of"
Holy Spirit, 3–4, 17, 124, 157, 160, 163, 191. *See also* "Baptism of the Holy Spirit"
  acquisition of, 183
  "channeling of," 134, 136, 209
  "Church of," xxxii
  descent of, 125
  "ecclesiology of," xxxi
  gift of the, 12, 122–23, 125–27, 144–45, 158, 162, 166, 182, 187
  grace of the, 186, 192
  "laughter of," 151–54, 212–18
  "New Age of," xxxiii, 143, 173, 192
  Old Testament manifestation of, 4
  "outpouring of," xxxiii, 121, 150, 166, 170
  "Third Age of," xxxiii
Howard-Browne, Rodney, 213–14, 218
Hubbard, Barbara Marx, 218
"humanoids," 91–96, 113
Huxley, Aldous, 21
Hynek, Dr. J. Allen, 82–95, 98, 101, 219
  cases examined by, 88
  chief consultant of Project "Blue Book," 82
  technical consultant, 91
  —*The Edge of Reality: A Progress Report on Unidentified Flying Objects,* 91n, 93, 99
  —*The Hynek UFO Report,* 86n, 88, 90
  —*The UFO Experience: A Scientific Inquiry,* 82n, 84–85, 84n, 86n, 87, 89, 92, 95–96
hypnosis, 95–97, 100, 129, 133, 202
hysteria, 152, 155

I Ching, 64
Iakovos, Archbishop of New York, xxviii, 182
Ifugao magic, 16
Ignatius (Brianchaninov), St., 68, 104, 111, 113, 144–46, 150, 154, 157, 159, 162, 165–67, 239
  —*On Miracles and Signs,* 111
Ignatius Loyola, 158
Illuminist sects, 3
Incarnation, Mystery of the, 4, 6
India, xvii, 13, 15, 19, 22, 30, 47, 50–51, 56, 61
Indonesia, "revival" in, 184–85
initiation
  into the New Age, 209
  into the psychic realm, 68
  into the realm of demons, 238
  Luciferian, 210, 225
  pagan experience of, xxii, 19, 47–48, 57, 101, 136, 152, 156, 188, 192, 205, 219
Inter-Church Renewal, 121, 163
Isaac of the Kiev Caves, St., 144
Isherwood, Christopher, 21
Ishmael, the son of Hagar, 5
Islam, xxv–xxviii, xxx, 2–3, 23

James the Apostle, St., 8
Javers, Ron
  —*The Suicide Cult,* 198n
Jerusalem, Temple of, 174, 177, 179
Jesus Christ, xxx, 2–6, 9, 20n, 24–26, 34, 62, 65–66, 122, 174–76, 178, 183, 188, 190–92, 232–35, 239
  Church of, xix, xxiii, xxv, xxvii, xxix, xxxi, 7, 37, 109, 114, 120–23, 128, 141, 146, 151, 158, 171–72, 174, 178–79, 186, 188, 191–92
  Cross of, 172, 211, 213
  Gospel of, 186
  incarnation of, 211, 231
  redemption by, 211, 213
  resurrection of, xii, xxv

GENERAL INDEX

Second Coming of, 179, 181n, 238
"Jesus Movement," 155, 175–76
Joachim of Floris, xxxiii
Joel, Prophet, 166
John Cassian, St., 146
John Climacus, St.
  —The Ladder of Divine Ascent, 149, 189
John of Kronstadt, St., 166
  —My Life in Christ, 189
Johnston, William
  —Christian Zen, 42, 44
John the Apostle and Theologian, St., 3, 5, 11, 111, 146, 154, 156, 166, 182, 189, 237
Jones, Jim, 195–96, 198
Jonestown, Guyana, xiv, 195–200
Journal of Shasta Abbey, The, 64, 65n
Judaism, xxviii, 2–3
Jung, Carl G., 210–11
  —Flying Saucers: A Modern Myth of Things Seen in the Skies, 71

Kabbalah, 204
Kali, goddess, 15, 20, 20n
Keel, John A., 112
  —UFOs: Operation Trojan Horse, 97n, 99, 102, 110n, 113
Kempis, Thomas à
  —Imitation of Christ, 145
Kennett, Jiyu
  —How to Grow a Lotus Blossom, 68n
Kilduff, Marshall
  —The Suicide Cult, 198
King, Pat, 115n
Kireyevsky, Ivan, xiii
Klass, Philip J., 84–85
  —UFOs Explained, 84n
Knox, Ronald A.
  —Enthusiasm: A Chapter in the History of Religion, 137n
Koch, Dr. Kurt, 126, 128, 130, 137–40
  —Between Christ and Satan, 131n
  —Day X, 181n
  —Occult Bondage and Deliverance,

130n, 131n, 133n, 156
  —The Revival in Indonesia, 185n
  —The Strife of Tongues, 128, 168
Kontzevitch, I. M., 145
Koran, 2
"Krishna consciousness" movement, 54–58, 68
Kuhlman, Kathryn, 214n

La Croix, 1
La Foi Transmise, 6
La Suisse, xxvi
laughter, "holy." See "holy laughter" movement; Holy Spirit, "laughter of"; Toronto Blessing
Lausiac History (Palladius), 189
laying on of hands, 117, 123, 126, 134, 139
  "charismatic" definition of, 136
LeMasters, Carol, 207
levitation, xxi, 50, 90
Lewis, I. H.
  —Ecstatic Religion, An Anthropological Study of Spirit Possession and Shamanism, 148n, 153
Lilli, D. G.
  —Tongues under Fire, 168
Lindsay, Gordon
  —Israel's Destiny and the Coming Deliverer, 177
liturgical experimentation, 120, 210–12
Lives of Saints, 37, 131n, 144, 148–49, 181, 220
Logos, The, xx, xxxiii, 13, 115n, 116, 121n, 123–24, 149, 152, 159n, 164, 166, 170, 173, 181
  as "herald of this new age," xxxiv
Logos Journal, 115n, 135, 161, 172, 177–78
Look, 95
Lucifer, 14, 18, 210, 224–25. See also devil; Satan
"Luciferian Initiation," 210, 225
Lundy, Mary Ann, 212

General Index

Lunn, Harry, 172
Lutheranism, 121, 128, 211

Macarius, St., Elder of Optina, 156, 158
Macarius the Great, St.
—*Homilies,* 189
Mackintosh, C. H.
—*The Lord's Coming,* 181n
magic, 16
  demarcations between science and, 76
  Druidical, 204
  manifestation of, 131n
"magnetic field," 132
    proper "flow" of the yogic, 60
    spiritistic, 134
Maharaj-ji, Guru, 56–58
Maharishi Mahesh Yogi, 46–51, 56
"Maitreya," 226
mantras, 19, 39, 48–49, 54, 60
  Pujabi, 59
  Sanskrit, 17, 19, 61
Manuel, David, Jr., 177
Martin of Tours, St. 104–5
Masonry. *See* Freemasonry
Maugham, Somerset, 21
McIntire, Carl, 177
meditation, xxxv, 39, 42–44, 50–51, 59, 187, 191
  agnostic character of, 44
  "Christian," 39, 52, 187–88
  convention on, 44
  Eastern, 35, 42, 45, 208
  experiences, 187
  music, 208
  on Scriptural passages, 149
  Roman Catholic, 41
  silent, 43
  various kinds of, 68
  workshops, 209
  Zen, xxi, 45
mediumism, 102, 104, 128–30, 131n, 134–36, 157, 162, 209, 223
  applying tests for, 133

central characteristic of, 35
  "Christian," xx, 130
  and discarnate entities, 198, 225
  modern spiritistic, 137
  passivity or submissiveness of, 131
  séance as a crude form of, 132
mediumistic
  possession, 157
  techniques, xiv, 110, 136
Merton, Thomas, xxvi, 21, 37
Methodism, 117, 132, 210–11, 215
"millennium," 179–80
  Orthodox interpretation of, 178–79
"Millennium '73," 57–58, 177, 179
miracles, false, 35, 58, 109, 111, 116, 144, 169, 184
  of antichrist, 111
  false, prepare the world for the false messiah, 183
  of God, 114
"miraculous healings," 97, 129
Mohammed, 2
monasticism, 63, 65, 149
  ascetic spirit of, xxxii
  Orthodox instructors in, 182
  Roman Catholic, 21, 73, 210
Monism, 22, 27, 202
monotheism, 1, 3–4
  ecumenists unite on the basis of, xxxiv
Motovilov, N. A., conversation of St. Seraphim with, 183
Muktananda, Swami, 217
Muller, Robert, 229
munbaki, 16
mutki (salvation), doctrine of, 15
"Mystery of Iniquity," 192

near-death visions, 68n
Nectarios of Pentapolis, St., 166
neo-paganism, xi, xii, xiv, 7, 203–4, 207, 210, 219, 233. *See also* paganism
New Age, 56–58, 221
  "Luciferian Initation" required to enter, 209

GENERAL INDEX

Messiah, 217, 225–26
movement, xiv, 15, 201–3, 207–11, 213, 217–27, 230, 232–33
"of the Holy Spirit," xxxii–xxxiv, 143, 166, 192
"Plan" for, 223–27
"new religious consciousness," xiv, xxii, 58, 68, 70, 77, 166, 188, 192, 202, 209, 223, 231–35, 238
of Berdyaev, 143
of the "charismatic revival," 143
seductive power of, 69
significance and goal of, xxxv
symptoms of, xi
New Religious Consciousness, The, 61
New World Order, xiv, 224, 227–28
New York Times, 198
Nicetas, Bishop of Novgorod, St., 144
Nicholas (Drobyazgin), Archimandrite, 30
Nilus of Sora, St., Life of, 106
Nilus, Sergei
—The Power of God and Man's Weakness (in Russian), 107n
—Svyatynya pod Spudom, 113n
Niphon of Constantia, St., 169

occult, xii, 51, 64–75, 77, 109n, 147, 204, 238
initiation rituals of, 101
interest in, 51
"mystical" overtones of, 73
phenomena, 97–98
realm, 99, 102–3, 110, 130, 219
occultism, 72, 131, 150, 204–7, 217, 223, 238
connection between "science" and, 76
contemporary, 141, 149
influence on events in Russia of, 30
"Omega Point," 29, 192, 232
Ordo Anno Mundi, 205
Ordo Templi Orientalis, 206–7
original sin, 9, 28, 237
Ortega, Ruben, 142, 155, 168
—The Jesus People Speak Out, 168

Orthodox Church, xxiii, 25, 36, 121, 124, 133, 145, 178, 184, 186, 216, 233. See also Jesus Christ, Church of
Orthodox Life, xxxii(n), 31
Orthodox Word, The, xx, xxii–xxiii, 7, 68, 104n, 140, 145n
Orthodoxy, xxiv, 7, 38, 182–84, 233, 239. See also Christianity, Orthodox
ascetical teaching of, 143–44
contemplative tradition of, 45
conversion from Hinduism to, xxxiv
Fathers of, 5–6, 11, 104–6, 112, 145–46, 149–50, 153–54, 158, 166, 169–70, 182–83, 189–91, 239
historical, xxxii
"new posture of," xxxiv
self-liquidation of, xxiv–xxv
tradition of, xxiv, 153, 174, 181–82
true spirituality of, 42
Ostrander, Sheila
—Psychic Discoveries behind the Iron Curtain, 74n, 83n
ouija-boards, 162–63

paganism, xxix, 56, 206–7, 210, 217, 233. See also neo-paganism; initiation, pagan experience of
experience of, 152, 171
gods of, 7, 105, 152, 217
interest in Western forms of, 204
religious experiences of, 156
shamanistic, 173
Pagan Federation, 206
Pagels, Elaine, 234
Paisius the Great, St., 189–91
Pan-Christianism, 27
pantheism, panentheism, 202, 207, 211, 232
papacy, xix
parapsychology, 76, 102
Parham, Charles, 117
Parliament of Religions, 21, 24, 229, 230n

passivity, 131–32, 189
  foreign to Orthodox spirituality, 133
  of mind, 157, 162
  pronounced in "charismatic" communities, 134
  of the spiritistic séance, 133
Paul VI, Pope, 1, 36, 118, 126, 137, 156, 186. *See also* Roman Catholicism
Pentecostal, 44, 125–27, 134–35, 161
  "channels," 135
  experience, 44
  "laying on of hands," 134
  movement, 116–17, 120, 136–37. *See also* "Charismatic movement"
  revival, 120
  sects, 116, 119, 124, 132
Pentecostalism, 120, 134, 142, 171, 212–15. *See also* "Charismatic revival"
  ecumenistic theories and practices of, 124
"People's Temple," 198
Philokalia, 38, 42, 45, 66, 112, 154
"planetary initiations," 225. *See also* initiation
Poe, Edgar Allan, 72
possession. *See* demonic possession
"post-Christian" age, 62, 66, 70, 73, 77, 110, 118, 203, 222
Prabuddha Bharata, 24
Pranayama, 19
prelest, 11, 41, 143–44, 149, 162
Presbyterianism, 135, 138, 211–12
pride, 9, 11, 66, 159
  basic sin of, 14
  may take the form of "humility," 149
  spiritual, 149
"Project Blue Book," 81–82, 89, 101
prophecy, xxxv, 144, 159–60, 166, 192
  concerning the last days, 178
  false, "accompanied by a vision," 161
  false, of Nicholas Berdyaev, 173
  of the future of mankind, 195
  of St. Niphon of Constantia, 169

satanic, 192
"prophesying," 141
"prophets," false, 175, 192
Protestantism, xx, 38, 52, 102, 181, 210–11, 215. *See also* revivalism, Protestant
  fundamentalist, xix, 120–21, 171, 177, 180, 181n
  pagans converted to, 184
psychedelic (hallucinogenic) drugs, 52, 202
psychic, 43, 68–69, 81, 103, 187, 219
  component in UFO sightings, 97
  devices, UFOs as, 99
  disciplines, 69
  disorders, 133, 157
  energy, 59
  experience, 11, 68
  experiments, 68
  games, dangerous, 127
  healing, 100
  hypotheses, 71
  and occult activities, 64
  parlor tricks, 18
  phenomena, 98–100, 102, 169
  power, 45
  reality, the boundaries of, 71
  realm, 68, 219
  researchers, 107
  sensitivity, 129
  states, 129, 136, 188
  technique, 49
psychotechnologies, 202
Puja (Hindu ceremony of worship), 84
purgatory, xix

Radix, 198n
Rainbow Gatherings, 208
Rajneesh, Bhagwan Shree, 217
Ramakrishna, xxvii
Ranaghan, Kevin & Dorothy, 125, 135, 151–52, 155, 158–60, 163–64, 178
  —*Catholic Pentecostals,* 168
"Rapture," the, 180

General Index

Raudive, Konstantin
—*Breakthrough: An Amazing Experiment in Electronic Communication with the Dead,* 110n
"Rave masses," 210
Rebus, 30
redemption, dogma of, 211
"Re-imagining" movement, 210–12, 232
reincarnation, 198, 202
religions, 13, 23, 67, 101, 199, 202, 207, 208, 221, 225–26, 229–37
"American," 61
of antichrist, 114, 188
comparative study of all, 13
"convergence" of, 223, 225, 228–30
Convocation of, for World Peace, xxv
"create a world community of," xxvii
Eastern, xiv, xvi, xxxiv, 9, 20n, 35, 38, 52–53, 55, 58, 61, 67, 69, 171, 188, 203–4
false, 113
of the future, xxii, xxxv, 67, 188, 195, 203–4, 225, 228, 234, 236, 238
new world, 172
non-Christian, 20n
primitive, 15, 128, 137
universal, 203, 225, 228, 231
religious
cults, Eastern, 52
"experiments," 188
"feelings," 163
ignorance of our times, xxxii
instructions, 10
"liberals," xxx
mentality of modern man, 237
"new experiences," 189
phenomena, contemporary, xi
"revival," 192
spectrum, American, 196
syncretism, xxviii
thought, contemporary, xxxiii
Religious News Service, xxvii–xxviii
revivalism, Protestant, xx, 116, 180, 182

Robbins, Jhan
—*Tranquility without Pills (All about Transcendental Meditation),* 46n
Roberts, Oral, 132, 133n, 218
Robertson, Pat, 215
Roerich, Nicholas, 224
"Rolfing," 67
Roman Catholicism, xix, 21, 23–25, 27, 37–38, 52, 209–11, 215–16. *See also* Paul VI, Pope; Vatican II
Rowling, J. K., 205
Ruppelt, Captain Edward, 82n
as first director of "Blue Book"
—*Report on Unidentified Flying Objects,* 82
Russia, xi, xv–xvi, 30, 106, 113, 216

Sabellius, 3
"sacred heart," xix
Safran, Grand Rabbi Dr., 2
Saint Herman of Alaska Brotherhood and Monastery, xi–xii, xv, xviii
Saint Peter's Cathedral, xxvi, 2, 9, 36–37
Saint Vladimir's Theological Quarterly, xxiv
Sakkas, Fr. Basile, 1, 6
Samadhi, 13, 43
Samhain, pagan feast of, 207
Sanskrit, 48, 54–55, 58
Sarov Monastery, Russia, 30
Satan, xxix, 12, 15, 36, 146, 199, 222, 224–26, 236, 238–39. *See also* devil; Lucifer
aerial realm as chief dominion of, 111
evident and brazen activity of, xxii
fantasies and illusions of, 12
servants of, 169
Satanic, 36, 188, 199
prophecy, 192
Satanism, 141, 149, 208, 236
Scherbachev, Mikhail, xvi
Schroeder, Lynn
—*Psychic Discoveries Behind the Iron Curtain,* 74n, 83n

Schweitzer, Albert, xxvii
science fiction, 72, 77, 91
  future "evolved" beings of, 74
  history of, 75–76
  myth behind, 74
  rooted in magic and mythology, 76
  totally secular universe of, 73
"Science of Mind," 67
"Scientology," 67
séances, 131–33, 161, 210
Second Coming of Christ, 179, 181n
Seraphim (Rose), Hieromonk, xi–xvii,
    201, 203–4, 209, 212–13, 216,
    219, 223, 227, 235–39, 238
  —The Kingdom of Man and the King-
    dom of God, xii
  —The Northern Thebaid, 106n
  —The Soul After Death, xvi, 104n
Seraphim of Sarov, St., 30, 158, 182–83
700 Club, 216
shamanism, 44, 137, 148, 153, 173
  as a "religious" expression, 128
  Native American, 152, 204
  powers, 148
  "speaking in tongues," 127
Shasta, Mount, xi–xii, 62
Shasta Abbey, 62–63, 65–66, 68n
Shelley, Mary Wollstonecraft
  —Frankenstein, or the Modern Prome-
    theus, 72
Sherill, John L., 124, 127, 134–35, 142,
    151–52, 154, 160
  —They Speak with Other Tongues, 168
Shri Guru Dev, 48
Siddhis, 18, 50
Sikh religion, 61
"Silva Mind Control," 67, 209
Siva Cave, 16–17
"Slain in the Spirit," 214, 214n, 216
Smena, 83, 83n
Sobornost, xxiv(n), xxx
Sodom and Gomorrah, 73
Sophia, goddess, 211–12, 233
sorcery, 75–76, 104, 131n
South America, 81, 195, 213

Soviet Life, 83n
"Space Civilizations," Soviet scientific
  conference on, 83
Spangler, David, 209, 223, 225–26
  —Reflections on the Christ, 225n
speaking in tongues, 117, 124, 126–29,
    134–37, 139–41, 155, 159, 166,
    170
  common "gift" of the possessed, 128
  not a gift but a technique, 136
  shamanistic, 128
  "supernatural" phenomenon of, 142
Spielberg, Stephen, 219
spiritism, 129, 131, 133, 137, 142, 161,
    202
  19th-century, 98
  automatic writing of, 107
  comparison of "charismatic revival"
    with, 171
  crude techniques of, 132
  "magnetic circles" in, 134
  mediumistic, 102
spirits, 129, 147, 153, 174
  "of devils," 183
  evil, 112, 148, 199
  fallen, xiv, 129, 162, 185
  "guardian," 209
  openness to the activity of, 133, 162
  at séances, 161
Spiritual Counterfeits Project, 48, 51n
Spiritual Counterfeits Project Journal,
    102, 231n
Spiritual Counterfeits Project Newsletter,
    205n, 210n
Sputnik, 74n
Sri Lanka (Ceylon), 31
Standing Conference of the Canonical
    Orthodox Bishops in the Americas
    (SCOBA), xxiii
Star Trek, 72, 75
Star Wars, 72–73
State of the World Forum, 231
Steiger, Brad, 101
Stephanou, Fr. Eusebius, xx, xxxiii,
    115–16, 121, 123n, 152, 152n,

GENERAL INDEX

164, 166, 170, 179–82

Strieber, Whitley, 219–23

Sufism, 236

suicide, 97, 112, 145

"revolutionary," 197, 199

Sulpicius Severus, 104

Swedenborg, Emanuel, 147

Swing, Bishop William, 230–31

Symeon the New Theologian, St., 112, 182

Symposium of Religions, 24

syncretism, xxv, xxviii, 38, 46, 69

Syrian Antiochian Archdiocese of New York, 140

Talbott, Strobe, 228

Talmudic traditions, 2

Tantra, 19, 27, 60, 202

Tari, Mel

—*Like a Mighty Wind,* 185n

telepathy, 75, 97

Temple of Jerusalem, 174, 177, 179

Temple of Understanding, Inc., xxvi, 229

Theophan the Recluse, St., 122–23

—*The Spiritual Life,* 123n

—*Unseen Warfare,* 189

Theosophical Society, 223, 224n

Theosophy, 132

"3HO," 61–62, 68

Tibetan Buddhism, 203–4

Time, 197n

Timofievitch, A. P., 31

TM in Court, 51n

tongues, speaking in. *See* speaking in tongues

Toronto Blessing, 212–18. *See also* "Holy laughter movement"; Holy Spirit, "laughter of"

 Airport Vineyard Church, Toronto, 215

Transcendental meditation, 45–47, 49–51, 56, 68

 centers, 47

transpersonal psychology, 208

2001: A Space Odyssey, 72

unidentified flying objects (UFOs), xvi, 70–71, 77, 79, 83, 101, 112–13. *See also* "close encounters"; "Condon Report"; Cults, UFO; "Project Blue Book"; psychic

"abductions," 95–97, 106, 220

contemporary researchers of, 107

"Daylight Discs," 86

debunking, 84

emotional response of witnesses, 87

encounters with, 81, 90, 100–102, 219–23

government investigation of, 81

groups, 82

"landings," 80–81, 93, 99

manifestations of, 102, 108, 219, 222

network of watchers of, 219–21

as "Nocturnal Lights," 86

observations made of, 85

"occupants" of, 100

phenomena, xiv–xv, 71, 78, 81, 89, 98, 100–103, 107, 112–13, 218–19, 222

"Radar-Visual" reports, 86

reports, scientific analysis of, 78

sightings of, 78, 84–85

wave of, 79–80

United Nations, 228–29

United Religions Initiative, 230–31, 237

University of Creation Spirituality, 210

Upanishads, 8, 27

U.S. News & World Report, 67

Vallee, Dr. Jacques, 78, 83, 92, 94, 97–101, 219

—*The Edge of Reality: A Progress Report on Unidentified Flying Objects,* 91n, 93, 99

—*The Invisible College,* 96–100, 108–9

—*Passport to Magonia,* 100n

—*UFOs in Space: Anatomy of a Phenomenon,* 78n, 94n

General Index

Van Dusen, Wilson
   —*The Presence of Other Worlds,* 148n
Vatican II, 37. *See also* Roman Catholicism
Vedanta, 10, 13, 14–15, 19, 24
   Advaita, 18, 22–23
   idolatry, 19
   message of, 21–22
   philosophy, 25, 203
   plagiarisms from, 27
   Societies, 13, 21
   teachings and practices of, 26
Vedanta and the West, 24
Vedanta Kesheri, 24
Vedantasara, 8
Verne, Jules, 72
visualization, 202, 213
Vivekananda, Swami, xxx, 15, 19–25, 28–29
   mission of, 26
   philosophy of, xxvii
   power behind, 25
   purpose of, for coming to the West, 22
   Universal Religion of, 26, 28–29
Von Daniken, Erich
   —*Chariots of the Gods?* 73
   —*Gods from Outer Space,* 73

Walsch, Neale Donald
   —*Conversations with God,* 237–38
Ward, Admiral Charles, 227
Weldon, John
   —*Close Encounters: A Better Explanation,* 102n
   —"UFOs: Is Science Fiction Coming True?," 102n
Welles, Orson, 79
Wells, H. G., 72, 224
   —*War of the Worlds,* 79
Wicca, 206–8, 210, 230n
"wicker man" sacrifices, 207
Wilber, Ken, 231–34
Williams, J. Rodman, 133–34, 136, 142, 160, 168

—*The Era of the Spirit,* 168
Wilson, Clifford
   —*Close Encounters: A Better Explanation,* 102n
   —"UFOs: Is Science Fiction Coming True?," 102n
witch doctors, 137
witchcraft, 133, 204–10, 230n
Witch's Voice (website), 205
wizards, 7
World Council of Churches, xxvi, xxx, 120, 211, 212
   Central Committee of, xxvii
   World Council Movement, 120

yoga, 38–40, 43, 48–49, 68–69
   Agni writings, 224
   bhakti, 55
   "Christian," 39, 41–42, 46–47
   hatha, 40
   kundalini, 59
   original purpose of, 33, 203
   practice of, 40, 61, 202–3, 208
   tantric, 59
Yogi Bhajan. *See* Bhajan, Yogi
Yonggi Cho, Paul, 213

Zaitsev, Dr. Vyacheslav
   —"Visitors from Outer Space," 74n
Zen Buddhism, 37, 43–44, 62, 64–66, 68, 133, 203–4
   agnostic, pagan experience of, 45
   "Christian Zen," 46–47
   Japanese, 43, 53, 63
   master, 22
      near-death visions of, 68n
      Western, 53, 203–4
   monastery, 62
Ziegel, Dr. Felix U., 83
   —"On Possible Exchange of Information with Extra-Terrestrial Civilizations," 83n
   —"UFOs, What Are They?," 83n
Zoroastrianism, xxx, 23

Scripture Index

Old Testament

Genesis
  Ch. 3: 5 238
      16: 1ff. 5
      17: 5. 5
      18: 1–2 4
Leviticus
  Ch. 20: 6 130
Deuteronomy
  Ch. 18: 10–12. 130
II Kings
  Ch. 13: 21. 129
Psalms
  Ch. 95: 5. 7
      109: 1 4
Sirach
  Ch. 21: 23. 153
Isaiah
  Ch. 5: 20–21 26
      14: 13–14 14
Jeremiah
  Ch. 29: 8–9 161
Daniel
  Ch. 3: 25. 4
      7: 13. 4
Joel
  Ch. 2: 28 . . . . xxxi, 202

New Testament

Matthew
  Ch. 5: 4 153

    7: 22–23 186
    16: 1 193
    24: 2 200
    24: 22. 193
    24: 23–27. 178
    24: 24 . . . . . . 175, 191
    24: 30. 111
Mark
  Ch. 14: 61–62 3
Luke
  Ch. 12: 32 . . . . . . 175, 192
      18: 8 170
      21: 11. 111
John
  Ch. 5: 43 178
      6: 29. 4
      8: 39. 4
      8: 56. 4
      10: 30 3
      12: 31 36
      14: 6, 9 5
      16: 33. 193
      17: 24 3
Acts of the Apostles
  Ch. 1: 11. . . . . . . 111, 179
      2. . . . . 125, 166
      2: 34. 4
      10. 125
      10: 34–35 36
      10: 34–48 37
      14: 17 36

19. 125
19: 12. 129
19: 15. 146
Romans
Ch. 4: 17. 5
8: 31 193
11: 4 184
I Corinthians
Ch. 12–14. 126
II Corinthians
Ch. 4: 4. xxix
6: 14–17. 37
11: 14. 149
Galatians
Ch. 1: 8–9. 186
3: 16. 5
3: 29. 5
5: 24 145
Ephesians
Ch. 1: 4–5 3
4: 14 xxiii
5: 15 xvii
Colossians
Ch. 3: 11 239
I Thessalonians
Ch. 4: 16–17 . . . . 181n
II Thessalonians
Ch. 2: 3–4, 9–12 175

2: 4. 58
2: 7 109
2: 8 238
2: 9 . . . . 171, 226
2: 10 188
2: 15 186
I Timothy
Ch. 4: 1 170
II Timothy
Ch. 4: 3–4 xxiii
James
Ch. 4: 6 8
5: 16 129
I John
Ch. 1: 1 5
2: 18 183
2: 23. 3
4: 1 . . . . . . 11, 116, 214
4: 3 237
Apocalypse (Revelations)
Ch. 3: 17 166
13: 13. 111
16: 14. 170
20: 3. . . . . 170, 188
20: 6 179
20: 7 188
20: 7–8 109
22: 20. 193

SAINT HERMAN OF ALASKA BROTHERHOOD

Since 1965, the St. Herman of Alaska Brotherhood has been publishing Orthodox Christian books and magazines.

View our catalog, featuring over fifty titles, and order online, at
www.sainthermanmonastery.com

You can also write us for a free printout of our catalog:

St. Herman of Alaska Brotherhood
P. O. Box 70
Platina, CA 96076
USA